VOYAGES

IN ENGLISH

Writing and Grammar

Elaine de Chantal Brookes

Patricia Healey

Irene Kervick

Catherine Irene Masino

Anne B. McGuire

Adrienne Saybolt

LOYOLAPRESS.

Grateful acknowledgment is given to authors, publishers, photographers, museums, and agents for permission to reprint the following copyrighted material. Every effort has been made to determine copyright owners. In the case of any omissions, the publisher will be pleased to make suitable acknowledgments in future editions. Continued on page 535.

Cover Design/Production: Loyola Press, Steve Curtis Design, Inc.
Cover Illustration: Jeff Parks
Interior Design/Production: Think Design Group, Loyola Press

ISBN-10: 0-8294-2099-1
ISBN-13: 978-0-8294-2099-9

Manufactured in the United States of America.

LOYOLA PRESS.

3441 N. Ashland Avenue
Chicago, Illinois 60657
(800) 621-1008
www.loyolapress.com

09 10 11 12 13 14 Web 10 9 8 7 6 5 4 3 2

CONTENTS

PART

Written and Oral Communication

PART 2

Grammar

What do all of these

people have in common?

They all use writing in their jobs.

How do you think that writing helps them in their everyday lives?

Written and Oral Communication

CHAPTER 1

California is a large stretch of land that borders the Pacific Ocean. California became a territory of the United States in 1848 after the Mexican-American War. Two years later, California became the 31st state, with Sacramento as its capital. Today more people live in California than in any other state. It is the third largest state in the country in area. Only Alaska and Texas are larger.

What are some things that you know about California?

Personal Narratives

To: Alan and Marina Wood <amwood@doubletrux.net>

From: Tanya <twood@campparker21.net>

Hi Mom and Dad,

It's a good thing you got me that waterproof watch to use at camp. If you hadn't, I might still be splashing around in Lake Parker!

It all started when Pete and I went kayaking on the lake. We decided to go all the way to the island in the middle. About halfway there, Pete started splashing water at me. I splashed back, and soon we had both gone tumbling into the water!

In all the commotion, we didn't hear the camp counselor call everyone in for dinner. Instead, we headed for the island and explored it. It wasn't until I looked at my watch that I realized we were late for dinner.

When we finally made it back, the counselor was a little angry with us. But he was also glad that we made it back safely. We were just glad they saved us some dinner!

Love,
Tanya

What Makes a Good Personal Narrative?

Our Wide Wide World

Native Americans have lived in California for over 10,000 years. Before Europeans came, one of the largest tribes was the Chumash. The Chumash lived along the southern coast of California. They built large canoes called *tomols* and used them for fishing and moving goods. The Chumash were excellent basket makers. They also made beads from shells and used them as money.

A narrative is a story. A personal narrative is a true story about something that happened to the writer. It could be a journal entry about the first day of school. It could be a letter describing an exciting trip. Here are some ideas for what makes a good personal narrative.

Topic

Anything that really happened to you can be a good topic for a personal narrative. It should be something you remember clearly. The topic might be something funny, exciting, or unusual.

Audience

The people who will read your story are your audience. Think of them when you choose your topic. Your friends might want to hear how you beat the newest video game. Your grandparents might be more interested in hearing about a family trip.

Point of View

Point of view shows who is telling the story. In your personal narrative, you are telling the story. This is called the first-person point of view. Use words such as *I, me, my, we,* and *our.*

Activity A

Read the e-mail on page 7 and answer these questions.

1. How can you tell that this is a personal narrative?
2. Why do you think the writer chose this topic?
3. Who is the audience of this narrative?
4. What is the point of view of this e-mail?
5. What words are used to show the point of view?

Activity B

Decide which topics would make good personal narratives.

1. the day I found a $20 bill
2. my first piano recital
3. my brother's trip to the zoo
4. a train ride I'll never forget
5. the day I was born
6. what I'd do if I were an astronaut
7. my unlucky day at the beach
8. a boring afternoon
9. my summer vacation to the Grand Canyon
10. when my sister broke her arm
11. my first trip in an airplane
12. the day of the big snowstorm

Writer's Corner

Write three things that happened to you that would make good personal narratives.

Time Order

The events in a personal narrative are told in the order that they happened. Tell what happened first near the beginning and what happened last near the ending. Use time words such as *first, next, after, then, finally,* and *last* to show the order of the events. Here is an example.

> First I got out of bed.
>
> Then I got dressed.
>
> After getting dressed, I ate breakfast.
>
> Next I waited on the corner for the bus.
>
> Finally the bus arrived.

• Activity C •

Below is a personal narrative about a trip to school in the morning. The first two sentences are given, but the other sentences are in the wrong order. Put the sentences in time order in paragraph form.

I woke up late this morning. I should have just stayed in bed.

1. After breakfast I headed for the bus.

2. When I looked in my closet, I found that all my favorite shirts were in the laundry.

3. I finally picked out a shirt, but I spilled juice on it at breakfast.

4. Next I missed my bus by a few seconds.

5. It was too late to finish eating.

6. When I got to school, I remembered that my homework was back at home.

7. I had to leave the bus stop when I realized I'd forgotten my lunch.

8. I begged my brother to drive me to school.

Activity D

Here is a paragraph that a fourth grader wrote about planting his first garden. Rewrite the paragraph. Add time words to help show the order in which things happened.

Finally	First	Next	Then

I was excited about planting a garden. ——————— I chose a nice sunny spot. ——————— I dug up the soil. ——————— I fertilized it. ——————— I planted the seeds and watered them. I can't wait for the flowers to grow.

Activity E

Revise the paragraph. Put the sentences in time order. Add at least two time words to show the order.

My brothers and I were stuck inside for yet another rainy day. She made an announcement. My mother was getting tired of our yelling. We spent the morning chasing one another around the house. "It's mud day!" she called out. We spent the next hour rolling in the mud and getting as dirty as we could. She told us to run upstairs and find our oldest clothes. When we finally came inside and changed our clothes, we were ready for a nap. She sent us to the backyard, where the rain had turned our lawn into a mud puddle.

Writer's Corner

Write what you did before school this morning in paragraph form. Use time words to show the order of events.

Introduction, Body, and Conclusion

A personal narrative has three main parts: the introduction, the body, and the conclusion. These are the beginning, middle, and ending of your story. Here are some tips for writing each part of a personal narrative.

Introduction

The introduction of your personal narrative is your chance to grab your reader's attention. The introduction should make the reader want to know more.

Body

The body, or middle, of your personal narrative tells what happened. It describes the events in time order, including everything important that happened. It should not include details that are not related to your personal narrative.

Conclusion

The conclusion of your personal narrative should tell how the story ended. You might tell something you learned or explain how you felt.

Activity A

The introduction of a personal narrative should grab the reader's attention. Choose the most effective introduction for each personal narrative.

1. I was doing well until I found myself at the top of a hill. Before I could stop, I was flying down the slope. Then my wheel hit a rock. Bam! Down I went! I bruised my leg and scraped my elbow, but luckily I wasn't hurt badly. Now I know why my dad insisted that I wear a helmet.

   a. I was riding my skateboard down Acorn Street.

   b. I had never tried to skateboard before.

   c. I was zooming along on my skateboard and feeling confident—maybe too confident!

2. My class went on a sleepover at the Museum of Natural History. First we explored an ancient Egyptian tomb by flashlight. It was really eerie! Next a troupe of African dancers performed. Then we curled up in our sleeping bags right beside the skeleton of a real dinosaur. I was fascinated by its sharp teeth. I decided then and there that I want to study dinosaurs when I grow up.

   a. I had an exciting weekend.

   b. Have you ever slept near a dinosaur? I have.

   c. Here's how I decided what I want to be when I grow up.

Writer's Corner

Think of something you tried for the first time. Write the introduction to a personal narrative about what happened. Grab the reader's attention with the first sentence.

Details

The body of a personal narrative should be filled with details. Good details make a personal narrative clearer and more real to the reader. However, details unrelated to the story can distract the reader. Make sure all your details add something to your personal narrative.

Juan Rodríguez Cabrillo was an explorer who worked for the Spanish government. In 1542 he became the first European to set foot in California. He landed in a beautiful body of water that is now known as San Diego Bay. During his journey he sailed all the way to the current border of Oregon and California. In 1913 a national monument was built on the San Diego coast in Juan's honor.

• Activity B •

Which two details in each group are not related to the same topic as the rest?

1. My parents said we could get a dog.
   My sister once had a goldfish.
   We went to the animal shelter.
   Our neighbor is allergic to cats.
   There were a lot of dogs waiting to be adopted.
   A little black and white dog was wagging her tail.
   We bought her a new red leash and took her home.

2. I went into the submarine.
   We went below the surface of the water.
   I like to water-ski.
   I could see oyster beds.
   I could see sea urchins and sea horses.
   I have a poster of sea horses on my bedroom wall.
   Some of the sea urchins were brightly colored.

• Activity C •

For each group choose the sentence that is part of the introduction, the sentence that is part of the body, and the sentence that is part of the conclusion.

1. I caught three big fish in just one hour.
   I never thought I would like fishing.
   After that experience, I can't wait to go fishing again!

2. By the time it was over, I realized it was the best Saturday of my life.
   We played in the fountains and went down the water slide.
   I got a big surprise from my parents last weekend.

Choose one personal narrative and find the unrelated detail. Then write a conclusion that explains how things ended.

A. The day after we moved to Minnesota was the most surprising day of my life. Until that day I had never seen snow.

   As soon as I woke up, I put on my warmest clothes, ran outside, and jumped into a drift. I couldn't believe how wet and cold it was!

   My brother and I played in the snow all morning. He's two years older than I am. Mom gave us socks to put on our hands so we could make a snowman. We used an old cardboard box to slide down a hill.

B. Dad has told me a million times to close the door of the hamster cage, and I usually remember to do it. Last Tuesday I forgot.

   The first thing Dad does when he comes home from work is change his clothes and shoes. On Tuesday when he picked up his shoe, he saw a ball of fluff curled up inside. It was Magpie, my hamster! Dad was so startled that he dropped the shoe. Magpie woke up and scooted under the bed. The bed was covered with my favorite blanket. I had to crawl under it and pull him out.

Writer's Corner

Think of something you made recently. Maybe you cooked a meal or built a birdhouse. List as many details as you can about the experience. Then write a conclusion to a personal narrative about your experience.

Time Lines

A time line is one tool that writers use to organize their ideas. It can help you think of all the important events in a personal narrative. A time line can also help you put your ideas in time order.

A time line is created by drawing a long line on a sheet of paper. The line can be drawn either up and down or across the paper. On one side the line is divided into equal periods of time. On the other side important events are listed in time order.

Here is a time line one student, Pedro, made for his personal narrative about tubing on the Delaware River.

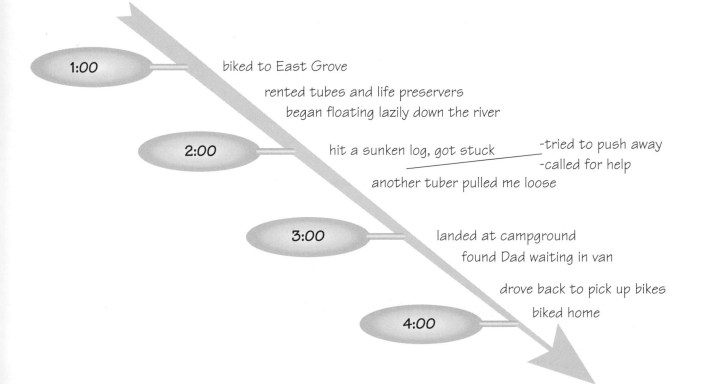

1:00 — biked to East Grove
rented tubes and life preservers
began floating lazily down the river

2:00 — hit a sunken log, got stuck — -tried to push away
-called for help
another tuber pulled me loose

3:00 — landed at campground
found Dad waiting in van

drove back to pick up bikes
biked home

4:00

Look at Pedro's time line. On the left side he divided it by hours, listing each hour at an even distance. On the right side he listed all the important events where they belonged on the line.

Do the same thing when you create your time line. On one side divide the line into equal periods of time, such as by minutes, hours, or days. On the other side put the events where they belong in time order. For example, if an event happened at 1:20, put it closer to 1:00 than to 2:00.

Activity A

Copy and complete the following time line about what you did one night this week. Add more times if necessary. Add events on the other side.

5:00

6:00

7:00

Activity B

Imagine you are Pedro writing a personal narrative. Using the time line on page 16, write two sentences about each part of your tubing adventure: starting the trip, getting stuck on the log, and ending the trip. Use time words to connect your ideas.

Writer's Corner

Make a time line of the classes that you have today. Make the opening bell your first event and the closing bell your last event.

Revising a Time Line

Once you finish a time line, it is a good idea to go back over it. Ask yourself the following questions: Did each event occur at the time shown on the time line? Should I rearrange any of the events? Have I included all the important details? Are there missing details I should add or unneeded details I should take out? Make any changes to the time line that you think are necessary.

Look at Pedro's time line on page 16. What details do you think Pedro added after making the time line?

● Activity C ●

Here are Jessica's notes about a trip to Philadelphia. Draw a time line on a sheet of paper. Put Jessica's notes on the time line, showing what she did with her family. Make up times for events if they are not included. Do not include unneeded details.

At 2:00 p.m. we each had a giant hot pretzel.

At 10:30 p.m. we saw a tremendous light show.

Next year we're going to Boston.

After breakfast we took a bus tour.

After lunch we went to the Benjamin Franklin Memorial.

Betsy Ross lived in Philadelphia.

When the tour was over, we went to Independence Hall.

At 9:00 a.m. we ate breakfast at a coffee shop.

We didn't have time to see the Liberty Bell.

For lunch we had Philly cheese steaks.

We went back to our hotel for dinner.

Philadelphia is called the "City of Brotherly Love."

Twenty-one missions were founded along the California coast between 1769 and 1823. The missions were set up by Spanish Catholics who wanted to bring Christianity to the people in California. Many farms were also set up with the help of the missions. Many of these missions are now open as landmarks. Some are still active parishes.

Activity D

Put these steps for making muffins into the time line. Leave out the unneeded detail. Then write the steps in paragraph form. Use time words.

6:10   I put the muffins into a 350° oven.

6:05   I stirred until the batter was smooth.

6:25   I checked on the muffins as they baked.

6:03   I added the milk and eggs.

6:08   I poured the batter into the muffin tins.

6:20   My brother came home.

6:00

I poured the muffin mix into a bowl.

6:15

6:30

I pulled the muffins out of the oven.

Activity E

What did you do last Sunday? Make a time line. Start with waking up in the morning. End with going to bed. Read over your time line. Add any missing details. Take out any unneeded details.

Writer's Corner

Use the time line you made in Activity E to write the body of a personal narrative about what you did last Sunday. Use time words to connect the details.

Exact Words

A writer paints a picture with words. If you use exact words, such as strong verbs and colorful adjectives, you will paint a clearer picture. When you use exact words, readers will enjoy your writing more.

Strong Verbs

A strong verb is a verb that shows the action of a sentence in an exact way. Read the following sentences:

> My friend and I walked up the hill.
> My friend and I *marched* up the hill.

> I ate my dinner and went outside.
> I *devoured* my dinner and *darted* outside.

Notice how the verbs in italics make each sentence more interesting. They paint a clearer picture of the action in the sentence.

When you revise your writing, look for any verbs that are too general or dull. Replace them with strong verbs.

• Activity A •

Think of a strong verb to replace each of the verbs below. Then choose three of the verbs you thought of. Write a sentence using each verb.

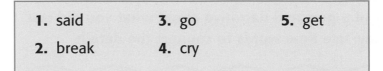

1. said	**3.** go	**5.** get
2. break	**4.** cry	

Activity B

Replace the italicized verb in each sentence with a strong verb from the list.

bragged	rattled	slid
grumbled	scooted	

1. The train *moved* along the track.

2. The playful otters *went* down the muddy riverbank.

3. Sean *said*, "I can't move this box."

4. I *ran* around the corner to hide from him.

5. "I scored the winning run!" *said* Nancy.

Activity C

Revise the paragraph. Change at least four verbs to strong verbs.

The engine sounded, and the boat went. I held on to the rope and went across the water on my water skis. "Look at me!" I said. My heart was beating fast. A spray of water hit my face. Then, as the boat turned, I lost my balance and went through the air. I hit the water and let go of the rope. As the boat came around to pick me up, I said, "Can I go again?"

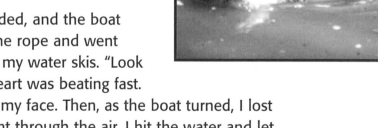

Writer's Corner

Rewrite the sentences in Activity B. Use different strong verbs from the ones given.

Our Wide Wide World

In 1848 James Marshall found a gold nugget in a river in northern California. Although he tried to keep his discovery a secret, the news quickly spread across the country. Over the next several years, more than a half million people came to California to find gold. Most gold seekers barely found enough gold to survive, but the Gold Rush changed California forever.

Colorful Adjectives

Just like strong verbs, colorful adjectives can bring your writing to life. Colorful adjectives describe something in an exact way. Colorful adjectives paint a clear picture of what is being described.

> The mean dog jumped at the gate.
> The *snarling* dog jumped at the gate.

Notice how the colorful adjective *snarling* makes the second sentence more interesting. When you revise your writing, look for places to add colorful adjectives.

Activity D

Replace the adjective in italics in each sentence with a colorful adjective from the list.

enormous	jagged	velvety
blinding	thrilling	rundown
charming	silent	booming

1. Suddenly the call of a crow echoed through the *quiet* forest.
2. The campers listened to the *good* story.
3. I tried to take a bite of the *big* sandwich.
4. He stroked the kitten's *soft* fur.
5. The forest ranger had a *nice* smile.
6. We tiptoed past the *old* shed.
7. The *loud* thunder scared everyone.
8. She tripped on the *rough* rock.
9. I had to squint in the *bright* sun.

Complete the sentences by filling in the blanks with colorful adjectives. Be as creative as you can.

1. The _____ sailboat glided on the _____ blue water.
2. A _____ squirrel darted behind a _____ tree.
3. Charlie's _____ pet scared his neighbors.
4. The _____ boys marched up the _____ hill.
5. Her _____ baby waved her _____ hands in the air.
6. The _____ smell of popcorn made me hungry.
7. One by one we dove into the _____ water of the _____ lake.
8. The _____ girls were lost in the _____ fog

• Activity F •

Complete the paragraph by filling in each blank with an exact word. The word in parentheses tells whether to use a strong verb or a colorful adjective.

The air grew thinner as we _____(verb)_____ up the mountain. __(Adjective)__ trees gave way to smaller plants. The __(adjective)__ wind was cold, and we _____(verb)_____ in our thin cotton jackets. __(Adjective)__ clouds threatened overhead. In the distance we could hear an eagle _____(verb)_____ . Suddenly there was a __(adjective)__ clap of thunder, and lightning _____(verb)_____ the sky. Because of the __(adjective)__ storm, we _____(verb)_____ for shelter.

Writer's Corner

Write a short personal narrative about something that happened last week. Use strong verbs and colorful adjectives.

Contractions with Pronouns

Sometimes two words can be combined to make one word called a contraction. The contraction is shorter than the two words because one or more letters are left out. An apostrophe takes the place of the missing letter or letters.

Some contractions are formed by joining a pronoun and a verb. Study this list of contractions. Name the missing letter or letters in each contraction.

I am	I'm	I will	I'll
he is	he's	he will	he'll
she is	she's	she will	she'll
it is	it's	it will	it'll
we are	we're	we will	we'll
you are	you're	you will	you'll
they are	they're	they will	they'll
I have	I've	I would	I'd
you have	you've	you would	you'd
we have	we've	we would	we'd
they have	they've	they would	they'd
he has	he's	he would	he'd
she has	she's	she would	she'd
it has	it's		

Activity A

Match each pair of words in Column A with their contraction in Column B.

Column A

1. they have
2. I would
3. we will
4. she is
5. I have
6. I am
7. it is
8. I will

Column B

a. I'll
b. we'll
c. I'm
d. they've
e. it's
f. I've
g. she's
h. I'd

Activity B

Use a contraction in place of the words in italics in each sentence.

1. *I have* never seen a pink flamingo.
2. *She is* going to eat split pea soup.
3. In the play, *I am* a talking dragon.
4. *We are* playing on the trampoline.
5. *I would* rather meet a cat than a tiger.
6. If you start to walk, *they will* follow you.
7. I think *it is* the same color as mine.
8. If we can, *we will* be there.

Writer's Corner

**Write about a game you played recently.
Use contractions in your sentences.**

Formal and Informal Language

Sometimes writing should be formal. You use formal writing when you write a letter to a business or a report for your teacher. At other times your writing can be informal, such as in an e-mail to a friend.

One way to make your writing formal is to avoid contractions. Informal writing often uses contractions, but formal writing does not. Think of your audience and your purpose before you write. If you are writing something formal do not use contractions.

Activity C

Make each sentence more formal by removing the contraction.

1. You said you'd help me.
2. She'll be there right after school.
3. I'd like more information about your book club.
4. We've never done this before.
5. I think it's going to rain.
6. She's requesting a refund.
7. I thought they'd be here by now.
8. They're not going to accept the offer.
9. It's been sunny all week.
10. He's going to finish the project by Friday.
11. I'm not going to be at the meeting.
12. You'll need permission from your teacher to attend.
13. They'll call the airline to make the reservation.
14. We're going to make the changes.
15. It's been a long time since I talked to them.

Activity D ●

This paragraph is from a friendly letter. Make it less formal by adding contractions. Words used to make contractions with pronouns are underlined.

<u>We are</u> having a great time here in North Conway. <u>I am</u> so excited! Today <u>we will</u> be going on the water slides. <u>I have</u> also gone swimming in the lake, and <u>we have</u> all had fun playing mini golf. <u>You will</u> wish that you had come. Do not worry. <u>I will</u> be sure to bring home pictures.

Activity E ●

These paragraphs are from a thank-you letter. Make it more formal by taking out contractions.

I'm writing to thank you for visiting our class last week. It's always a pleasure to talk to a real firefighter. I'm sure you're a busy person, and we're honored that you decided to visit our class. You're always welcome in our classroom.

You've inspired many of us to become firefighters when we grow up. If possible, we'd like to visit you at the fire station. It would be interesting to see the fire trucks and other equipment up close.

Writer's Corner

Write a formal note requesting something from your teacher or principal. Use formal language and avoid contractions.

Speaking and Listening Skills

Oral Personal Narratives

When you get home from school, do you tell your family what happened during the day? At school do you tell your friends what you did over the weekend? When you do, you are giving an oral personal narrative.

An oral personal narrative has the same parts as a written personal narrative. Keep the same tips in mind.

Introduction

Your opening should grab your listeners' attention. You might start with a question or a sentence that hints at what your personal narrative is about.

Body

Tell the main part of your personal narrative in time order so your listeners can follow it easily. Add enough details to make your story interesting, but do not include things that aren't important. Details that are not important to the story will distract your listeners.

Conclusion

Be sure to let your listeners know that the story is finished. Tell them how the experience ended and how you felt about what happened.

Voice

Change your tone of voice to make parts of your personal narrative sound exciting or important. You might speak faster or louder at an exciting part. You might speak slower or softer at a scary part. Remember that this is your own story. Let your personality shine through.

• Activity A •

Think of something good that happened to you at school recently. Write a good first sentence for an oral personal narrative about the event. Practice saying the sentence in different tones of voice.

• Activity B •

Read each sentence aloud twice with a partner. Show a different emotion each time. You might read it as if you were happy, surprised, frightened, angry, or sad.

1. It's just around the corner.

2. I didn't expect that.

3. Is that really for me?

4. I think it's going to be here soon.

5. I don't think you should do that.

Speaker's Corner

Tell a partner about the experience you chose for Activity A. Include all of the details that you think are important. Ask your partner which details he or she thinks are the most interesting. Do the same for your partner's experience.

California is known for its earthquakes. The worst California earthquake in modern history was the San Francisco earthquake of 1906. It happened along the San Andreas Fault. Lasting nearly one minute, it caused fires that destroyed almost the entire city of San Francisco. The earthquake was the first major natural disaster to be recorded in photographs.

Practice

Speaking in front of the whole class can be scary. One way to calm your nerves is to practice ahead of time. The better you know your story, the calmer you will feel.

Write out your introduction and conclusion on note cards. Write each detail of your personal narrative on a separate card. Use key words and phrases to help you remember the details. Put the cards in time order. Read them over carefully to make sure all the details are important.

Practice telling your story several times. You might stand in front of a mirror, or you might ask a friend or family member to listen to you. Look at your note cards to help you remember what you want to say, but don't just read them aloud. Use a tone of voice that shows how you felt about the experience.

Listening Tips

In an oral personal narrative, the listener is as important as the speaker. Follow these tips when you listen to another student's personal narrative.

- Look at the speaker so he or she knows you are paying attention.

- Listen to the introduction and try to guess what the narrative will be about.

- Picture the story in your mind as the speaker talks.

- Listen for the speaker's tone of voice to know how he or she felt about the experience.

- Give the speaker some positive feedback at the end of his or her presentation.

Activity C

Choose one of these ideas or think of one of your own. Think of a good introduction that would grab the attention of your audience. Think of a conclusion that tells how the experience ended. Write the introduction and conclusion on note cards. Then think of important details for the body and write them on separate note cards.

A. a time you surprised your family

B. something exciting that happened on vacation

C. making something with a friend or your family

D. something that didn't turn out as you expected

E. a funny thing a pet did

Activity D

Work with a partner. Take turns telling each other about the experience you chose in Activity C. When it is your turn to talk, practice using your voice in different ways to show different emotions. When it is your turn to listen, help your partner decide which tone of voice worked best to tell his or her story.

Speaker's Corner

Prepare to tell about the event you chose in Activity C. Be sure your notes are in time order. Practice using your voice to make the story interesting. Finally, present your personal narrative to the class.

Personal Narratives

Prewriting and Drafting

What funny, exciting, or strange things have happened to you? What stories from your life do you like to tell? One way to share these stories is to write a personal narrative.

Prewriting

Prewriting is the time a writer spends exploring ideas and planning. Andy, a fourth grader, spent time prewriting before writing a personal narrative. He brainstormed to help him choose a topic, free wrote, and then made a time line.

Brainstorming

Brainstorming is listing ideas quickly. Andy began choosing a topic by brainstorming a list of things that had happened to him. Here is his list.

getting lost on the way home from school

getting an A on my math test

hanging out with my friends over the summer

making a bird sanctuary with my mom

going to the beach

After he had completed his list, he thought about each topic. He wanted to write a narrative with a beginning that gets readers' attention, and a clear ending. He also wanted a story that would be interesting to his audience, his classmates. He decided to write about making a bird sanctuary with his mother. Since some of his friends had seen his sanctuary and asked him about it, he thought they would be interested in reading about it.

Your Turn

Brainstorm a list of interesting things that have happened to you. Did you go on an exciting trip? Did you do something you are proud of? When you have completed your list, choose a topic that you will enjoy writing about. Your topic should also be interesting to your audience, your classmates.

Free Writing

After choosing a topic, Andy spent five minutes free writing. He wrote down all the ideas and details he remembered about his topic. He wrote in words and phrases.

Your Turn

Spend some time free writing. List all the ideas and details about your experience you can think of. Write quickly. Pay attention to your ideas.

Making a Time Line

After free writing, Andy decided to organize his ideas with a time line. He drew his time line across a sheet of paper. On one side he divided his line into hours. On the other side he filled in the important events in the narrative from his free writing.

When he was finished, he reviewed his time line. He added a detail that seemed important and crossed out one detail that did not seem important. The time line he made is below.

Your Turn

Make a time line to organize your notes. What happened first? What happened next? How did the experience end? Put your notes in order on the time line.

Read your time line. Can you think of any important details you forgot? Are there any details that are not related to your topic? Revise your time line if necessary.

10:00 — went to garden center
picked out birdbath,
two bird feeders
looked at plants, flowers.

12:00 — put birdbath under tree
put bird feeders in tree
filled birdbath with water

added seeds, nuts, frute

~~ate peanut butter~~
~~sandwiches for lunch~~

2:00 — birds came to eat and drink

Drafting

Andy was ready to write the first draft of his narrative. He used his time line to guide his writing. As he wrote, he thought of more details to add. He used time words to help his readers understand his narrative. Here is Andy's draft.

My Bird Sanctuary

This sumer my mom and I made a bird sanctuary in our backyard. First we went to the garden center. We picked out a nice birdbath. We bought two bird feeders too. We looked at a lot of plants and flowers, but we didn't buy any.

When we got home, we put the birdbath under a tree by the hedge the birds can hide in the hedge. Next I put the bird feeders in the tree. I put seeds, nuts, and frute in the feeders. Then my mom got the hose and filled the birdbath with water. The sanctuary was ready

Later that afternoon my mom called me to the window. There were birds eating at the feeders. A bluebird was taking a drink from the birdbath. I was happy that w'ed made the sanctuary. The birds seemed happy too.

Your Turn

Look over your notes and your time line. Then begin writing your draft. Double-space so you will have room to edit and make changes later.

Write an introduction that grabs your reader's attention. In the body give details in time order about what happened. Write a conclusion that tells what you learned from your experience or how you felt about it.

As you write, add details to make your narrative more interesting. Do not include any details that do not relate to your topic.

Writing a Title

Have you ever read a book or an article because the title caught your attention? A good title catches a reader's attention and gives a hint about the topic.

A good title should be short but interesting. Use strong and colorful words that make a reader want to know more. Try using words that start with the same sound to give your title a punch. For example, "Bobby's Birthday Blast" sounds better than "Bobby's Party."

Personal Narratives

Content Editing

Andy enjoyed writing his first draft, but he knew he could make it better. First, he checked the ideas and details in his draft by content editing.

Content editors read a draft to make sure that all the important ideas are included. They also make sure there are no unnecessary details. Andy made his corrections with a red pencil so that the changes would be easy to see.

After looking over his draft, Andy asked his friend Karla to read it. Because Karla had not heard about his bird sanctuary, she would notice if any important details were missing. Karla used this Content Editor's Checklist to help her.

Content Editor's Checklist

✓ Does the introduction grab the reader's attention?

✓ Are the details told clearly and in time order?

✓ Are all the important details included in the body?

✓ Have unnecessary details been left out?

✓ Does the conclusion tell what the writer learned or how the writer felt?

Karla read the draft once all the way through. Then she read it more carefully, checking each item on the checklist. She read the introduction to see if it grabbed the reader's attention. As she read the body, she looked for details that were unnecessary or out of order. She checked the conclusion to see if it was effective. Karla shared her suggestions with Andy.

Karla first told Andy what she liked about his personal narrative. She found the topic very interesting. She liked the conclusion and found that all the details were in time order. Then she gave Andy these suggestions.

- The introduction tells what your topic is, but it didn't really grab my attention.

- I don't think you need to tell that you didn't buy any plants or flowers.

- Maybe you could tell why you put different kinds of food in the bird feeders. I thought all birds eat seeds or insects.

- It might be interesting to know what kind of tree you put the bird feeders in.

Andy thanked Karla for her suggestions. He liked most of them and knew that he would use her ideas when he revised his draft.

Your Turn

Read your draft, looking carefully at the Content Editor's Checklist. Write your ideas on your draft. Then work with a partner and read each other's narratives. Check one item from the checklist at a time. Take notes on a separate sheet of paper. Then meet with your partner and respectfully make suggestions for improvement. Remember to share what you like about your partner's work.

After hearing your partner's suggestions, decide which ones you want to use in your revision.

Personal Narratives

Revising

This is how Andy used Karla's suggestions and his own ideas to revise his narrative.

Backyard
My ∧ Bird Sanctuary

Watching birds in the wild can be fun, but why not make the birds come to you?
∧This sumer my mom and I made a bird sanctuary in our backyard. First we went to the garden center. We picked out a nice birdbath. We bought two bird feeders too. ~~We looked at a lot of plants and flowers, but we didn't buy any.~~

When we got home, we put the birdbath under a tree
from other animals
by the hedge the birds can hide ∧ in the hedge. Next I
Different kinds of birds eat different kinds of food, so
put the bird feeders in the tree. ∧ I put seeds, nuts, and
frute in the feeders. Then my mom got the hose and filled the birdbath with water. The sanctuary was ready

Later that afternoon my mom called me to the
some chickadees and a cardinal
window. There were ∧ ~~birds~~ eating at the feeders. A bluebird was taking a drink from the birdbath. I was happy that w'ed made the sanctuary. The birds seemed happy too.

Look at what Andy did to improve his personal narrative.

- He took Karla's suggestion about his introduction. He thought his classmates would want to read about how they could attract birds to their yards.

- He also decided to take out the sentence about the plants and flowers because it wasn't necessary in his narrative.

- He added some information about why he put out different kinds of food.

- Andy didn't think that telling the kind of tree was important. Instead, he decided to name the kinds of birds he saw on the feeders.

Andy looked over his draft again. He decided to add the phrase *from other animals* to explain why the birds would want to hide.

The last thing Andy did was to improve his title. He thought the two *b* sounds gave it a real punch.

Your Turn

Use your partner's suggestions and your own ideas to revise your narrative. When you have finished, go over the Content Editor's Checklist again. Be sure you can answer yes to all the questions.

Personal Narratives

Copyediting and Proofreading

Copyediting

When you copyedit, you check every sentence to make sure it is clear and makes sense. Copyeditors also check that all the words have been used correctly.

Andy knew that his revisions had improved his writing. His new introduction would interest readers, and the body included all the important details. He knew, however, that he could make his draft better by copyediting.

As Andy copyedited his draft, he used this Copyeditor's Checklist.

Copyeditor's Checklist

✓ Are all the sentences complete sentences?

✓ Are there any run-on sentences?

✓ Have exact words been used to paint a picture in the reader's mind?

✓ Are time words used to show time order?

✓ Have any words been repeated too often?

Andy found some changes he wanted to make. He noticed that he had used the word *nice* to describe the birdbath. He decided to use colorful adjectives to help the reader picture the birdbath. He also noticed that he had used the verb *put* three times in the second paragraph. He changed one of them to *hung*, which was a stronger verb.

Andy also noticed that he had written two sentences as one sentence. Can you find his run-on sentence?

Your Turn

Read your personal narrative again and copyedit it, using the Copyeditor's Checklist. Be sure you have used complete sentences and avoided run-on sentences. Check that you used words that help your reader understand your narrative and picture the events.

Proofreading

After copyediting, Andy asked his classmate Tom to proofread his draft. Proofreading is checking a draft for mistakes in grammar, spelling, or punctuation. Writers always ask someone else to proofread their work.

Tom used this Proofreader's Checklist as he read Andy's draft.

Proofreader's Checklist

✓ Are the paragraphs indented?

✓ Have any words been misspelled?

✓ Is the grammar correct?

✓ Are capitalization and punctuation correct?

✓ Were any new mistakes added during editing?

Tom was happy to proofread Andy's narrative. He realized the words *summer* and *fruit* were misspelled. He also found a missing period and a misplaced apostrophe. Can you find them?

Your Turn

Read your draft carefully, using the Proofreader's Checklist. First look to make sure all the paragraphs are indented. Next look for misspelled words. Continue question by question through the list. Use proofreading marks to make changes.

When you have finished proofreading your own narrative, trade papers with a partner. Go over your partner's paper in the same way.

Proofreading Marks		
Symbol	**Meaning**	**Example**
¶	begin new paragraph	over.¶Begin a new
◯	close up space	close u͜p space
∧	insert	students ∧ think *(should)*
℈	delete, omit	that the ~~the~~ book
/	lowercase letter	M̸athematics
∩	letters are reversed	letters are reve(sr)ed
≡	capitalize	w̲ashington
⌄⌄	quotation marks	⌄I am⌄ I said

Personal Narratives

Publishing

Andy was almost ready to share his personal narrative with his audience. He checked it over once more before typing it into a computer. He put the title in the top center of the paper with his name below it. After printing out his personal narrative, he posted it on a bulletin board for his classmates to read.

My Backyard Bird Sanctuary

By Andy Hawkins

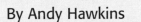

Watching birds in the wild can be fun, but why not make the birds come to you? This summer my mom and I made a bird sanctuary in our backyard. First we went to the garden center. We picked out a shallow stone birdbath. We bought two bird feeders too.

When we got home, we put the birdbath under a tree by the hedge. The birds can hide from other animals in the hedge. Next I hung the bird feeders in the tree. Different kinds of birds eat different kinds of food, so I put seeds, nuts, and fruit in the feeders. Then my mom got the hose and filled the birdbath with water. The sanctuary was ready.

Later that afternoon my mom called me to the window. There were some chickadees and a cardinal eating at the feeders. A bluebird was taking a drink from the birdbath. I was happy that we'd made the sanctuary. The birds seemed happy too.

Your Turn

Publishing is your chance to share your personal narrative with your audience. You can share your personal narrative with your classmates, friends, and family.

To publish your personal narrative, print it on a computer or write it neatly on a sheet of paper. Place the title in the top center of the paper and put your name under the title. Then check over your personal narrative one final time. Make sure that all your mistakes have been corrected and that no new mistakes have been made.

Along with your teacher and classmates, decide how to share your personal narratives. One way would be to post them on a bulletin board for everyone to read. You might include a drawing or photograph to post beside your narrative. Visuals like these will draw readers into the narratives and help them picture in their minds what happened.

Reading your classmates' personal narratives may teach you some surprising things about your classmates. And when your classmates read your personal narrative, they may learn something surprising about you!

CHAPTER 2

In 1845 Texas became the 28th state of the United States. It had once been part of Mexico and had even been an independent country before being annexed. Today Texas is the second largest and second most-populous state in the country. Its nickname is the Lone Star State, and its capital city is Austin. What are some things you know about Texas?

Formal Letters

4325 West Pine View Street
Danville, IA 50012

May 14, 20–

Thomas Meloni
Director of Fan Relations
Danville Dandies
1404 Stadium Road
Danville, IA 50012

Dear Mr. Meloni:

August 3 is my birthday. My father has promised to take me to the Dandies game for my birthday present. Would it be possible for me to be your guest batboy on August 3?

I have been a Dandies fan since I was very young. I go to at least 10 home games every season. I can name all the players on last year's team, and I know the batting averages of most of them. My friends are all Dandies fans too, but I am the biggest one.

I know what the batboy's duties are because of all the games I have seen. It would be a dream come true if I could sit in the dugout with the players.

Thank you for reading my letter.

Sincerely,

Hector Garcia

Hector Garcia

What Makes a Good Formal Letter?

Formal letters are used when companies or people write about business matters. Formal letters present information in a specific way. In formal letters all writing starts at the left side of the page. Here are the parts of a formal letter.

The **heading** is your address with the date below it. The heading goes at the top left corner of the letter.

The **inside address** shows the name of the person receiving the letter and that person's job title. The inside address also shows the name and address of the company that the person works for.

The **greeting** is next. It should begin with *Dear* followed by the person's name. If you don't know the person's name, the greeting should be *Dear Sir or Madam*. All greetings should end with a colon (:).

The **body** is the main part of the letter. It explains your reason for writing.

The **closing** of a formal letter should be short and polite. You can use *Sincerely* or *Respectfully*. The closing ends with a comma. If you are typing, skip several lines and type in your name.

Always sign your name after the closing. If you type your letter, add your **signature** between the closing and your typed name. Include both your first and last names.

4325 West Pine View Street
Danville, IA 50012

May 14, 20–

Thomas Meloni
Director of Fan Relations
Danville Dandies
1404 Stadium Road
Danville, IA 50012

Dear Mr. Meloni:

August 3 is my birthday. My father has promised to take me to the Dandies game for my birthday present. Would it be possible for me to be your guest batboy on August 3?

I have been a Dandies fan since I was very young. I go to at least 10 home games every season. I can name all the players on last year's team, and I know the batting averages of most of them. My friends are all Dandies fans too, but I am the biggest one.

I know what the batboy's duties are because of all the games I have seen. It would be a dream come true if I could sit in the dugout with the players.

Thank you for reading my letter.

Sincerely,
Hector Garcia
Hector Garcia

The Body

The body is the main part of the letter. First you should explain your problem or situation. Next you should ask the reader to help you. Explain what you would like the company or organization to do. Finally you should thank the reader for his or her help.

Activity A

Arrange each list in the proper order for the heading of a formal letter.

1. St. Louis, MO 63139; 275 E. King Street; May 10, 20–

2. June 7, 2004; 1830 Birch Road; Akron, OH 45210

3. 8122 Copper Street; Calumet, MI; 49913; July 2, 20–

4. your own address, today's date

Activity B

Rewrite each greeting using correct capitalization and punctuation.

1. Dear sir or madam:

2. Dear Ms Guzman;

3. dear dr Thomas—

4. Dear mr. hughes,

Writer's Corner

Write parts of a formal letter from your school to your family, leaving the body blank. Use your school's address and today's date for the heading. Write your own address as the inside address. Write the name of a family member in the greeting. Sign your own name in the closing.

Using Formal English

In a formal letter, it is important that the reader understand exactly what the writer needs. That is why formal letters use language that is understood by most people. American businesses use formal English when they communicate in writing.

Formal English is polite. It uses proper grammar and correct spelling. It also uses words that most people know. If you aren't sure about a word, check a dictionary. If the word isn't in the dictionary or if it is labeled *slang*, don't use it in a formal letter. You should avoid contractions such as *I'm*, *I'll*, *you're*, or *you've*.

Activity C

The following sentence pairs should not be in formal letters. Some are impolite, and some are not in formal language. Rewrite the sentences so that they can be used in formal letters.

1. Your kids' museum is wicked good! Do you give tours to fourth-grade classes?

2. The dumb directions are impossible to follow. It took me forever to figure them out.

3. Me and my buddies shop at your store a lot. You need to start selling Thor basketball shoes.

4. I want my money back. Your ad didn't say the model plane was made out of crummy cardboard.

5. I'm writing a report on the Alamo. Send me all the free stuff you have about that battle.

Our Wide Wide World

Before Europeans began settling in Texas, one of the largest Native-American groups was the Caddo. The Caddo were farmers who lived in eastern Texas. They grew corn, beans, and squash. They are well-known for the large, cone-shaped, grass huts in which they lived. They are also noted for their beautiful ceramic pottery. The name *Texas* comes from a Caddo word meaning "friends."

Caddo Lake

The formal letter below is filled with mistakes. There is a mistake in the heading, the inside address, the greeting, and the closing. See if you can find them all. Then read the body. Find two sentences that do not use formal English.

2404 Oak Terrace
Roman, OK 73013

Juan Marquez
Ardmore Eraser Company
2500 Francis St.
Ardmore, OK 73050

Dear Mr. Marquez,

I am writing to request new erasers for our class. The erasers we bought are totally bad. They leave black marks on the paper when we try to erase.

Our class bought 30 erasers from your store. Can't you send us some new erasers or something? If not, please refund us the $14 we spent on the erasers.

Thank you for your help.

Sincerely
Melanie McLaughlin
Melanie McLaughlin

Writer's Corner

Write the body of a short formal letter to your teacher. You might ask for something special for you or your class, such as less homework or a new desk. Use formal English.

Types of Formal Letters

There are two main types of formal letters that you might write. You might write to a company to complain about a product, or you might write to an organization to request information. Both types of formal letters follow the rules that you learned in Lesson 1.

Letters of Complaint

You might write a letter of complaint to a company because a product that you purchased from them does not work or is incomplete. In the body of your letter, first state what the problem is. Then explain how you would like the company to solve the problem.

Remember that this is a formal letter. You should use polite language, even if you are unhappy with the company. Successful businesses usually try to keep their customers happy and will work to solve your problem.

Activity A

Read the name of each product. What kind of problem might you have with that product? Tell why you might write a formal letter about each one.

1. box of cereal

2. CD player with headphones

3. football cleats

4. cell phone

5. backpack with several pockets and zippers

Activity B

The greeting and body on the right are from a letter of complaint. The writer has used language that will not make the business eager to help. Rewrite the letter using formal language.

Hey:

What kind of cheesy operation are you running? On November 29 I placed an order at your shop for *The Hawk that Dared Not Fly by Day* by Scott O'Dell. The clerk promised it would be sent to me within 10 days, but I haven't received it yet. I'm really getting ticked off.

I want to give this book as a holiday gift. I was hoping for this Christmas, not next Christmas. You better call me as soon as possible to tell me when I'll get my book. My phone number is 606-555-6342.

A really mad customer,

Hannibal Jones

Writer's Corner

Think of a product that didn't work as you expected it would. Write answers to these questions: *What is the product? What is the problem? To whom can you write to solve the problem? If you don't know, how can you find out?*

Letters of Request

You may sometimes need information for a school project or for a family vacation. Often you can find what you need on the Internet. If you can't find exactly what you need there, you may have to write to someone who can give you more personal help. Government agencies or other organizations supply this type of information for free. You could write one of them a letter of request.

As in all formal letters, first state the reason that you are writing. Then tell how you would like the agency or organization to help you. Keep your letter short and polite.

• Activity C •

Choose two of the following situations. Write the body of a formal letter for each product or service needed. Explain clearly and formally what you would like. Be sure to thank the person for helping you.

A. Your family will be driving across South Dakota. You would like information about Custer State Park.

B. Your school chorus wants to have T-shirts made. You would like to know the price for printing 35 T-shirts.

C. Your school band wants to travel to a concert in a nearby town. You would like to know how much it costs to charter a bus and how many passengers each bus holds.

D. Your favorite toothpaste is offering a free book of knock-knock jokes. You must send in four proof-of-purchase seals and a stamped, self-addressed envelope.

Activity D

Some of the following sentences are from letters of complaint. Some are from letters of request. Read each sentence and decide which is which.

1. Please send me a copy of the latest Tangerine Man comic book.
2. The problem is that the wheels of the skateboard are lopsided.
3. I hope you will find the time to send me an autographed picture.
4. I found that the model airplane did not come with directions for putting it together.
5. Do you want to meet me at my house for a video game marathon?
6. I would be grateful if you would send me some information about places to stay near Mount Washington.

Activity E

This is a writer's first draft of a letter of request. The language is too informal. Rewrite the letter to make the language formal and polite.

Hi. How are you? My soccer team will be visiting Prairie City next week. Any chance we can take a tour of your dairy? There will be about 25 of us. Thanks.

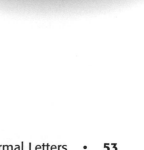

Writer's Corner

Think about the product you wrote about in the Writer's Corner on page 51. Write the beginning of the body of a letter of complaint. Clearly and politely explain the problem.

Compound Sentences

To many, Stephen F. Austin is considered to be the "Father of Texas." He was the leader of the first American colonists to inhabit Texas. Austin met with the Spanish governor, Antonio María Martinez, and obtained his permission to settle in the area. In 1823 approximately 300 families and business partners followed Austin and developed a rich colony along the Brazos River. Those early inhabitants are remembered today as the "Old Three Hundred."

Some writers use too many short sentences in their writing. Writing is more interesting when the sentence lengths are varied. Often two short sentences with related ideas can be combined, or joined, to make a longer sentence. The longer sentence is called a compound sentence. The short sentences can be combined by using a comma and a conjunction such as *and*, *but*, or *or*.

Here are some sentence pairs that have been combined to make compound sentences. Notice how the compound sentences are more interesting and less "choppy."

One leg is missing. The top is scratched.
One leg is missing, and the top is scratched.

I changed the batteries. It still doesn't work.
I changed the batteries, but it still doesn't work.

We can go Tuesday. Friday is OK if that's better for you.
We can go Tuesday, or Friday is OK if that's better for you.

Where are we going? How do we get there?
Where are we going, and how do we get there?

Should we wait until the movie ends? Would you rather go now?
Should we wait until the movie ends, or would you rather go now?

Activity A •

Write each compound sentence with correct punctuation.

1. I read all the instructions but I still have a few questions.

2. You can mail the tickets to us or we can pick them up at the box office.

3. I enjoy reading your magazine and I would like to order a subscription.

4. We would like to take the tour but we won't arrive until the afternoon.

5. We will be there for five days and we would like some information on nearby parks.

Activity B •

Combine each pair of sentences to form a compound sentence. Use the conjunction in parentheses.

1. The basket is new. The handle broke off. (but)

2. I will send it back. You can pick it up. (or)

3. The bottle is closed. The liquid leaks out. (but)

4. The plastic is cracked. The color is faded. (and)

5. My mom called. My dad sent a fax. (and)

6. I've called for help. I only get a busy signal. (but)

7. The switch is on. The toy will not start. (but)

8. You can fix it. You can send me a new one. (or)

9. I wanted to buy your game. The store had run out. (but)

10. You can send me a new copy. You can refund my money. (or)

Writer's Corner

Write two compound sentences for each of the conjunctions *and*, *or*, and *but*.

Choosing the Correct Conjunction

You can combine sentences only when they are about related ideas. There are different ways that ideas can be related. You need to use the conjunction that shows how the ideas are related.

Study this chart to know when to use *and*, *but*, and *or*.

and	connects ideas that are alike in some way Carla can swim, **and** she can ride a bike.
but	connects ideas that are different Tomas can swim, **but** he can't ride a bike.
or	connects ideas that give a choice Later I can swim, **or** I can ride my bike.

Activity C

Combine the first part of a compound sentence in Column 1 with the correct second part in Column 2. Write the sentences using the correct conjunctions.

Column 1

1. Dad must use sunscreen,
2. Jeb has a fever,
3. Todd took the bus,
4. We were going to play tennis,
5. Fido slipped out of his collar,
6. The baby must have his blanket,

Column 2

a. he still went to school.
b. he met us at the museum.
c. it started to rain.
d. he will get burned.
e. he will start to cry.
f. it took an hour to catch him.

Activity D

There is a conjunction missing in each of these sentences. Tell the best conjunction that could complete each sentence.

1. You can call me, _____ you can send me an e-mail instead.
2. I like the jacket, _____ the buttons are too large.
3. The lamp works, _____ the bulb is burned out.
4. The pearls are real, _____ they are expensive.
5. We can go there by car, _____ we can take a bus.

Activity E

Write each pair of sentences as a compound sentence.

1. The backpack is new. The zipper ripped out.
2. The bag is closed. The pieces fall out anyway.
3. The clock is slow. The alarm doesn't work.
4. The chain fell off. The paint is scratched.
5. We can eat our big meal now. We can have it tonight.
6. Come visit us anytime. Be sure to call first.
7. I like to garden. I have never grown squash before.
8. Would you like some tea? Would you like coffee instead?
9. I have a new puppy. I need information on caring for her.
10. We can sleep in a cabin. We can stay at the lodge.

Writer's Corner

Work with a partner. Choose a topic. Each of you write three sentences about the topic. Each sentence should have five words or fewer. Then trade papers and add a second idea to each of your partner's sentences to make it a compound sentence.

Mailing a Formal Letter

State Abbreviations

Alabama	AL
Alaska	AK
Arizona	AZ
Arkansas	AR
California	CA
Colorado	CO
Connecticut	CT
Delaware	DE
District of Columbia	DC
Florida	FL
Georgia	GA
Hawaii	HI
Idaho	ID
Illinois	IL
Indiana	IN
Iowa	IA
Kansas	KS
Kentucky	KY
Louisiana	LA
Maine	ME
Maryland	MD
Massachusetts	MA
Michigan	MI
Minnesota	MN
Mississippi	MS
Missouri	MO
Montana	MT
Nebraska	NE
Nevada	NV
New Hampshire	NH
New Jersey	NJ
New Mexico	NM
New York	NY
North Carolina	NC
North Dakota	ND
Ohio	OH
Oklahoma	OK
Oregon	OR
Pennsylvania	PA
Rhode Island	RI
South Carolina	SC
South Dakota	SD
Tennessee	TN
Texas	TX
Utah	UT
Vermont	VT
Virginia	VA
Washington	WA
West Virginia	WV
Wisconsin	WI
Wyoming	WY

Addressing the Envelope

When you have finished writing your letter, you want to be sure it gets to the right person. It is important to address the envelope correctly. Look at the following envelope.

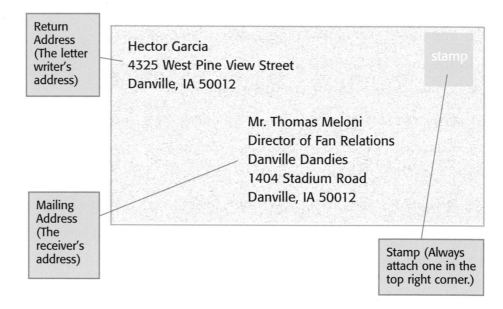

Return Address (The letter writer's address)

Hector Garcia
4325 West Pine View Street
Danville, IA 50012

stamp

Mr. Thomas Meloni
Director of Fan Relations
Danville Dandies
1404 Stadium Road
Danville, IA 50012

Mailing Address (The receiver's address)

Stamp (Always attach one in the top right corner.)

Your return address goes on the top left corner of the envelope. Write your name, street address, city, state, and zip code. If the letter cannot be delivered, the Postal Service will know where to return it.

In the middle of the envelope, write the name and the address of the person receiving the letter. This is the mailing address. Copy this information from the inside address on your letter, using the same capitalization and punctuation.

State Abbreviations

The United States Postal Service has assigned abbreviations to the names of the states. The abbreviations are listed on page 58. Use them to help the Postal Service deliver your mail.

Activity A

Put the following return addresses in the correct order. Write them as they should be written on envelopes.

1. Juliet F. Jefferson; Honolulu, HI 96800; 724 Palm Street

2. Keokuk, IA 52632; Charles Singh; 14 Front Street

3. 314A Gross Point Road; Anne Gray; Big Bar, ID 83678

Activity B

Put the following mailing addresses in the correct order. Write them as they should be written on envelopes.

1. Director of Customer Service; Mr. Khalid Azarra; Skaters' World; 664 Hampton Road; St. Louis, MO 63197

2. Ms. Hannah Morgan; President; 67 Natchez Boulevard; Loopy Toy Company; Los Angeles, CA 90048

3. Mr. John Cicero; Lagrange, IL 60525; Cicero Canoes; Manager of Customer Relations; 12 Lake Street

Writer's Corner

Draw an envelope on a sheet of paper. Address the envelope to your school principal. Add your return address and draw a stamp in the correct corner.

Folding Your Letter

There is a correct way to fold a formal letter. First, fold the bottom third of the paper a little more than half of the way up. Then fold the top third down. Be sure to keep the left and right edges even. Then place the letter into the envelope with the last fold on the top.

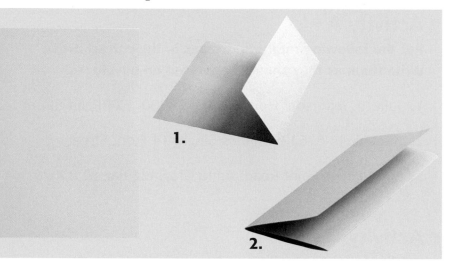

● Activity C ●

Use the list of state abbreviations on page 58. Write the state or district that each of the following abbreviations stands for.

1. ND	12. GA	23. CO	34. CT	45. KS
2. FL	13. TX	24. KY	35. IA	46. PA
3. MO	14. WV	25. HI	36. OR	47. WY
4. LA	15. AK	26. AZ	37. MN	48. ID
5. IL	16. CA	27. IN	38. NH	49. VA
6. SC	17. MI	28. WI	39. AL	50. NE
7. AR	18. WA	29. DE	40. NM	51. DC
8. OK	19. NJ	30. UT	41. OH	
9. NV	20. VT	31. MS	42. MT	
10. TN	21. ME	32. MD	43. MA	
11. NY	22. RI	33. SD	44. NC	

Activity D

The information in each of these addresses is not in the correct order. Draw envelopes on a sheet of paper. Address the envelopes correctly. Design and draw your own stamps.

Return Address	Mailing Address
1. 501 Adams Avenue Kelly Schmidt New Orleans, LA 70101	672 South High Street Advertising Director Mrs. Ann Saldo Happy Toy Company Arlington, VA 22213
2. Chicago, IL 60657 Pat Parker 656 West George Street	P.O. Box 6789 Ms. Jean Jaklin Portland, OR 97228 Vice President Skateboards Plus
3. Frank Martineau Edison NJ 08816 342 Lincoln Lane	Business Manager Krafts for Kids Reston, VA 20190 Mr. Carlos Suarez 1150 Briar Square

Writer's Corner

Look at the Writer's Corner on page 51. Write the address for the company in the form you would write it on an envelope.

Word Study

Antonyms

Antonyms are pairs of words that have opposite meanings. Here are some antonyms.

wide/narrow	thick/thin	fixed/broken
poor/rich	yes/no	better/worse
fast/slow	true/false	tidy/messy

You might use antonyms when you write a letter of complaint. Antonyms can describe what is wrong with a product. They can also describe how you want the problem to be solved. Here are some examples.

The coat looks <u>thick</u> in your ads, but it's really very <u>thin</u>.

The toy arrived <u>broken</u>, and I'd like to have it <u>fixed</u>.

I thought the roses would be <u>real</u>, but they were <u>artificial</u>.

Activity A

Read each word. Give an antonym for it.

tight	sharp	happy	kind
strong	warm	sweet	over
high	open	dry	little
off	wrong	loud	bent

Activity B

Match each word in Column A with its antonym in Column B. Use a dictionary if you need help.

Column A	Column B
1. large	a. common
2. high	b. asleep
3. right	c. young
4. old	d. easy
5. awake	e. dim
6. rare	f. take
7. difficult	g. low
8. bright	h. idle
9. busy	i. small
10. give	j. left

Activity C

Write *yes* if the underlined words in each item are antonyms. Write *no* if they are not.

1. The <u>hilly</u> road became <u>flat</u> when we got to the desert.

2. We left a <u>neat</u> cabin, and it was <u>clean</u> when we got back.

3. A <u>fast</u> car is no help when traffic is <u>slow</u>.

4. I thought the leather would be <u>real</u>, but it is <u>fake</u>.

5. The opening is too <u>wide</u> and <u>long</u>.

Writer's Corner

Choose three pairs of antonyms from page 62. Write a short letter to a friend, using each pair of antonyms.

• Activity D •

Choose an antonym for the underlined word from the words in parentheses.

1. The <u>rich</u> man could not afford a ticket. (poor/happy/honest)
2. My shirt is too <u>big</u>. (wrinkled/dirty/small)
3. Eddie spilled juice on the <u>old</u> rug. (green/new/tattered)
4. The clay is not supposed to <u>soften</u> so quickly. (grow/break/harden)
5. The lid will not <u>shut</u>. (open/bend/twirl)
6. Let the soup <u>heat</u> for five minutes. (burn/cool/cook)
7. I thought the bat would be <u>heavier</u>. (lighter/smaller/bigger)
8. Jenny <u>lost</u> her book in the park. (read/bought/found)
9. The crowd cheered when the shortstop <u>dropped</u> the ball. (caught/threw/held)
10. The <u>gentle</u> rain cooled down the runners. (icy/hard/blowing)

• Activity E •

Finish each compound sentence. Use an antonym for the underlined word.

1. Backpacks are supposed to be <u>light</u>, but _____.
2. The ad showed a shirt with <u>long</u> sleeves, but _____.
3. I thought the model car would be <u>fast</u>, but _____.
4. I need a <u>bright</u> flashlight for camping, but _____.
5. Ed asked for a <u>sweet</u> drink, but _____.

Activity F

Use an antonym in place of each underlined word. Write the new sentence.

1. The alarm is too <u>quiet</u>.

2. When I returned it, you said I was too <u>early</u>.

3. The left wheel is <u>crooked</u>.

4. The manager was <u>polite</u>.

5. This is the <u>best</u> pudding I ever had.

Activity G

Some words have more than one antonym. Choose the best antonym for the underlined word to complete each sentence.

1. The lever is <u>hard</u> to pull, and we asked for one that is (soft/easy/simple).

2. Dad can eat only <u>mild</u> foods, but the pizza was (strong/sharp/spicy).

3. I need <u>strong</u> tent poles, but these (weak/feeble/sick) poles bent the first time I used them.

4. The bag of markers was <u>full</u>, but the box for the cards was (vacant/blank/empty).

5. Our dancers ordered <u>long</u> skirts, but you sent (short/wide/brief) ones.

Writer's Corner

Write a sentence for each of three different letters of complaint. Use a pair of antonyms in each one.

Oral Complaints and Conflicts

Everyone gets angry once in awhile. Sometimes we get hurt feelings or have a reason to complain. Yet, if you have heard friends disagree, you probably know that talking about complaints and conflicts is difficult. Here are some ways to resolve conflicts by talking things over.

Cool Off

Take a deep breath. Before you try to talk about a conflict, take some time to clear your head. Think about what happened and why it happened. Take a walk around the block. Let your feelings quiet down. You'll be glad you did.

Use Ground Rules

Ask a grown-up to help you both come up with rules that you can follow to keep your conversation positive. Here are some rules that work pretty well.

- Be respectful.
- Wait your turn to speak.
- Work together for a fair solution.
- Tell the truth.

Remember, both people in a conflict think that they are right. Try to be polite to the other person.

Win/Win Guidelines

How do you talk with a person about a problem? Try these guidelines.

Use "I Messages."

If you were mad your younger brother lost your basketball, you might say "I am angry that my brother lost my ball. I wish he'd have asked me if he could borrow it first."

Try to see the other person's point of view.

Put yourself in the other person's shoes. You might say "I guess I never let you borrow anything, and you did need a ball to try out for the team."

Know you were part of the problem.

Knowing how you were part of the problem might help you understand how the problem started and how another problem might be avoided in the future.

Activity A

Choose a side for each conflict and write an "I Message."

1. Robert drops his pencil during a test. Simon picks it up and starts using it because his own pencil is broken.

2. Chad has his science project on his desk. Kate accidentally knocks it over with her backpack.

3. After music class, Allison teases Earl about his singing.

4. Jo forgets to ask Jenny to come to her birthday pool party.

Speaker's Corner

State the problems in Activity A as they might be seen from the opposite point of view. Then tell a story about each conflict. Tell both sides of the story.

Coming to a Solution

Now that you're talking, you can talk about a solution, or compromise, that works for both of you. In the case of the lost basketball, the younger brother might agree to save up to buy his older brother a new basketball. The older brother might agree to let his younger brother borrow the basketball in the future as long as he asks first.

Tips for a Resolver

On a different day you might become part of a conflict and not even be involved in the problem. Two friends might ask you to help them solve a conflict that they are having. Or you might be asked to be on a conflict resolution team. Here are some tips to help you:

- Pay attention to both people.
- Be sure you understand the problem.
- Focus on the problem and don't get off the subject. Don't talk about other problems these people might have had in the past.
- Be fair. Don't take sides.
- Speak calmly and politely.
- Work toward a solution.

If a problem is too big for you to help resolve, make sure you ask for help from a teacher or another adult.

Activity B

Pretend that you are either Simon, Kate, Allison, or Jo in each of the situations in Activity A. Write how you might be responsible for the problem. Then meet with a partner and practice saying how you are responsible for the problem.

Activity C

Read this story written from Xander's point of view. Pretend that you are Xander and follow the Win/Win Guidelines. Write "I Messages," how you think Xavier sees the problem, and how you think you might be part of the problem.

My best friend Xavier won a chance to meet our favorite snowboarder after his Saturday competition. Xavier was allowed to bring a guest, and he asked me to come along. I said yes and I told my indoor soccer coach that I would not be able to play in the game on Saturday. Then on Saturday morning Xavier told me that his parents wanted him to take his sister Francesca instead. I didn't get to meet the snowboarder. Even worse, I was not allowed to start in the soccer game because my coach had told another player that he could start in my place. I am mad at Xavier, and I haven't talked to him for three days.

Speaker's Corner

Plan a conflict-resolution skit with two other students. Come up with a nonviolent problem that two students might have with each other. Plan and practice a presentation that includes the Win/Win Guidelines and a solution based on compromise. Then present it to your classmates.

Formal Letters

Prewriting and Drafting

When you buy a product, you expect it to work. If it doesn't, you should tell the company that made it or sold it to you. Then the company can fix the problem. A good way to tell the company is in a formal letter of complaint.

Prewriting

Before writing a formal letter, a writer spends time prewriting to gather ideas. The prewriting steps include choosing a topic and planning the letter.

Choosing a Topic

Jocelyn is a fourth-grade student who was asked to write a letter of complaint for a class assignment. She began by making a list of things she had bought or received recently. Then she listed any problems she had found with them.

Jocelyn had bought a camera that didn't take very good pictures in the dark. She had also received some socks that had worn out quickly. Then she thought of an I Go Bingo game she had bought while visiting cousins in New Jersey. When she opened it,

she saw that the game was missing its playing cards. She decided to write a letter to the Timely Toy Company.

Your Turn

Make a list of things you have bought or received recently. Try to think of things that had problems with them. Make a T-chart to organize your list. Begin by drawing a large T on a sheet of paper. List the products down the left side of the chart. List the problems on the right side. When your chart is complete, circle one that you'd like to write about.

If none of the things you listed had any problems, imagine a problem that one of them might have had. Use this idea to start your letter of complaint.

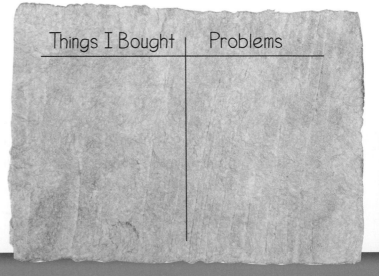

Things I Bought | Problems

Planning the Letter

After choosing her topic, Jocelyn began planning her letter. She started by writing down the address of the Timely Toy Company from the game box. She wasn't sure to whom she should send her letter, so she decided to address it to the Customer Service Department. This is the address Jocelyn wrote down.

Customer Service Department
Timely Toy Company
99 Highpoint circle
Cypress, PA 90630

Next, Jocelyn wrote her writing plan. She knew her letter would have three sections: a beginning, a middle, and an ending. She wrote ideas for each section in her plan.

For the beginning, she took notes about the problem or situation. For the middle she explained how she wanted the company to fix the problem. For the ending she thanked the company for its help. Here is Jocelyn's writing plan.

<u>Beginning</u>
Problem: bought I Go Bingo while visiting cousins in New Jersey. Game was missing deck of cards. Can't take it back to store.

<u>Middle</u>
Suggestions for Fixing Problem: send deck of cards or refund money to buy a new game

<u>Ending</u>
Thank you for your help.

Your Turn

Write an address for your letter. Look for it in the package or instructions for the product. If you do not find it, you might search the Internet for the address. If you cannot find the company's address, use your school's address and use your teacher's name.

Next, make a writing plan for your letter. For the beginning, write ideas describing the situation or problem. For the middle, write suggestions for fixing the problem. For the ending, write what you will say to thank the company for its help.

Drafting

Jocelyn wrote her letter to the customer service department of a big toy company. It was a formal letter, so she used formal language.

She wrote a first draft, using her writing plan as she worked. She double-spaced lines to leave room for changes and corrections when she revised her writing.

October 5, 20–

Customer Service Department

Timely Toy Company

99 Highpoint circle

Cypress, CA 90630

Dear Sir or Madam:

I was visiting my cousins in New Jersey. We played your I Go Bingo game.

I liked it so much that we went to Max's Toy City in the Century Mall, and

I baught my own I Go Bingo. When I got back home to Cincinnati, I opened

the box the deck of cards was missing.

I can't play I Go Bingo without the cards. I'm writing to ask that you either

send me the cards or refund my money so I can buy I Go Bingo at another

store. I cannot take the game back to the store where I got it. It is in New

Jersey and I live in Ohio.

Please respond as soon as you can so I can begin to enjoy your teriffic

game. Thank you for your help.

Sincerely

Jocelyn Morrissey

Your Turn

Look at your writing plan and write your first draft. Keep in mind that you will probably rewrite your letter several times. Double-space lines so you will have room to make changes later on.

Keep your audience in mind as you write. Be sure your writing is clear and to the point. Include details that the person needs to know.

Remember that the beginning of your letter should state the situation and the problem. The middle should tell how you want the problem solved. The ending should thank the person for taking the time to help you.

Using Details to Make Your Message Clear

When you write a letter of complaint, it is important to be brief. Do not add unnecessary details, but do not leave out important details. Be sure that you include details that will help the company solve your problem quickly and the way you want. The following information will make your message clear to the reader:

- the exact problem with the product

- the date you bought the product

- ways you have tried to solve the problem

- suggestions for how to solve the problem

Formal Letters

Content Editing

Jocelyn knew that she would revise her letter before she mailed it. Maybe she would rewrite the letter several times before it sounded right to her. The first thing she wanted to be sure of was that the content of her letter was correct. Did she include all the parts of a letter? Does the letter explain the problem clearly? Did she say what she wants the company to do?

Jocelyn used a checklist like this as she read over her letter. She also used a different pencil color so that she could see her changes more easily. Jocelyn read over the first draft of her letter. It looked good, but she was afraid she might have missed something. Jocelyn wanted a friend to read the first draft of her letter. She asked Paul to read it.

Paul and Jocelyn often studied together and checked each other's homework. They both knew that they should point out problems to make the writing better, not to make their partner feel bad.

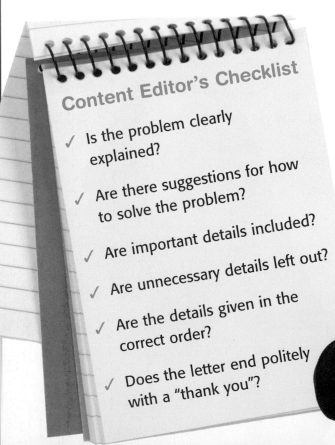

Content Editor's Checklist

✓ Is the problem clearly explained?

✓ Are there suggestions for how to solve the problem?

✓ Are important details included?

✓ Are unnecessary details left out?

✓ Are the details given in the correct order?

✓ Does the letter end politely with a "thank you"?

Paul read Jocelyn's letter through a few times and checked it against the Content Editor's Checklist. Then he and Jocelyn met.

First Paul told Jocelyn about things that he liked. Her letter clearly explained the problem. She also suggested ways to solve the problem. But Paul saw some ways that her letter could be improved. Here are his comments.

- When did you buy the game? If it was a long time ago, they might not help you. Add this detail.

- You don't need to tell them that Max's Toy Store is in the Century Mall. They just need to know that it is not in Ohio.

- How much did you pay for your game? Do you have a receipt? You should send a copy of the receipt with your letter.

- I think the detail about not being able to return the game to the store should go earlier in the letter. It's part of the problem, not what you want the company to do.

Jocelyn knew that Paul's suggestions were good ones, so she decided to follow most of them. She revised her draft, using his ideas and some of her own.

Your Turn

Read over your first draft and check it, using the Content Editor's Checklist. Write your ideas on your draft.

Then trade letters with a partner. Read your partner's letter several times, using the Content Editor's Checklist.

When you have finished reading your partner's first draft, give your honest opinion of how you think the letter could be improved. Be sure to comment on the good things that you read. Your partner will do the same for you.

Revising

Here is Jocelyn's revision of her letter.

October 5, 20–

Customer Service Department

Timely Toy Company

99 Highpoint circle

Cypress, CA 90630

Dear Sir or Madam:

Last week
I was visiting my cousins in New Jersey. We played your I Go Bingo game.
                                                    the next day
I liked it so much that ~~we went to Max's Toy City in the Century Mall and~~
                              I got it at a store near my cousins' house.
I baught my own I Go Bingo. When I got back home to Cincinnati, I opened

the box the deck of cards was missing.
I enjoy your game, but I can't play it
~~I can't play I Go Bingo~~ without the cards. I'm writing to ask that you either

send me the cards or refund my money so I can buy I Go Bingo at another

store. I cannot take the game back to the store where I got it. It is in New

Jersey and I live in Ohio. I am including a copy of my receipt. As you can see,
I paid $9.47 for the game.
Please respond as soon as you can so I can begin to enjoy your teriffic

game. Thank you for your help.

Sincerely

Jocelyn Morrissey

Look at what Jocelyn did to improve her letter.

- She added information to show that she had bought the game recently.

- She crossed out the name of the store and the mall and made it clear that she bought the game in New Jersey.

- She added information about how much the game cost. She would make a copy of the receipt and put it into the envelope.

- She didn't move the detail about the store being too far away to take the game back. The sentences seemed OK where they were.

The last thing Jocelyn did was to make her letter a bit more polite. She mentioned that she wanted the cards because she really enjoyed playing I Go Bingo. She hoped this would encourage her reader to respond quickly.

Your Turn

Use your own ideas and suggestions that you got from your content editor to revise your letter. Like Jocelyn, you don't have to follow all of your partner's suggestions. Follow only the suggestions that make your letter better.

When you have finished, go over the Content Editor's Checklist again. Can you answer yes to each question?

Formal Letters

Copyediting and Proofreading

Copyediting

Jocelyn saw that her letter was greatly improved by following Paul's suggestions. She was sure that it contained all the necessary information. Now she had to make sure she followed the correct form for a formal letter. She wanted to be sure that she used formal language and that her sentences flowed together smoothly. She used the following checklist.

Copyeditor's Checklist

✓ Are all the parts of a formal letter included and complete?

✓ Is only formal language used in the letter?

✓ Are all the sentences complete sentences?

✓ Are compound sentences used to make the writing more interesting?

✓ Do the sentences flow together smoothly?

Jocelyn checked over her letter to make sure all the important parts were there. Most of one part was missing. Review Jocelyn's letter. Do you know which part it was?

Jocelyn was missing most of the heading. She forgot to put in her own address. She added it above the date:

456 Wyomiss Lane
Cincinnati, OH 45201

Jocelyn saw that she had used some contractions. She replaced them to make her letter more formal.

Jocelyn checked to make sure her sentences were correct and varied. She didn't like the way the first two sentences sounded. How would you combine them?

Jocelyn also spotted a run-on sentence. Can you find it? How would you fix it?

Your Turn

Look over your revised draft. Be sure that all the parts of the letter are there. A good way to catch these mistakes is to compare your letter with one that you know is correct. Use the Copyeditor's Checklist to copyedit your draft.

Proofreading

Before writing the final copy of her letter, Jocelyn proofread the draft to check for spelling, punctuation, capitalization, and grammar.

Jocelyn used this checklist to help her proofread.

Proofreader's Checklist

✓ Is correct capitalization used including the first word of each sentence and all proper nouns?

✓ Is correct punctuation used including commas before conjunctions in compound sentences?

✓ Is each word spelled correctly?

✓ Is the grammar correct?

✓ Were any new mistakes added during editing?

Writers usually ask someone else to proofread their work for spelling, grammar, capitalization, and punctuation errors. A proofreader will often catch errors that the writer missed.

Jocelyn asked another classmate, Deena, to proofread her letter. Deena followed the Proofreader's Checklist. She found that the word *circle* in the inside address should have been capitalized. She found that the closing needed a comma. She also found two misspelled words. See if you can find them.

Your Turn

Read your letter carefully against the Proofreader's Checklist. Answer each question on the list separately. Check the body of the letter to make sure each sentence begins with a capital letter. Continue with the other questions on the checklist.

When you have gone through the whole checklist, trade letters with a partner. Go through your partner's letter in the same way. Be sure to use a dictionary if you are unsure of the spelling of a word.

Formal Letters

Publishing

Jocelyn revised her letter several times. Each time she made it better. When she felt that her letter was ready, she carefully typed it onto a clean sheet of paper and signed it.

She addressed an envelope, placed the letter and a copy of her receipt inside, added a stamp, and sent it. A deck of cards arrived in the mail just six days later!

456 Wyomiss Lane
Cincinnati, OH 45201

October 5, 20–

Customer Service Department
Timely Toy Company
99 Highpoint Circle
Cypress, CA 90630

Dear Sir or Madam:

Last week I was visiting my cousins in New Jersey, and we played your I Go Bingo game. I liked it so much that the next day I bought my own I Go Bingo. I got it at a store near my cousins' house. When I got back home to Cincinnati, I opened the box, but the deck of cards was missing.

I enjoy your game, but I cannot play it without the cards. I am writing to ask that you either send me the cards or refund my money so I can buy I Go Bingo at another store. I cannot take the game back to the store where I got it. It is in New Jersey, and I live in Ohio. I am including a copy of my receipt. As you can see, I paid $9.47 for the game.

Please respond as soon as you can so I can begin to enjoy your terrific game. Thank you for your help.

Sincerely,
Jocelyn Morrissey
Jocelyn Morrissey

Your Turn

Any time you share writing with your audience, it is publishing. Once you drop a formal letter into a mailbox, you can no longer correct mistakes. You want to be sure that everything in your letter is correct.

Look over your draft one more time to make sure all the mistakes have been corrected. Then address the envelope. The address on the envelope should match the inside address. Then place your letter inside the envelope, stamp it, and mail it.

If you are mailing your letter, first make a copy of it. Use the copy to create a class bulletin board with the other letters. Your teacher can call the board the "Reply Hall of Fame." Follow these steps:

1. Post your letters on the bulletin board.

2. As the letters are answered, display the replies next to the original letters.

After several replies come in, have a class discussion. Which letters got responses? Were they the ones with the most sensible suggestions for solving the problem? Were they the neatest letters or the most polite ones? Talk about your ideas. Perhaps you can use what you learned to write an even better letter the next time!

Jocelyn Morrissey
456 Wyomiss Lane
Cincinnati, OH 45201

Customer Service Department
Timely Toy Company
99 Highpoint Circle
Cypress, CA 90630

CHAPTER 3

The first people to meet European settlers in what is now Virginia were the Powhatan. More than 9,000 Powhatan people lived near the Chesapeake Bay when the first English settlers arrived. Powhatan homes were made of thatched mats and tree bark. The people grew fruits and vegetables in gardens near their homes. They also caught fish and hunted such animals as turkeys and deer.

Descriptions

The Burrowing Owl

The **burrowing owl** is about 9 inches long. Its back, head, and wing feathers are brown with white spots. Its belly feathers are whitish with brown stripes. It has yellow eyes and a dark band around its neck.

This owl's long legs and bullet-shaped head give it a strange appearance. Its stilt-like legs serve a purpose. They allow the owl to peek up over the grass that covers the prairies where it lives. They help it to run down the insects on which it feeds. The bird also eats small rodents. That is why farmers welcome this "ground owl" in their fields.

Although the owl is capable of digging its own nest, the bird usually seeks out holes made by prairie dogs, badgers, and other small mammals. It then lines the holes with grasses, roots, and dung. The female deposits 7 to 10 eggs near the bottom of the hole.

This owl has many different calls. The main song is a hoo-hooo-uh, hoo-hooo-uh, which the male uses to attract a mate. Other common calls are a raspy chuckle and a screech similar to car brakes squealing. When they sense danger, owlets in the nest make a sound that resembles a rattlesnake's warning.

The burrowing owl is native to southern Canada and the plains of the western United States. It has become endangered in some areas because of the destruction of its habitat.

What Makes a Good Description?

People write descriptions for many purposes. You can read descriptions in books, advertising, and newspapers. The description on page 83 is from a field manual about birds. Lively descriptions often use sensory language to help readers picture the people, places, things, and events in stories.

Descriptions usually have a beginning that names the topic, a middle that provides most of the details, and an ending that sums up the main idea or completes the information about the topic.

Choose a Topic

It is important to choose a topic that you know well. Your topic should be something you have seen, heard, smelled, touched, or tasted.

Choose a topic that is broad enough for you to write a description of more than one or two sentences. However, your subject should be limited enough to describe in the time that you have for writing.

Picture the Topic

Form a picture of your topic in your mind. Think about everything that you see, hear, smell, taste, and touch. Then describe the topic in as much detail as you can. Use sensory language.

Think About Your Audience

Remember your audience when you choose a topic. Will your readers be grown-ups or children? Will they know a lot about your topic, or will they know nothing about it? Keep these things in mind when you choose a topic.

Also remember your audience when you choose your words and phrases. Language that is too difficult or language that is too simple can make readers lose interest in what you have to say. You want to catch their interest right away and hold it. Choose words that match your audience.

Activity A

Read each of the following pairs of topics. Choose which of the two is a better topic for a description. Then tell whether the other topic is too limited or too broad to be a good topic for description. Explain your answers.

1. Grandfather's old dog
   hunting dogs

2. how I like my pancakes
   my idea of a good breakfast

3. a really messy bedroom
   things that I found under the couch

4. outside my bedroom window
   my hometown

5. my favorite musical performer
   rock 'n' roll music

Writer's Corner

Think of five topics like those in Activity A. Write them down. Tell whether each one is too broad, too limited, or a good topic for a description. Share your list with a classmate. Ask whether he or she agrees with you.

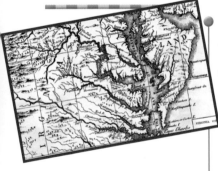

Organizing Your Description

Decide on the way that you want your audience to see what you are describing. Readers can more easily picture a description in their minds if it is written in an organized way. Here are some of the ways to organize descriptions.

Space Order

When you use space order, you describe things from one direction to another; for example, from left to right, from top to bottom, or from near to far. When you organize by space, keep the details in order. Don't jump back and forth.

Time Order

When you are writing about an event, organize your description by the order that things happen or in the order that you notice them. If you write about a trip to a bakery, you might notice the smells first, then the displays of baked goods, then the taste of the treat that you buy.

Activity B

Tell how best to organize a description of the following subjects. Would you use space order or time order?

1. the American flag
2. a visit to the barber
3. making breakfast
4. your family kitchen
5. a baseball diamond
6. a birthday party
7. your favorite animal
8. the clothes you wore to school today
9. washing a car or a pet
10. the pieces of your favorite board game

Activity C

The following sentences describe Mr. Jones. Write the sentences so that the description is organized in space order, from top to bottom.

1. He wears a bright red bandana around his neck.
2. He usually wears cowboy boots.
3. Mr. Jones has copper-red hair.
4. A shiny gold tooth gleams in his mouth.
5. He always wears jeans.
6. All his shirts are plaid flannel.
7. His bushy moustache is also red.

Activity D

Tell whether each of the following topics is better for grown-ups or for children. Then tell whether you would describe them in space order or time order. Explain why you think so.

1. the latest video game
2. a worker's toolbox
3. a classical music performance
4. the dashboard of a sports car
5. my favorite teddy bear

Writer's Corner

Picture the last meal that you ate with your family. Write the middle of a space order description of the foods as they were on the table. Then write the middle of a time order description of the foods as you ate them. Which type of organization uses which senses most often?

Sensory Language

Our five senses tell us about the world. Seeing tells us about rainbows and clouds. Hearing tells us about music and barking dogs. Touching tells us about kittens' fur. Smelling tells us about pies in the oven. Tasting tells us about cherries in our mouths.

Many of the things that you know you learned from your five senses. When you describe things, use words that appeal to the five senses to help people understand what you already know. The more senses you appeal to in your description, the more your audience can picture what you describe.

Read these two sentences.

A. The old gate opened noisily.

B. The rusty gate creaked loudly and scraped on the cracked sidewalk.

In sentence A the writer tells you what happened. In sentence B the writer not only tells you what happened, but also how it happened. Which sentence makes you feel more like you are there? Can you name the senses that the writer appealed to in sentence B?

Activity A

Tell which senses you would use to describe these subjects. Tell how each sense adds to the description.

1. buying new shoes

2. toasting marshmallows over a campfire

3. wrapping presents

Activity B

Use the sense in parentheses to write one sentence that describes each item.

1. an ostrich (sight)
2. bacon (sight)
3. a water faucet (sound)
4. you, as you run (sound)
5. a woman's purse (sight)
6. the wind (smell)
7. water in a swimming pool (taste)
8. burnt toast (taste)
9. buttered popcorn (touch)
10. rain (touch)

Activity C

Write the sense that you think would be used most in a description for each of the locations.

1. a bowling alley
2. a tennis court
3. a hot dog stand
4. the lobby of a movie theater
5. a sandy beach on a hot day

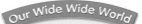
Our Wide Wide World

In the 1600s and 1700s, the American colonists believed that they were being treated unfairly by the British government. Colonists from Virginia played a major role in the American Revolution, the fight to gain independence from Britain. What do you know about these Virginians: Patrick Henry, Thomas Jefferson, and George Washington?

Writer's Corner

Choose a location from Activity C and write sensory words and phrases that describe it. Use many senses to make your description come alive.

• Activity D •

Tell which sense each of the sentences appeals to.

1. The new shoes gave my foot a painful blister.

2. Red and blue kites wheeled and bobbed in the sky.

3. Paolo's stomach ached from hunger.

4. Those gym socks need to be washed.

5. Their tasty hamburgers are cooked just right.

6. The skateboards' wheels rumbled on the sidewalk.

7. The sour milk ruined my cereal.

8. Only six or seven coins rattled in the bank.

9. My clothes got all smoky from the burning leaves.

10. The cup of hot chocolate warmed my numb fingers.

• Activity E •

Match each sensory word to the subject that it could describe. Tell what sense the word appeals to.

1. spicy		a. photograph
2. icy		b. apples
3. jagged		c. water
4. stinky		d. garbage
5. jingling		e. caramel
6. musty		f. fire
7. blurred		g. bells
8. sour		h. basement
9. sticky		i. pizza
10. crackling		j. mountaintops

The underlined sensory words in the following paragraphs got mixed up. Rewrite the sentences that have the misplaced words. Put the sensory words in the correct places. Use each sensory word just one time.

We dropped our <u>blood-curdling</u> backpacks onto the ground. I was hungry from hiking all morning, and I was looking forward to a <u>scared</u> lunch. We found a <u>hungry</u> spot to have a picnic. Just as we were unpacking our sandwiches, we heard a <u>crooked</u> growl coming from the bushes. Eddie jumped to his feet and ran back down the trail, yelling, "Bear!"

I didn't know if he was right or not, but I was too frightened to take any chances. I jumped up and followed Eddie back down the <u>heavy</u> path. We flew down the <u>tasty</u> hill like <u>steep</u> rabbits. I passed Eddie. Then he passed me. We both passed another group of hikers <u>stampeding</u> up the hill. Eddie yelled again, "Bear!" Soon there were eight of us <u>trudging</u> down the path. By the time we got back to the trail head, there were almost 20 of us.

Tomorrow Eddie and I may go back for our backpacks if we feel a little braver than we do right now. We'll be on the lookout for any more <u>shady</u> bears, however.

Writer's Corner

Briefly describe a place, using at least five sensory words. Underline the words. When you have finished, trade papers with a partner. Replace your partner's underlined words with new sensory words. Read the new paragraphs aloud.

Suffixes

A suffix is a word part added to the end of a base word. A suffix changes the meaning of the base word or makes a new word. Be sure to use suffixes correctly in your writing. Using the correct suffix can make your writing clear. Using the wrong suffix can confuse a reader.

Study the chart of common suffixes. Look at each suffix and its meaning. Notice how the base word changes when the suffix is added.

Common Suffixes

Suffix	Meaning	Base Word	Example
-ful	full of	cheer	cheerful
-less	without	help	helpless
-y	like; full of	thirst	thirsty
-er	person who	bake	baker

Read the paragraph below. Find the suffixes in the words in italics. Can you explain how each suffix changes the meaning of the base word?

Martin is a rock *climber*. He is *careful* to follow all of the rules he learned in his training. Martin knows that he is not just *lucky* when he has a good climb. Following safety rules is the key. Martin is not *careless*, so he has many good climbs.

**Write the sentences. Circle the words with suffixes.
Then underline the suffixes.**

1. My dad is a builder of homes.

2. Kia is thankful for your help.

3. The child's parents were hopeful that he would get well.

4. Exercise keeps me healthy.

5. The nurse said that the shot is painless.

6. I feel guilty when I tell lies.

7. The orange grower lost his crop.

8. It was a cloudy day.

9. Gina is a fearless athlete.

10. Are you a football player?

11. The doctor's advice was helpful.

12. She is blameless in this situation.

● **Activity B** ●

**With a partner take turns naming the base
word in the words you circled in Activity A.
Explain how the meaning of the base word
changes when the suffix is added.**

Writer's Corner

**Work with a partner to write ten sentences.
Each sentence should contain a word that ends in
one of the following suffixes: *-ful, -less, -y, -er*.**

Spelling Changes

Sometimes the base word changes its spelling when a suffix is added. Be sure to check a dictionary if you want to add a suffix to a word and you are unsure of the spelling.

Suffix	Base Word	Example
-ful	beauty	beautiful
-less	penny	penniless
-y	fog	foggy
-er	run	runner

• Activity C •

Choose a word from the box to replace the words in parentheses. Write each new sentence.

teacher	hopeless	thirsty	beautiful
greedy	graceful	timeless	helper

1. The dancer was (full of grace).

2. That story is (without time).

3. I like my (person who teaches).

4. Jana's mom is a lunchroom (one who helps).

5. After running, he was (full of thirst).

6. The wedding gown was (full of beauty).

7. King Midas was (full of greed).

8. Paul felt (without hope) as he looked at his messy bedroom.

Activity D

Add the correct suffix to the base word in italics in each sentence. Change the spelling of the base word if necessary. Write each new sentence. Use a dictionary if you need help.

1. When I grow up, I want to be a *write*.

2. Kendra is the most *power* hitter on our team.

3. My shoes got *mud* in the rain.

4. His pale face was almost *color*.

5. Latrel is a good *swim*.

6. Mozart was a great *compose* from Vienna.

7. I'm hoping for a *sun* afternoon.

8. The baby is quite a *cry*.

Activity E

Add *-ful*, *-less*, *-y*, or *-er* to each word. Then write a sentence for each word.

1. care
2. wind
3. use
4. storm

5. peace
6. mind
7. play
8. clue

Writer's Corner

Write a description of the best outdoor meal you ever experienced. Tell about some of the wonderful things that you saw, heard, smelled, touched or tasted. Use three or more words with suffixes.

Similes and Metaphors

Similes

You can use sensory language to describe people or things. Another way to describe people or things is by comparing them to other people or things.

A simile uses the words *like* or *as* to compare two different things. Read the sentences below. What does each sentence say about Ramona? What does she do well?

A. Ramona runs like a deer.

B. Ramona is as fast as lightning.

Sentence A compares the way that Ramona runs to the way that a deer runs. We know that a deer runs fast, so Ramona must run fast too. In sentence B Ramona is compared to lightning. Lightning is so fast that it is over almost as soon as it starts. Both sentences say that Ramona is fast.

Be careful when you choose the thing that you compare your subject with. Choose something that is different from your subject except for the part you want to point out. If you say your parakeet eats like a bird, readers will think that is a silly thing to say. All parakeets eat like birds. If you say that Ramona eats like a bird, readers will know that Ramona does not eat a lot.

Readers should also know enough about the two things being compared to understand what is meant. Most people know that a deer runs fast. However, many people haven't seen a zebra run. If you write that Ramona runs like a zebra, your readers might not understand what you mean.

Activity A •

Tell what two people or things are being compared in these similes. Then tell what is being described in each sentence.

1. Willie was as hungry as a bear.
2. Mr. Jones laughs like a hyena.
3. The hungry workers ate like starved wolves.
4. The lake is as smooth as glass.
5. You're as lazy as a slug.

Activity B •

Match each subject in Column A with an idea in Column B to make a simile. Then write three descriptive sentences using three of the pairs.

Column A

1. children arguing
2. sweaty gym shoes
3. icicles
4. cheering friends
5. fear
6. cat eyes
7. tough steak
8. storm clouds
9. a hilly road

Column B

a. a roller coaster
b. leather
c. dirty marshmallows
d. glowing emeralds
e. a skunk
f. chattering monkeys
g. a knot in the stomach
h. beautiful music
i. a glass necklace

Our Wide Wide World

The Appalachian Trail is a hiking path stretching from Maine to Georgia. You would have to walk about 2,174 miles to cover the entire trail! Virginia has more miles of the trail than any other state, over 500 of them. Parts of the trail go through Shenandoah National Park and the Blue Ridge Mountains. The hills and valleys of this area are especially beautiful in spring and fall.

Writer's Corner

Write a simile to describe each topic below. Try to paint a word picture with your similes.

joggers   an elephant   balloons   traffic

Metaphors

Like a simile, a metaphor describes by comparing. A metaphor is different from a simile because a metaphor does not use the words *like* or *as*. "Ed's car is a pile of junk" is a metaphor. It compares Ed's car to a pile of junk.

As with similes, the two things being compared in metaphors must be different. "Mr. Wong is a clever old bird" is a metaphor. "The crow is a clever old bird" is not.

• Activity C •

What two people or things are being compared in these metaphors? Tell what person or thing is being described.

1. Edna is a demon on the tennis court.

2. The candidate was a pit bull in the debate.

3. Adil is an Einstein in science class.

4. The sun was a blazing torch in the sky.

• Activity D •

Complete each sentence. Use a word from the word box that would make a good metaphor for each sentence.

mountain	king	stain	heaven
music	pretzel	window	

1. The fantasy book is a _____ into another world.

2. This chocolate cake is a piece of _____.

3. The winding road was a _____.

4. Yesterday's absence was the only _____ on my attendance record.

5. The snowdrift was a white _____ on the sidewalk.

6. The sound of the car pulling up was _____ to my ears.

7. My dog Sandy is the _____ of the neighborhood.

Activity E

Copy these sentences on a separate sheet of paper. Circle the person or thing being described. Draw a line under the word that the person or thing is being compared to. Then tell if the description is a simile or a metaphor.

1. Clouds floated in the ocean of the sky.

2. The cat's fur stood up like porcupine quills.

3. The corn was as sweet as candy.

4. The unfinished work is a thorn in my side.

5. The skyscrapers make downtown a concrete canyon.

6. Shadows stretched like fingers across the lawn.

7. The kitten's teeth were tiny needles jabbing my fingers.

Activity F

The following sentences have similes and metaphors. Write new sentences using the underlined part of each simile or metaphor. The first one is done for you.

1. Seeds dropping from the branches whirled <u>like tiny helicopters</u>.

   Hummingbirds hovered beside the flowers like tiny helicopters.

2. The fireflies were <u>stars</u> that escaped from the night sky.

3. A squirrel, holding her acorn <u>like a trophy</u>, chuckled loudly.

4. In the distance a dog howled out a <u>sad song</u>.

5. The old man's hands were <u>as twisted as tree roots</u>.

Writer's Corner

Choose a person or thing to describe. Write a short description using sensory language, a simile, and a metaphor. Read your description to the class.

Graphic Organizers

When you write a description, it helps to picture in your mind what you want to describe. Think about how it looks and how it sounds. Remember how it feels, how it smells, and how it tastes. Write down the details you remember. That way you will be less likely to forget them when you write your description. There are two good ways to organize the information. You can make a five-senses chart or you can make an idea web.

Five-Senses Chart

A five-senses chart lets you gather details according to each sense. This chart is for a cherry soda.

Cherry Soda				
Sight	**Sound**	**Smell**	**Taste**	**Touch**
tall glass with bubbling red soda	fizzing	hint of cherry aroma	deep cherry flavor	cold and wet
	clinking of ice cubes in glass			fizz tickles the nose
ice cubes			sweet	
straw sticking up				

A cherry soda appeals to all five senses, so each column has something written in it. Many topics will not have something in every column. Some topics will have many items listed under one sense. For example, a chart for a music CD could have many sounds in the Sound column but nothing in the Smell or Taste columns.

Activity A

The details in this five-senses chart are mixed up. Copy the chart on a separate sheet of paper. Put the details into the correct columns.

Football Game				
Sight	**Sound**	**Smell**	**Taste**	**Touch**
cheers and boos	hot dogs	whistles	thud of players crashing together	soft drinks
crisp autumn air	hard seats	cheerleaders jumping up and down		crowd jumping up
	players moving up and down the field		excited fans	football flying through the air

Activity B

Draw a five-senses chart to record details about a food court at a shopping mall. Think of the many food choices offered and the way the foods are presented. Think about the sights and sounds of the dining area. Add as many sensory details as you can.

Writer's Corner

Work with a partner. Decide on a topic to describe. Make a five-senses chart for that topic.

Idea Web

Another way to gather details is to use an idea web. Idea webs can help you organize ideas when you write.

First, write your topic in an oval in the center of a sheet of paper. Think of ideas that the topic suggests to you. Write the main ideas in ovals around your topic. Space out the ovals so that you will have room to add other ovals with more information.

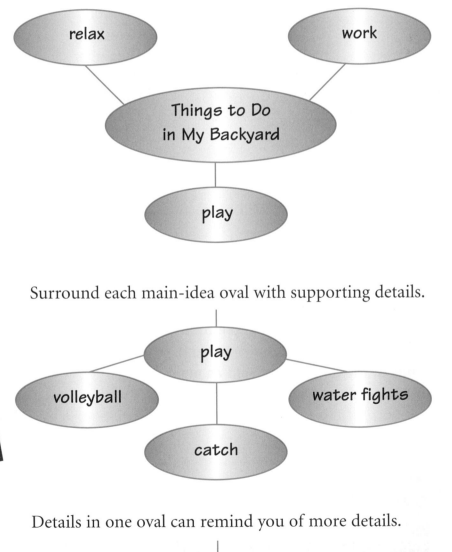

Surround each main-idea oval with supporting details.

Details in one oval can remind you of more details.

Copy the following ovals onto a sheet of paper. Fill them
in with details related to a school gym.

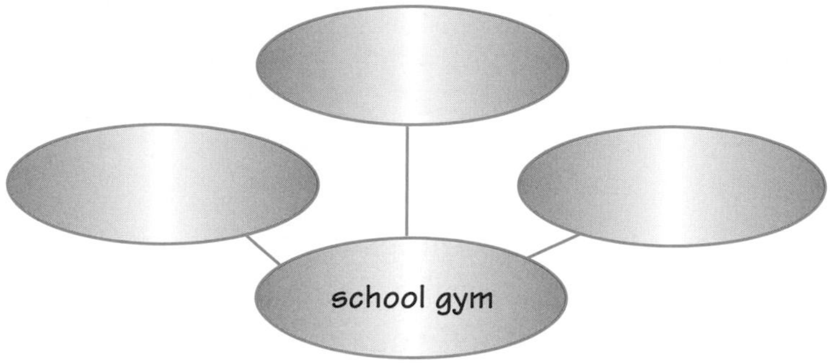

school gym

Copy the idea web for the topic, Favorite Desserts.
Use the words in the word box to fill in ideas and details.

apple	banana cream	peppermint
cake	devil's food	

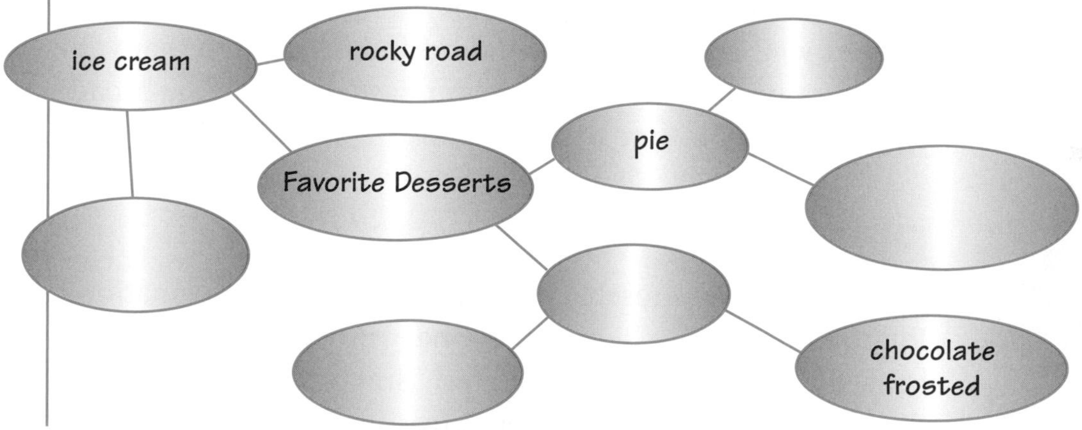

ice cream

rocky road

pie

Favorite Desserts

chocolate frosted

Writer's Corner

Make an idea web for the topic that you and your
partner chose for the five-senses chart on page 101.
When you have finished, compare the two graphic
organizers.

Oral Descriptions

You probably describe several things every day even if you don't realize it. You might describe a television program or movie to friends. You might tell your mother what you ate for lunch in school. These descriptions are informal.

Oral descriptions in school are more formal. For this kind of description, you prepare what you want to say. Then you practice saying it.

Choose a Topic

First choose a topic to talk about. It should be a topic that you are familiar with. Your topic should be one that will interest your audience. It should be limited enough that you can describe it in the time that you have. It should be broad enough to spend time describing it.

Picture the Topic

Once you have chosen a topic, gather your information. Picture your topic. Remember what you see and what you hear. Think about what you feel, smell, and taste. Write down what you can remember. A five-senses chart or an idea web can help you.

Organize the Information

Decide if you can describe your topic best by using space order or time order. Copy your notes from the five-senses chart or idea web onto note cards in the order you think works best.

Practice

Use your notes as you practice your oral description. Don't try to remember everything you wrote word for word. Use note cards to help you remember the main ideas. Practice your description many times until you feel comfortable. As you practice, think about these things.

- Speak loudly enough for everyone to hear.
- Look at all of your audience as you speak.
- Stand up straight. Do not move around a lot.
- Look at your note cards if you forget what to say.

Activity A

Tell which of these topics would be good for an oral description and which would not. Explain why.

1. a family car
2. London
3. a best friend
4. a bicycle
5. favorite socks

Activity B

Make a five-senses chart or an idea web for your favorite breakfast. Include as many senses as you can. Then organize the information into time order. Use note cards.

Speaker's Corner

Use the notes that you wrote for Activity B. Practice giving your description at least three times. Present it to a partner. Listen to your partner's description.

Assateague Island lies off the coast of Maryland and Virginia. Wild horses have lived on the island for centuries. Each July, saltwater cowboys help some of the horses swim across shallow water to Chincoteague Island. Hundreds of visitors watch the horses swim, and some visitors then choose a horse to buy. Chincoteague ponies can now be found in all 50 states and in many countries in the world.

Listening Tips

It is hard to stand up in front of a group of people and give a talk. It is even harder if the audience is not paying attention. That is why it is important for the audience to be polite. Here are some things to remember when you are listening to someone speak.

- Pay attention to the speaker. Take notes of interesting things the speaker says or interesting words he or she uses.

- Sit still. Do not move around in your seat.

- Do not talk. You would bother the speaker and the other people in the audience.

- Try to picture in your mind what the speaker is describing. Listen for sensory words, similes, and metaphors.

- If you have a question, wait until the speaker has finished. Then raise your hand to ask your question.

Activity C

Take turns with a partner. Choose an object in the classroom. Don't tell your partner what you chose. Describe the object. When you have finished, your partner will draw a picture of your object. Discuss your partner's picture. Did you give a complete description? Did your partner listen closely to what you said?

• Activity D •

Copy the five-senses chart on a separate sheet of paper. Add at least six details to the chart. Use your chart to prepare a short oral description of your favorite restaurant. Organize your description by time order or space order. Write your notes on note cards. Practice saying your speech. Be prepared to present your description to a partner.

My Favorite Restaurant				
Sight	**Sound**	**Smell**	**Taste**	**Touch**

• Activity E •

Take turns describing your favorite restaurant with a partner, using the notes you took in Activity D. Then ask questions to help your partner think of new sensory details. For example, you might ask, "Is the restaurant noisy or quiet?" or "What do the hamburgers taste like?" Use your partner's questions to help you think of sensory details. Add the new sensory details to your note cards.

Speaker's Corner

Present to the class the description that you gave to your partner in Activity E or in the Speaker's Corner on page 105. Try to include improvements that your partner suggested. Listen to new suggestions from your classmates.

Chapter 3 Writer's Workshop

Descriptions

Prewriting and Drafting

It is time to use the writing process to write a description. You may choose to describe a person, a place, a thing, or an event. Your audience will be your classmates.

Prewriting

Prewriting is the time that you explore topics that you could write about. It is the time to decide how you want to organize your description.

Choosing a Topic

Carmen is a fourth-grade student. The students in her class have been given an assignment to write a description of a summertime experience. Carmen had done so many things over the summer that she had trouble deciding what to write about. Her family had visited the state capital. She had gone to summer camp. Relatives from Costa Rica had come to visit for a week.

Carmen felt that she didn't know enough about the state capital to write a good description. Besides, she thought it was boring. She didn't think that her classmates would be interested in hearing about her

relatives. There wasn't enough time to write everything about her stay at the summer camp. After she thought for a while, Carmen decided to write about one activity at the camp. She would write about the canoe trips she took.

Your Turn

Think about people, places, things, or events that are interesting to you. Consider them in the same way that Carmen thought about the topics that she could write about. Which ones do you know well enough to write about? Which ones are limited enough to write a good description in the time that you have? Which ones will be interesting for your classmates to read? When you have narrowed your list, choose the topic that interests you the most.

Organizing Ideas

Carmen had many memories of her canoe trips. She wanted to be certain that she included all of the important details in her description.

Carmen created a five-senses chart to help her think of sensory details. The chart helped to organize her ideas into sight, sound, smell, taste, and touch.

Once she had gathered her details, Carmen thought about how she would organize her description. She decided to use space order. She would start with the first lake the canoers paddled on and then describe the second and third lakes.

Your Turn

Think of all the details you can about your topic. To help you think of sensory details, use a five-senses chart like the one Carmen created or use an idea web to help you think of more details.

Once you have thought of plenty of sensory details, think of how you will organize your description. Will it be easier to describe your topic in time order or space order?

Five Nations Canoeing Trips

	Sight	Sound	Smell	Taste	Touch
first lake	bass, muskie	campers' noises			icy water
second lake	deer, beavers, raccoons, woodchucks	wild turkeys, crows, woodpeckers		wild raspberries	prickly thorns
third lake		croaking frogs	decaying plants		

Drafting

Carmen used her five-senses chart to write the first draft of her description. She double-spaced her lines to leave room for changes when she revised her writing.

My favorite activity at Five Nations Summer Camp is canoeing. The camp used to be an old rock quarry. When they dug out the stone, they left three deep holes that became lakes. The water is deep. It is icy cold and as dark as ink. You can't swim in it, but if you take out a canoe, you will see some beautyful scenery.

It takes about 20 minutes to paddle across the first lake. You won't see as much wildlife here as in the other lakes. There are a lot of fish, such as bass and muskie. You won't see them, though, unless they go after bugs on the water's surface. When you get to the end of the first lake, you have to portage your canoe.

Now you begin to see and hear more wildlife. In the distance you can often hear three or four different woodpeckers. They are the drumers of the forest. You can hear their rat-a-tat pounding. They are looking for bugs in the oak trees that surround the lakes. You can also hear the calls of other birds echoing through the trees. You'll recognize the cawing of crows and the "gobble gobble" of the wild turkeys. Besides birds, you may also see deer, racoons, beavers, and woodchucks.

The portage to the third lake is pretty long. Several patches of wild raspberries make the hike worthwhile. It is easy to spend a half hour or so cramming the delightfuly sweet fruit into your mouth. By the time you are full, your hands will be stained a dark red. Be careful, though. Raspberry bushes have needle-sharp thorns. It's too bad there aren't wild blueberries. They don't have thorns.

The third lake has a shallower shoreline than the first two lakes have. The tall grass and cattails around the edges make an ideal hiding place for thousands of frogs. Late in the day they join in a croaking chorus that fills the air. Something else fills the air here. There is a rotten stink along the shore.. After 15 minutes in the foul air, most campers are ready to turn around and head back home. The entire trip lasts only four hours, but you will remember it your whole life.

Your Turn

Use your idea web or five-senses chart to write your first draft. Double-space your lines so that you will have room to make changes later. Keep your audience in mind as you write. Use words that your readers will understand and that will hold their interest.

Similes and Metaphors

Most good descriptions include similes and metaphors. They are not used in every sentence, however. Too many similes and metaphors can confuse the reader. A writer should choose the most memorable similes and metaphors, ones that paint clear pictures in the reader's mind.

Descriptions

Content Editing

When writers complete their first draft, they want to make sure that all of the important information is included and that it is correct. It is just as important to be certain that unnecessary information is left out and that the ideas are presented in an order that is easy to follow.

Content Editor's Checklist

✓ Will the audience be interested in the topic?

✓ Are sensory details included?

✓ Is all the necessary information included?

✓ Is unnecessary information left out?

✓ Are the details presented in an order that is easy to follow?

✓ Are similes or metaphors used to help the reader picture the description more easily?

✓ Does the ending sum up the description?

Carmen used the Content Editor's Checklist to make sure that her description did all of these things.

Carmen asked her friend Mathias to look over her paper. Mathias and Carmen often checked each other's writing. She trusted his opinions and knew that he would make good suggestions.

Mathias used the checklist to go over Carmen's description. He made a list of ways that he thought Carmen could improve her description. Then they met to discuss what he found. Mathias told Carmen that he really enjoyed her description and thought her audience would be interested in the topic. He thought the description was well organized and full of sensory details, including similes and metaphors. He also thought the ending summed up the description nicely.

Then Mathias made these suggestions for improvement.

- The opening doesn't say what your paper is about. Your description is about nature, but it sounds like you will be talking about canoeing.

- Why don't you see much wildlife around the first lake?

- What do you mean when you say you must portage your canoe?

- You say that the reader will recognize the cawing of crows and the gobbling of wild turkeys. Not everyone will know how these birds sound. Maybe you should leave that part out.

- The sentences about wild blueberries aren't necessary if you don't see them on the trip.

- What causes the rotten stink along the shore of the third lake? Are there skunks nearby?

Carmen was pleased with Mathias's suggestions. She could see that they would improve her paper, so she decided to follow most of them. She didn't agree with the suggestion about dropping the birdcalls. Carmen decided to leave that sentence as it was.

Your Turn

Reread your first draft several times. Use the Content Editor's Checklist to help you remember what to look for. Don't try to check all the items on the Checklist at once. Look for just one item at a time.

When you feel that your description is as good as you can make it, trade papers with a classmate. Look over your partner's paper as carefully as you did yours. Use the Content Editor's Checklist. Write notes about ways that you think your partner's paper could be improved.

Meet with your partner to suggest your improvements. Be sure to point out the good things as well as things you think should be changed.

Descriptions

Revising

This is how Carmen revised her description, using Mathias's suggestions and her own ideas.

The best way to see nature up close is from a canoe. I learned how to canoe last year ∧ ~~My favorite activity~~ at Five Nations Summer Camp ~~is canoeing~~. The camp used to be an old rock quarry. When they dug out the stone, they left three deep holes that became lakes. The water is deep. It is icy cold and as dark as ink. You can't swim in it, but if you take out a canoe, you will see some beautyful scenery.

It takes about 20 minutes to paddle across the first lake. You won't see as much wildlife here as in the other lakes.∧ The activity around the camp scars most of it away. There are a lot of fish, such as bass and muskie. You won't see them, though, unless they go after bugs on the water's surface. When you get to the end of the first lake, you have to portage your canoe.∧ That means you must carry it over a stretch of land to the next lake.

Now you begin to see and hear more wildlife. In the distance you can often hear three or four different woodpeckers. They are the drumers of the forest. You can hear their rat-a-tat pounding. They are looking for bugs in the oak trees that surround the lakes. You can also hear the calls of other birds echoing through the trees. You'll recognize the cawing of crows and the "gobble gobble" of the wild turkeys. Besides birds, you may also see deer, racoons, beavers, and woodchucks.

The portage to the third lake is pretty long. Several patches of wild raspberries make the hike worthwhile. It is easy to spend a half hour or so cramming the delightfuly sweet fruit into your mouth. By the time you are full, your hands will be stained a dark red. Be careful, though. Raspberry bushes have needle-sharp thorns. ~~It's too bad there aren't wild blueberries. They don't have thorns.~~

The third lake has a shallower shoreline than the first two lakes have. The tall grass and cattails around the edges make an ideal hiding place for thousands of frogs. Late in the day they join in a croaking chorus that fills the air. Something else fills the air here. There is a rotten stink along the shore. ^Dead plants are decaying and causing the smell. After 15 minutes in the foul air, most campers are ready to turn around and head back home. The entire trip lasts only four hours, but you will remember it your whole life.

Look at some of the things that Carmen did to improve her description.

- She rewrote the first sentence to hint that her description would be about nature.

- She explained that the noise from the summer camp scared wildlife away from the first lake.

- She explained what the word *portage* means.

- She took out the sentences about the blueberries.

- She explained that rotting plants caused the stink along the shore of the third lake.

Your Turn

Use your partner's comments and your own ideas to revise your draft. When you have finished, go over the Content Editor's Checklist again. Can you answer yes to each question?

Descriptions

Copyediting and Proofreading

Copyediting

When you copyedit, you make sure that you have used the right words for what you want to say. You also want your sentences to flow smoothly. There shouldn't be too many long sentences or too many short ones.

Carmen used the Copyeditor's Checklist to finish editing her description. Carmen read her paper aloud and listened to how the sentences sounded. The first two sentences in the paragraph about the raspberries didn't sound quite right. Carmen decided to combine them to make a compound sentence. How would you combine the two sentences? She decided to combine two of the sentences about woodpeckers to make the writing flow more smoothly.

Your Turn

Look over your revised description. Use the Copyeditor's Checklist to make sure that your writing is interesting and easy to read. Read your description aloud or ask someone else to read it aloud while you listen.

Proofreading

Incorrect capitalization, punctuation, or grammar make readers think that a writer is careless. After you have finished editing and revising your work and you feel that your sentences and ideas are clear, you are ready to proofread. A checklist can help you catch all of these mistakes.

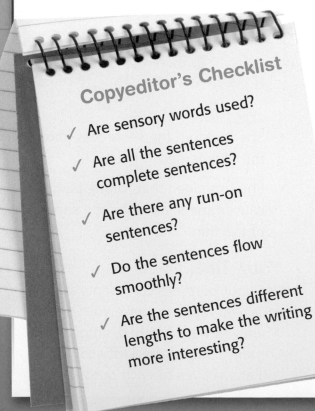

Copyeditor's Checklist

✓ Are sensory words used?

✓ Are all the sentences complete sentences?

✓ Are there any run-on sentences?

✓ Do the sentences flow smoothly?

✓ Are the sentences different lengths to make the writing more interesting?

Proofreader's Checklist

✓ Are all the paragraphs indented?

✓ Are all the words spelled correctly?

✓ Is the grammar correct?

✓ Are capitalization and punctuation correct?

✓ Were any new mistakes added during editing?

Carmen used the checklist to proofread her description. She caught two misspelled words, *beautyful* and *delightfuly*. What is the correct spelling of these words? She also noticed that one revision added another misspelled word. Can you find it? Finally, Carmen saw a paragraph that needed to be indented. Can you spot it?

Carmen was pleased that she found the mistakes. Now she wanted her friend Deana to give her description one final proofreading. It is a good idea to have another person proofread your paper after you have proofread it yourself.

Deana read Carmen's description three times, using the Proofreader's Checklist. She found two more misspelled words and a sentence with two periods. Can you find these mistakes?

Your Turn

Read your paper carefully, using the Proofreader's Checklist. Look for only one kind of mistake at a time. You might not see some mistakes if you look for too many things at once. If you read your paper several times, you have more opportunities to catch mistakes. Use the proofreading marks that you learned in Chapter 1 to mark changes on your paper.

When you have finished proofreading your description, trade papers with a partner. Proofread your partner's paper just as carefully as you did your own. Use proofreading marks to point out corrections.

Publishing

Publishing is the time that you share your finished work with an audience. You know it is your best work. You might read it aloud in class, put it on a bulletin board, or turn it in to your teacher.

Carmen had revised her description several times. She had copyedited and proofread it herself and asked a classmate to proofread it also. After all the work, Carmen added a title and was eager to share her description with her class.

Paddling into Mother Nature's Home

The best way to see nature up close is from a canoe. I learned how to canoe last year at Five Nations Summer Camp. The camp used to be an old rock quarry. When they dug out the stone, they left three deep holes that became lakes. The water is deep. It is icy cold and as dark as ink. You can't swim in it, but if you take out a canoe, you will see some beautiful scenery.

It takes about 20 minutes to paddle across the first lake. You won't see as much wildlife here as in the other lakes. The activity around the camp scares most of it away. There are a lot of fish, such as bass and muskie. You won't see them, though, unless they go after bugs on the water's surface. When you get to the end of the first lake, you have to portage your canoe. That means you must carry it over a stretch of land to the next lake.

Now you begin to see and hear more wildlife. In the distance you can often hear three or four different woodpeckers. They are the drummers of the forest. You can hear their rat-a-tat pounding as they look for bugs in the oak trees that surround the lakes. You can also hear the calls of other birds echoing through the trees. You'll recognize the cawing of crows and the "gobble gobble" of the wild turkeys. Besides birds, you may also see deer, raccoons, beavers, and woodchucks.

The portage to the third lake is pretty long, but several patches of wild raspberries make the hike worthwhile. It is easy to spend a half hour or so cramming the delightfully sweet fruit into your mouth. By the time you are full, your hands will be stained a dark red. Be careful, though. Raspberry bushes have needle-sharp thorns.

The third lake has a shallower shoreline than the first two lakes have. The tall grass and cattails around the edges make an ideal hiding place for thousands of frogs. Late in the day they join in a croaking chorus that fills the air. Something else fills the air here. There is a rotten stink along the shore. Dead plants are decaying and causing the smell. After 15 minutes in the foul air, most campers are ready to turn around and head back home. The entire trip lasts only four hours, but you will remember it your whole life.

Your Turn

It is time to publish your description. When you write a paper in school, you publish by sharing it with your teacher and your classmates. Make sure that your work is in its best form before you publish it. Follow these steps to publish your description:

- Look over your draft one last time to make sure there are no mistakes. If you can, use your computer's spell checker.

- Use your neatest handwriting or a computer to make the final copy.

- Keep your work safe from tearing or wrinkling.

- If you have any photographs of the topic that you described, you may want to include them with your paper. That way readers can compare the pictures with your description.

Have a discussion with your classmates and your teacher about ways that you can publish your descriptions. One way could be to put together a book of descriptions. If your class makes a book, put in any of the photographs that students have included with their descriptions.

Your teacher can keep the book in the classroom so that students can read their classmates' descriptions. Take time to read some of the descriptions. Good writers read other writers' work for ideas to improve their own work.

CHAPTER

4

At 630 feet high, the Gateway Arch in St. Louis, Missouri, is the tallest national monument in the United States. This giant arch represents the importance of Missouri in the settling of the West. Visitors can take a four-minute train ride to the top of the arch, from which they can see for 30 miles both to the east and to the west. What other national monuments do you know?

How-to Articles

Make Your Own Kazoo

It takes years of experience and great skill to make a guitar or a violin. However, it takes just a few minutes to make a homemade kazoo.

To make your kazoo, you will need a cardboard tube, a sheet of wax paper, a rubber band, and a pair of scissors.

First cut a square piece of wax paper that's about three inches larger than the opening of the cardboard tube. Wrap the wax paper over one end of the tube.

Next put the rubber band over the wax paper to fasten it to the tube. Finally put the open end of the cardboard tube up to your mouth and hum a tune. Notice how the kazoo buzzes and vibrates, changing the sound of your humming.

Play your kazoo for anyone who will listen. Now you have a new instrument to delight (or annoy) your friends!

What Makes a Good How-to Article?

A how-to article teaches the reader how to do something. The instructions for a board game are a kind of how-to article. So is a set of directions to your school. Here are some things to remember when you write a how-to article.

Introduction

The introduction of a how-to article tells what the reader will learn from the article. The introduction should be informative. It might even be catchy if the writer thinks the audience needs to be "hooked."

Body

The body of a how-to article tells how to complete the task. All the necessary materials are listed. Next the steps are clearly explained in time order. The body should not include any unnecessary information. Each step is written as an imperative sentence, which is a sentence that gives a command.

Conclusion

The conclusion of a how-to article sums up what has been taught. It might also tell how the information will help the reader.

Activity A

Look over the how-to article "Make Your Own Kazoo" on page 121. Then answer the questions below.

1. Which paragraph makes up the introduction?

2. Which paragraph tells what materials are needed?

3. Are all the important steps included?

4. Which paragraph makes up the conclusion?

5. Think of another introduction or conclusion the writer might have used for this article.

Activity B

Decide which of the following sentences would make a good introduction for a how-to article about model airplanes. Explain your answers.

1. Model airplanes are made of plastic.

2. Building a model airplane is easy and fun.

3. Never build a model airplane without an adult to help you.

4. I'm afraid to ride in airplanes.

5. With a little patience and work, you can build a model airplane that looks just like the real thing.

Writer's Corner

Write a list of three easy things that you know how to do. Choose one and write an introduction for a how-to article about that topic.

Time Order

The body of a how-to article tells how to do something step by step. The directions are given in time order. If some of the directions are out of order, your readers might get confused. They may not be able to complete the task.

The body of a how-to article on writing a letter is written below. Can you find the steps that are out of order?

Fold your letter into three parts. Write the heading and the inside address at the top of the page. Then write the closing and sign your name. Write your greeting and the body of your letter. Put the letter into an envelope. Seal the envelope and drop it in the nearest mailbox. Write the receiver's address and your address on the envelope and add a stamp.

• Activity C •

Revise the paragraph above, using time order. The first sentence has been done for you.

Write the heading and the inside address at the top of the page.

• Activity D •

Arrange the steps for taking down a flag in the correct order.

1. Unhook the flag from the flagpole.

2. Fold the flag carefully with your partner.

3. With a partner, hold the flag by the corners.

4. Put the flag in a safe place.

5. Bring the flag down the flagpole.

Activity E

The following sentences are from a how-to article about making a sock puppet. Decide which sentence is the introduction and which is the conclusion. Then arrange the steps in time order.

1. Draw a face around the eyes and glue the yarn above them for hair.

2. Now you're ready to put on a show for your friends.

3. Making a sock puppet is simple and fun.

4. Then glue the googly eyes to the front of the sock.

5. Put your hand into the finished sock puppet.

6. Gather a sock, two googly eyes, some yarn, and a permanent marker.

Activity F

Choose one of the topics below. Write three steps for the body of a how-to article about this topic. Use time order.

A. how to take a photograph

B. how to make a peanut butter and jelly sandwich

C. how to play hopscotch

D. how to make your bed

E. how to wrap a present

F. how to make a scrapbook

G. how to give your dog a bath

Writer's Corner

Add any steps that are missing for a how-to article about the topic you wrote about in Activity F. Then write an introduction and a conclusion for the article.

Important Details

A how-to article should be complete. This means that all the necessary information should be included. If an important detail is left out, the reader may not be able to complete the task.

As you write a how-to article, you should also make sure that you leave out any details that are not necessary. Any unimportant details will distract your reader.

Read the how-to paragraph below. Can you find any details that are not needed?

Dive Away!

Diving off a diving board is not as hard as you might think. First stand at the end of the diving board with your toes coming just off the edge. It could be an indoor pool or an outdoor pool. Bend your knees and lean your head forward. Raise your hands over your head. You won't be doing one of those fancy dives like you see in the Olympics. Push off with your legs and lean forward so that you go headfirst into the water. When you come up, you'll be glad you took your first dive.

The sentence "It could be an indoor pool or an outdoor pool" is not needed. It distracts the reader. The sentence "You won't be doing one of those fancy dives like you see in the Olympics" is also unnecessary.

Activity A

Each group of sentences below is from a how-to article. Which sentence in each group is not an important detail?

1. **A.** When you hear a fire alarm, get up from your seat.

   B. Line up single file.

   C. Walk calmly and quietly out the door.

   D. Many fire alarms are drills, not real fires.

2. **A.** Put all the dirty dishes in the dishwasher.

   B. Using a dishwasher is easier than washing the dishes yourself.

   C. Put soap in the dishwasher.

   D. Close the door and turn the knob to "wash."

3. **A.** To train for a marathon, you should start at least six months before.

   B. The Boston Marathon is one of the most famous marathons.

   C. Start by running just a few miles each day.

   D. Increase your runs by about one mile every week.

Writer's Corner

Write a few sentences telling how to get somewhere in your school. Trade your writing with a partner. See if your partner has left out any important details.

Being Specific

The details you give in a how-to article should always be specific. This means telling your readers exactly what they need to know. When giving travel directions, be sure to tell whether to turn right or left. In a recipe tell how much of each ingredient to add and how long to cook the dish.

What specific information is missing from this paragraph?

> To get to the police station go down Haverhill Street and turn. Go straight down Winston Street for a while until you reach the store. Turn at the store and go down the hill. Pass a few stop signs and turn right on Main Street. The police station will be on the side of the street.

This paragraph is missing important details. The writer does not say which direction to turn from Haverhill Street or which way to turn at the store. The writer does not give the name of the store or tell which side of the street the station is on. Phrases such as "a while" or "a few" are also not helpful. Instead, the writer should say exactly how far to go or how many stop signs to pass.

● Activity B ●

The how-to article below is missing some specific information. Discuss what details should be more specific in order to make the fruit smoothie.

Here's what you need to do to make a fruit smoothie. You will need a blender, milk, yogurt, and fruit. First pour the milk, the fruit, and the yogurt into the blender. Then turn the blender on. Set it high enough to make the smoothie. When you know it's done, pour it into a cup.

Activity C

The note below is a how-to article written for someone who took over a friend's paper route. Read the list of details after the note. Which details should be included in the note? Which ones are not important? Decide where each important detail should go in the note.

Thank you for offering to help deliver my papers this week! Here's what you need to do. Get the newspaper sections from the driveway and put the papers together. Put all the newspapers into your newspaper sack. Go to each house on the list and deliver the newspapers. Pick up any money envelopes you see and put them in the sack. Hold on to them until I get back.

Thanks again!
Danny

1. Lots of people have signed up for the newspaper this year.

2. Put the papers together by sliding the sports section inside the main sections.

3. I just got a new newspaper sack a month ago.

4. Put the newspaper inside the screen door of each house.

5. The envelopes are usually taped to the door.

6. With any luck, all the customers will leave big tips in their envelopes.

7. You should start at 6:30 a.m.

Writer's Corner

Think of a game you like to play. Write the directions for playing the game. Be sure to give specific details.

Prefixes

A prefix is a word part that is added to the beginning of a base word. A prefix changes the meaning of the base word. Three common prefixes are *dis-*, *pre-*, and *under-*.

Here are the definitions of these prefixes and examples of how they are used. Can you use each of the example words in a sentence?

Prefix	Meaning	Base Word	Example
dis-	not, opposite of	like	dislike
pre-	before, earlier	cook	precook
under-	below, less than	foot	underfoot

Sometimes you might come across an unfamiliar word that has a prefix. If you know what the prefix and the base word mean, you might be able to guess what the word means.

• Activity A •

Think of a word that fits each meaning. Each word should begin with the prefix *dis-*, *pre-*, or *under-*.

1. not allow

2. view before

3. make a line below

4. pay before

5. not favor

6. arrange before

7. not pleased

8. below the proper age

Add the prefix *dis-*, *pre-*, or *under-* to each word in parentheses to complete the sentences.

1. When Sandra said she had not taken a cookie, she was being (honest).

2. When we first turned on the radio, we found that some stations had been (set).

3. Remember to wear a button-up shirt on top of your (shirt).

4. The submarine took Captain Jack and his crew on their first (sea) adventure.

5. Mr. Jones tried not to (judge) who had told the truth before he knew all the facts.

6. Because we were given less time to take the test, we had a (advantage).

7. The tiny rabbit hid from the fox by hiding in the (brush).

8. The band of trolls plotted their attack from their (ground) hideout.

9. We thought the television program was being shown live, but the truth is that it was (recorded).

10. My dog Rex may not be smart, but he is never (loyal).

Writer's Corner

Choose five of the words from Activity A or B. Use each word in a sentence.

• **Activity C** •

Choose the word from the word box that best completes each sentence below.

disagree	preheat	underdress
disbelief	prehistoric	underhand
displease	preschool	undersized
disrespect	preteen	underwater

1. Before starting kindergarten, my brother has to go to _____.

2. The _____ catcher's mitt is too small to fit on my hand.

3. The umpire says that the ball went through the goal, but I _____.

4. Before you put the cookies in the oven, be sure to _____ the oven for 15 minutes.

5. After the amazing magic trick, we all shook our heads in _____.

6. Because I hurt my shoulder, I could only throw the ball _____.

7. The student's rude comment to the teacher was a sign of _____.

8. The bones in the cave show that there was a group of _____ settlers in the area.

9. It will _____ Ruana to find out that you forgot her birthday.

10. The class of fifth graders looked for books intended for a _____ audience.

11. Remember to hold your breath when swimming _____.

12. You will _____ for the wedding if you do not wear a jacket and tie.

Activity D ●

Write the meaning of each of the words below.

1. underweight
2. disbelieve
3. predate
4. disprove
5. underarm

6. dishonor
7. premix
8. underfoot
9. pregame
10. disobey

Activity E ●

Read the paragraphs below and find the words with the prefixes *dis-*, *pre-*, or *under-*. Choose five of the words and write the meaning of each word.

Mr. McSweeney wondered what had happened to all his apricots. Before jumping to a conclusion, he took the precaution of counting them. When he did, he knew that he had not underestimated how many there had been. Some of the apricots had disappeared.

His first thought was that one of his customers had been dishonest. The idea that a customer would steal really displeased him.

Then Mr. McSweeney sat in disbelief as he saw a squirrel dart out from the underbrush near the fruit stand. It hopped up from the underside of the stand, took an apricot, and ran off. Mr. McSweeney was glad to find that the thief was a squirrel and not a disloyal customer!

Writer's Corner

Look through a book for five or more words with the prefixes from this lesson. Write a sentence for each of these words.

Dictionary

Do you know what a quark is? What about sassafras? The best way to find out what a word means is by looking in a dictionary. A dictionary can tell you the meanings of words. It can also tell you where the word comes from, how it is spelled, and more.

Alphabetical Order

A dictionary is arranged in alphabetical order. This makes it easy to find the word you are looking for. When you look for a word, think of the part of the alphabet that the first letter of the word is in: the beginning, the middle, or the end. Flip to that part of the dictionary to look for your word.

Guide Words

Guide words can help you find a word in the dictionary. Two guide words are found at the top of each page. They tell you the first and last words on that page. To find your word, look for the guide words that are closest to your word in alphabetical order. If your word fits between the two guide words, you will find it on that page. Here is the top section of a dictionary page with guide words.

141 lightning • locate

light•ning (līt′nĭng) *n.* A flash of electricity in the sky.

Activity A •

Arrange each list of words in alphabetical order.

1. below
over
after
toward

2. street
crosswalk
traffic
light

3. cloud
star
moon
horizon

4. cup
bowl
saucer
knife

Activity B •

Arrange each list of words in alphabetical order. If the first letter is the same, use the second letter. If the first two letters are the same, use the third letter.

1. pizza
pancakes
potatoes
peanuts

2. hymn
harp
hoard
hefty

3. spear
spin
spot
spread

4. breakfast
brand
bring
brook

Activity C •

Look at the sample guide words below. Decide whether each word would be on that page, before it, or after it.

Guide Words: ligament • lofty

1. lamp
2. train
3. limp
4. mast

5. love
6. look
7. kind
8. lint

9. jewel
10. lose
11. lure
12. load

Writer's Corner

Turn to a page in the dictionary and write down five words in random order. Trade lists with a partner. Put your partner's list in alphabetical order. Then find your partner's page in the dictionary. Write sentences using your partner's words.

Dictionary Meanings

The most important part of a dictionary entry is the meanings. Some words have just one meaning, while others have more than one. Often a dictionary will give a sample sentence to help you understand the meaning. Look at the dictionary entry below. How many meanings does the word have?

jog (jŏg) **1** *v.* to move by shoving or bumping. *She jogged her friend to see if she was awake.* **2** *v.* to shake up and remember, especially a memory. *The photograph jogged my memory.* **3** *v.* to run at a steady, slow pace. *I jog around town to keep in shape.* **4** *n.* a steady, slow trot. *We went for a jog.*

Did you know all the meanings of the word *jog*? Reading a dictionary entry can help you learn more about a word. It can also help you become a better reader, writer, and speaker. The more words and meanings you know, the easier it will be for you to say what you mean.

• Activity D •

Look at the entry above for the word *jog*. Decide which meaning is being used in each sentence below.

1. The woman jogged me when the subway train suddenly stopped.

2. I was worn out after jogging for two miles.

3. The smell of wildflowers jogged my memory of the walk in the woods.

4. The football players start off every morning with a jog around the park.

5. When Brian started daydreaming, Stacy jogged his arm to make him pay attention.

6. Finding my old tennis racket jogged my memory of the many hours that I'd spent practicing my serve.

Activity E

Find each word in a dictionary. Tell how many meanings each word has. Then choose two of the words and write a sentence that uses each word.

1. exercise
2. crank
3. steel
4. strain
5. needle
6. outline
7. handle

Activity F

Look up each word in a dictionary. Write the meaning of the word. Choose two words and use each in a sentence.

1. jest
2. plateau
3. scuttle
4. bewilder
5. replenish
6. graffiti
7. abandon

Our Wide Wide World

In 1847 an enslaved man named Dred Scott sued to become a free man. The case went from St. Louis, Missouri, to the U.S. Supreme Court, the country's highest court of law. Sadly, the Court decided that African Americans could not become U.S. citizens and therefore could not sue in federal court. With the end of the Civil War, however, that decision was overturned. Dred Scott's brave action showed other people the injustice of slavery and helped lead to its end.

Writer's Corner

Find a word in the dictionary that has at least three meanings. Write three sentences, each using a different meaning. Trade sentences with a partner. See if your partner can guess the meaning of the word in each sentence. Do the same for your partner's sentences.

Time Words

Have you ever read a paragraph in which the sentences did not seem to fit together? If so, the paragraph might have needed time words. Time words help a writer connect ideas so that they flow together. These kinds of words are often placed at the beginning of a sentence. Here are some examples.

after	next
before	second
finally	then
first	third
later	while

Read the following paragraphs. Notice how time words help the sentences to flow more smoothly in the second paragraph.

Here's how to do the laundry. Put all the laundry into a basket and take it to the washing machine. Separate the white clothes from the dark clothes. Open the washing machine and add one cup of detergent. Put the white clothes into the machine. Turn the knob to "wash." Wait about 25 minutes for the machine to wash your clothes.

Here's how to do the laundry. First put all the laundry into a basket and take it to the washing machine. Separate the white clothes from the dark clothes. Next open the washing machine and add one cup of detergent. Put the white clothes into the machine. Then turn the knob to "wash." Finally wait about 25 minutes for the machine to wash your clothes.

Activity A

Add time words to this how-to article.

Here's how to make a pompon ant. You will need three pompons, four craft stems, two googly eyes, some craft glue, and scissors.

_____ glue two pompons together, using just a bit of glue. This will make the body of the ant. _____ glue a third pompon to the other pompons to make the head.

_____ cut four craft stems so that they are each about four inches long. Glue one underneath the front of each pompon. Curl them so they look like legs sticking out each side.

_____ bend the fourth craft stem in the middle and curl each end upward. Glue it to the top of the head to make two antennae.

_____ glue the googly eyes to the front of the head.

_____ put your pompon ant in a special place to amuse you and your friends!

Writer's Corner

Describe what you do when the school day ends, using time words. Read it aloud. Then read it without the time words. Which one sounds better?

George Washington Carver, who was born in Diamond Grove, Missouri, in 1864 was a brilliant scientist. Carver studied plants of the southern United States, including peanuts and soybeans. He is famous for inventing many of the products that we use today— including peanut butter!

• Activity B •

Choose one of the paragraphs below. Revise it by adding at least three time words.

A. To make chicken soup, you will need a can of soup, a can opener, a pot, some water, and crackers. Open the can with the can opener. Pour it into the pot. Fill the can with water and add the water to the pot. Put the pot on the stove and turn the knob to "medium." Stir the soup often. After about five minutes, pour the soup into a bowl. Crumble some crackers over the top of the soup.

B. Here's how to brush your teeth. Take your toothbrush out and run the brush under cool water. Spread toothpaste on the brush. Make sure you squeeze the tube from the bottom! Gently brush your teeth for three minutes. Start with your front teeth and work your way to the back. Spit the toothpaste into the sink. Take a sip of water to rinse out your mouth. Rinse off the brush and put it away.

C. To make s'mores at a campfire, you will need graham crackers, a chocolate bar, marshmallows, and a stick. Break a graham cracker into two equal squares. Break off a piece of chocolate and put it on one cracker. Slide a marshmallow onto the stick and hold it over the campfire. Hold it there until it turns a golden brown. Press the marshmallow onto the chocolate. Put the other graham cracker on top like a sandwich and slide the stick out. Be sure to eat the s'more while it's still warm.

D. It's easy and fun to make your own pizza. You will need a 10-inch pizza crust (ready-made kind works fine), tomato sauce, shredded cheese, and whatever toppings you like, such as mushrooms, pepperoni, sausage, or olives. Spread the tomato sauce on the pizza crust. Sprinkle some cheese on top of the sauce. Put the toppings on. Add another layer of cheese. Put the pizza in the oven, and bake it according to the directions on the pizza crust package. The pizza is done when the cheese turns golden and bubbly.

Activity C

Put these sentences from a story in time order. Add time words. The first sentence of the story is given.

    For space-traveler extraordinaire Jenna Moonbeam, it was time to say goodbye.

1. She radioed to the control tower to begin the countdown.

2. She put on her helmet and stepped toward the ship.

3. Zach gave her the signal that he was ready to fly.

4. As the engines roared, she listened to the countdown over the radio.

5. Jenna looked out the window as the earth grew smaller and smaller in the distance.

6. Jenna took her seat at the controls and fastened her seatbelt.

7. The countdown ended, and she could feel the ship lifting off.

8. "We hear you, Moonbeam," came the voice from the tower.

9. Jenna heard the sound of the engines firing up beneath her.

10. She zipped up her space suit and kissed her family goodbye.

11. Her copilot, Zack Solaris, followed behind her as she stepped inside.

Writer's Corner

Revise the paragraph you chose from Activity B using different time words. Which paragraph sounds better?

How-to Talks

Have you ever taught someone how to play a game? Have you told a friend how to get to your home? When you tell someone how to do something, you are giving a how-to talk. Here are some tips for giving a good how-to talk.

Topic

When you plan a how-to talk, choose a topic that your audience might not know but will be interested in learning about. Choose something that is easy to explain in a few steps.

Introduction

Begin your talk by telling what you will teach. You might also want to get your audience's attention with a question or a catchy first sentence.

Body

In the body go through all the steps needed to complete the task. Begin by listing anything your audience will need, showing examples if you can. If possible, show how to complete the task by doing it yourself as you explain. If not, you might show a picture, diagram, or other visual aid.

Conclusion

The conclusion of your talk should sum up what has been taught. You might show your audience what you made or did. Leave time for questions at the end.

Activity A

**Which of the topics below do you think would
be most interesting to a class of fourth graders?**

1. how to play dodge ball

2. how to tie your shoes

3. how to make a banana split

4. how to change the oil in a car

5. how to build a house

6. how to use a video camera

7. how to plan a party

8. how to pack a suitcase

Activity B

**Choose two of the topics below. List three steps you might
include in a how-to talk about each topic. Describe how
you would show the steps, such as by using a visual aid.**

A. how to color Easter eggs

B. how to sharpen a pencil

C. how to do a cartwheel

D. how to get to the library

E. how to make lemonade

F. how to play miniature golf

G. how to arrange flowers

H. how to hang a picture on a wall

Speaker's Corner

**Think of a topic for a how-to talk you would like to give.
Make a list of the steps needed to complete this task.
Think of a way to show the steps during your talk.**

Prepare

To prepare for a how-to talk, first list all the important steps. Think of an informative introduction and a good conclusion for your talk. Write your introduction and conclusion on separate note cards. Then write each step on a separate note card. Also make notes of when to show your visual aids.

Next prepare any visual aids. If you will be showing a picture or drawing, make it big enough for everyone to see. If you are bringing in materials, gather everything you need.

Practice

Before giving your how-to talk, practice in front of a friend or family member. Try to look at the person and not just read from your note cards. Remember to speak slowly and clearly.

Practice with your visual aids if you're using them. If you will be showing how to follow the steps in your talk, go through them a few times. Practice each step until you can do it smoothly.

As you practice your talk, ask yourself these questions:

- Am I speaking slowly and clearly?
- Am I speaking loudly enough?
- Does my introduction catch my audience's attention?
- Have I included all the necessary materials?
- Have I included all the important steps?
- Do I show my visual aids at the right time?
- Does my conclusion sum up what has been taught?

Listening Tips

When someone gives a how-to talk, it is important to be a good listener. Keep in mind these points as you listen to your classmates' talks.

- Look at the speaker to show that you are listening.
- Have a pencil and a sheet of paper ready in case you want to take notes.
- Listen for the introduction to find out what is being taught.
- If you cannot see a visual aid or do not understand a step, raise your hand. Politely ask the speaker for help in seeing the visual aid or in understanding the steps.
- After the talk, ask the speaker any questions you have.
- Tell the speaker one thing you liked about the talk.

Activity C

Prepare and practice the how-to talk you chose for the Speaker's Corner on page 143. Write the introduction, the steps, and the conclusion on note cards. Prepare your visual aids. Then present the talk to a partner. Talk about ways you could improve your talk. Listen to your partner's talk and give suggestions for improving it.

Speaker's Corner

Present your how-to talk to the class. Remember to speak slowly and clearly. Show any visual aids so that everyone can see them. When you have finished, invite your audience to ask questions or to make comments. When your classmates give their talks, keep in mind the listening tips.

How-to Articles

Prewriting and Drafting

What things do you know how to make or to do? Can you build a snow fort or make a necklace? By writing a how-to article, you can share your skills with others.

Prewriting

Kim was asked to write a how-to article for her fourth-grade class. Before she began writing, she did prewriting. First she chose a topic. Then she organized her ideas by listing the materials needed and the steps.

Choosing a Topic

Kim had lots of ideas for how-to articles. She had made all sorts of crafts at summer camp. Her older sister Mara had taught Kim how to play lots of games. She made these lists of all the fun things she knew how to make and to do.

Crafts:
friendship bracelets
placemats
Christmas ornaments
jigsaw puzzles
snow globes
kites

Games:
checkers
tick-tack-toe
Crazy Eights
hopscotch
musical chairs

After looking at her lists, Kim decided that a craft would be more fun to describe. Her favorite thing to make was friendship bracelets. However, she thought that it would be much easier to show how to make them. Some of the steps would be hard to describe in writing.

Kim also liked making snow globes. Explaining how to make snow globes would be easy to do in a how-to article. She decided that this would be the topic of her article.

Your Turn

Make a list of things that you know how to make or to do. You could list crafts and games, as Kim did. You could list food that you know how to cook. You could list anything else that you know how to do.

Look over your list. Choose one topic that would be fun and easy to explain. Choose a topic that you think would interest other people too.

Organizing Your Ideas

After she chose her topic, Kim made a list of all the materials needed for making a snow globe. Then she wrote down all the important steps.

Materials needed:
jar with lid
small plastic toy or other object
silicone sealer
glitter
corn syrup
paints

Steps:
1. Pick out a plastic object to go inside the snow globe.
2. Glue it to the jar lid.
3. Fill the jar most of the way with corn syrup.
4. Sprinkle glitter inside the jar.
5. Screw the lid on tight.
6. Spread a strip of silicone sealer around the top of the jar.
7. Paint the top of the globe if you want.
8. Turn over the jar so the lid is the base and the toy is right-side up.

Kim looked at her lists. First she looked to see if she had forgotten anything from the list of things needed. She saw that glue was used in the second step. She added it to the materials list.

Next Kim looked at her steps. She tried to imagine making the snow globe. She realized that the silicone sealer needed to be added before screwing on the lid. She changed the order of the steps.

Your Turn

Make a list of all the materials needed for the topic you chose. Next, write down all the important steps.

When you have finished, read over what you have written. Make sure you have included all the materials. Check that all the important steps are included and in the right order. Make changes to your list if you find any mistakes.

Drafting

Kim was ready to turn her prewriting notes into a first draft. She wrote her steps out in sentence form, adding an introduction and a conclusion.

How to Make a Snow Globe

A snow globe is a pretty decaration, did you know that you can make one yourself? Here's how to do it.

You will need a jar and lid, glue, corn syrup, glitter, silicone sealer, paint, and a plastic toy that fits inside the jar. Choose a plastic toy that would look nice inside a snow globe.

To make the globe, glue the plastic toy to the jar's lid. Fill the jar most of the way up with corn syrup. Pour in some glitter.

You could use eggshells instead of glitter, but that's messier and doesn't look as nice. You would have to boil the eggs. Then you would have to peel the eggshells and break them up to look like snow. I would just use glitter.

Spread some silicone sealer over the top of the jar. Screw the lid on tightly. If you want, you can paint the top or bottom of your globe to make it more colorful.

Turn over the jar so the lid is the base and the toy is right-side up. To test the globe, shake it.

Your Turn

Look at the prewriting notes you made for your how-to article. Think of an introduction that tells what you will be teaching. You might want to think of a catchy first sentence to get your readers interested.

Next write the body of your how-to article in time order. Start by listing any materials that are needed. Then list the steps in paragraph form. Use time words to help the sentences fit together.

Finally add a conclusion. Sum up what you taught. You might want to tell the result of following the steps. For example, you might tell your readers what they can do with what they made.

Being Specific

When you write a how-to article, it is important to be specific. It can be easy to forget that your audience might not know what you mean.

If you list materials in your how-to article, look at how you describe them. Could your readers misunderstand and use the wrong material?

For example, Kim said a jar was needed for her snow globe. However, she forgot to mention that the jar needs to be a clear glass jar. Try to think of any important adjectives you should use when describing your materials.

Read over each step to make sure it is clear. Try to think of any way your audience could get the step wrong. If you can think of one, you will need a clearer way to say what you mean.

How-to Articles

Content Editing

Kim liked the draft she had written. However, she knew she could make it better by editing. She read her draft again, seeing if it was clear, complete, and correct. As she edited, she used this Content Editor's Checklist.

After editing her draft, Kim gave it to her friend Justin. Since he had never made a snow globe, she thought he would be able to find any missing steps.

Justin read Kim's draft twice. He read it through all the way once. Then he used the checklist to look it over more carefully. He took notes on what changes Kim might make. Then he shared his notes with her.

Content Editor's Checklist

✓ Does the introduction tell what is being taught?

✓ Does the body list all the materials that are needed?

✓ Does the body include all the important steps?

✓ Are the steps given in time order?

✓ Have all unimportant details been left out?

✓ Are all the details specific and clear?

✓ Does the conclusion sum up what has been taught?

Justin began by telling Kim how interesting he thought her topic was. He had never heard of someone making a homemade snow globe. He told her that all the materials seemed to be listed and most of the steps were clear and in time order. He also liked the introduction. Then Justin gave Kim these suggestions.

- Can you give an example of what kind of plastic toy might look nice in a snow globe?

- I don't know if kids would have silicone sealer. Where can you buy it?

- I don't think you need all the stuff about eggshells. If you don't use them, why tell about them?

- Shouldn't you let the glue dry before you put the lid on?

- I think the end comes too fast. You might want to add a better conclusion.

Kim listened to Justin's suggestions. She thought he had some good ideas. She thanked Justin and decided to use his ideas when she revised her draft.

Your Turn

Read your draft carefully and answer the questions on the Content Editor's Checklist. Take notes of the changes you would like to make.

Trade drafts with a partner. Read your partner's draft and answer the questions on the checklist. You might want to read the draft more than once. Think of any ideas that might improve your partner's draft.

Share your ideas with your partner. Start by telling what you like about the draft. Then give some ideas of what your partner might change.

Listen to your partner's ideas for your draft. Make any changes that you think will improve your draft.

Revising

Here are the changes that Kim made after meeting with Justin.

How to Make a Snow Globe

A snow globe is a pretty decaration, did you know that you can make one yourself? Here's how to do it.

You will need a ^clear glass^ jar and lid, glue, corn syrup, glitter, silicone sealer, paint, and a plastic toy that fits inside the jar. Choose a plastic toy that would look nice inside a snow globe. ^such as a person, an animal, or a tree.^ You can find silicone sealer at a ^hardware store.^

To make the globe, glue the plastic toy to the jar's lid. Fill the jar most of the way up with corn syrup. Pour in some ^one teaspoon of^ glitter.

~~You could use eggshells instead of glitter, but that's messier and doesn't look as nice. You would have to boil the eggs. Then you would have to peel the eggshells and break them up to look like snow. I would just use glitter.~~

Spread some silicone sealer over the top of the jar. Screw the lid on tightly. ^You should let the glue dry first.^ If you want, you can paint the top or bottom of your globe to make it more colorful.

Turn over the jar so the lid is the base and the toy is right side up. To test the globe, shake it. The glitter should float inside the globe and fall down slowly like snow. Find a special place where you can put your homemade snow globe.

Look at some of the ways Kim revised her how-to article. She used Justin's ideas, as well as her own, to improve her how-to article.

- She added a few examples of plastic toys that might look nice in a snow globe.

- She explained where a reader might be able to find the silicone sealer.

- Kim agreed that the part about eggshells was not an important detail. She deleted that paragraph.

- She realized that she should add a step about waiting for the glue to dry.

- Kim decided to add more to the conclusion. She explained the result of shaking the globe. She also gave an idea of what to do with the globe.

Finally Kim made a few other changes that she thought were important. She decided to be more specific by telling the audience to use one teaspoon of glitter. She also decided to describe the jar as a "clear glass jar."

Your Turn

Look at your partner's suggestions and your own ideas for improving your draft. Choose the ones you think will make it better. Make the changes to your draft. When you finish, go over the Content Editor's Checklist again. Be sure you can answer yes to each question.

How-to Articles

Copyediting and Proofreading

Copyediting

Kim thought her revisions had made her draft better. However, she knew there was more to do. She still had to copyedit her draft to make sure every sentence was written clearly and correctly. She used this Copyeditor's Checklist to help her.

Copyeditor's Checklist

✓ Are all the sentences complete sentences?

✓ Are there any run-on sentences?

✓ Do all the words have the right meaning?

✓ Are the directions clear and specific?

✓ Are any words repeated too often?

✓ Are time words used correctly?

Kim found more changes to make. Her first sentence was a run-on sentence. She made it into two sentences.

In the second paragraph, she thought she didn't need to use the word *plastic* twice. She took it out of the second sentence.

Next she thought that some of her directions were not specific enough. Saying that the silicone sealer went on the "top of the jar" seemed confusing, so she called it the "rim." Just to be sure, she said that the rim was where the lid goes.

Finally, Kim noticed that she had not used any time words. She added the words *then* and *next* to make the sentences fit together better.

Your Turn

Read your how-to article again. Copyedit it, using the Copyeditor's Checklist. Look for any incomplete sentences or run-on sentences. Make sure that you have used words that mean exactly what you want. See if there are any places where you can add time words to make the sentences fit together better.

Proofreading

Kim was glad she found so many ways to improve her article. She knew that a proofreader might find any mistakes she had missed. Kim asked a classmate, Mariano, to check her draft for spelling, grammar, and punctuation. He used this Proofreader's Checklist.

Proofreader's Checklist

✓ Are the paragraphs indented?

✓ Have all the words been spelled correctly?

✓ Is the grammar correct?

✓ Are capitalization and punctuation correct?

✓ Were any new mistakes made during editing?

Mariano enjoyed reading Kim's article about snow globes. He thought he might make one himself. He also noticed a few mistakes that Kim had made in her draft.

First, Mariano noticed that the word *decaration* looked strange. He checked a dictionary and found that it was spelled *decoration*.

Mariano thought that Kim should say to which side of the lid the toy should be glued. Kim wished she had noticed that mistake herself during copyediting. However, she was glad Mariano noticed it now.

Finally, Mariano saw a mistake in one of Kim's changes. The sentence about waiting for the glue to dry was not in time order. He thought she should add it earlier in the how-to article.

Your Turn

Read your draft, using the Proofreader's Checklist. Look for any mistakes you may have made. Then give your draft to someone else to check. Listen to the changes your proofreader suggests. Make the changes that improve your draft.

How-to Articles

Publishing

Kim's how-to article was almost completed. She looked it over one more time. Then she typed it on her computer. She typed the title at the top and put her name below it. Then she printed out her how-to article.

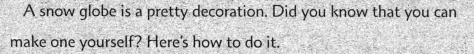

How to Make a Snow Globe

By Kim Aiello

A snow globe is a pretty decoration. Did you know that you can make one yourself? Here's how to do it.

You will need a clear glass jar and lid, glue, corn syrup, glitter, silicone sealer, paint, and a plastic toy that fits inside the jar. Choose a toy that would look nice inside a snow globe, such as a person, an animal, or a tree. You can find silicone sealer at a hardware store.

To make the globe, glue the plastic toy to the inside of the jar's lid. Let the glue dry. Then fill the jar most of the way up with corn syrup. Pour in one teaspoon of glitter.

Next, spread some silicone sealer over the rim of the jar, where the lid will go. Screw the lid on tightly. If you want, you can paint the top or bottom of your globe to make it more colorful.

Turn over the jar so the lid is the base and the toy is right-side up. To test the globe, shake it. The glitter should float inside the globe and fall down slowly like snow. Find a special place where you can put your homemade snow globe.

Your Turn

Look over your draft one more time. Make sure all the changes have been made correctly.

Add a title and your name at the top if you haven't already done this. Print out your article on a computer or write it neatly on a sheet of paper.

To publish your article, make a class how-to manual. Put everyone's articles together. Arrange them by subject in alphabetical order. Make a table of contents that shows the order of the articles.

Add a title page too. The title might be *The Fourth-Grade How-to Manual*. To decorate the cover, draw pictures of the things that are the topics of the articles.

Place your manual in a binder. Display it in the school library or office. Then everyone in the school will be able to read your how-to article.

CHAPTER
5

Before European settlers arrived in what is now Massachusetts, several different Native American peoples lived in the area. The Wampanoag people were one such group. These people were the first ones to meet the Pilgrims when they arrived. The Wampanoag taught the newcomers their methods for hunting, fishing, and farming. What would you teach someone who has moved to your area from another country?

Persuasive Writing

Experienced Babysitter for Hire

Do you need someone to watch your toddlers or young children while you run errands on weekends? My babysitting service is just what you need. My name is Debbie Krantz. I am a 13-year-old girl. I look after my six-year-old brother and four-year-old sister on Saturdays and Sundays. I keep close watch on them as they play in our backyard or playroom. I can look after two or three more children at the same time.

I have been babysitting for two years. My customers are always happy. I have a lot of experience with children of different ages. I know how to change diapers and how to prepare baby formula. I can make healthy meals that children like. I know how to play many games that older children enjoy.

My rates are reasonable. Prices for babies in diapers are $4 per hour. Prices for older children are $3 per hour. I will look after children who are between the ages of one and eight years. My service is available on Saturdays from 8:30 a.m. until 4:30 p.m. and on Sundays from 10:30 a.m. until 4:00 p.m.

If you want to call some of my customers, I will give you their phone numbers. My phone number is 555-3705. Please call me if you are interested.

What Makes Good Persuasive Writing?

Persuasive writing tries to convince readers to think or act in a certain way. Sometimes it is used to get people to buy a particular product or to urge people to vote for a political candidate.

Choosing a Topic

When writing a persuasive article, it is important to choose a topic that has two sides. For example, your topic might be your school's music program. The way you feel about the topic is your point of view. You feel strongly that your school should continue to fund the music program. You play the piano and hope to be part of a famous orchestra someday.

Introduction

State your topic and point of view clearly in the introduction. Write what you want your readers to believe or how you want them to act. In the model Debbie says she wants parents to allow her to babysit their children.

Body

In the body give reasons to support your point of view. Reasons help the audience understand why you feel a certain way. They convince your readers that your point of view is correct. Some reasons are facts and some are opinions. Debbie says that she has been babysitting for two years, that she can change diapers, and that she charges reasonable rates.

Conclusion

Sum up your persuasive article with your strongest reasons. Don't add any new reasons in the conclusion, but restate your point of view in a clear and positive way. Your conclusion might include things your readers can do if they agree with you.

Activity A

Read each topic and decide if you are for or against it. Write your point of view about the topic.

1. exploring space

2. limiting cell phone usage

3. being a vegetarian

4. recycling

5. protecting our natural forests

Activity B

The following are possible points of view. Decide if each point of view is either appropriate or inappropriate for a persuasive article.

1. The town should fix the potholes on Main Street.

2. Life on Mars would be fun.

3. The local library ought to have more computers.

4. My cat, Osiris, is the best cat in the world.

5. People should walk instead of drive their cars at least one day a week.

Writer's Corner

Write down three topics that you have strong feelings about. After each topic explain why it is important to you.

Audience

It is necessary to know your audience when writing a persuasive article. The reasons and language you use will change depending on who you are writing for. Debbie's advertising flyer is aimed at parents. The reasons she gives for using her babysitting service are important to them.

Activity C

Each of the following pairs of sentences is from an advertisement. The audience is either adults or students. Decide for what audience you think each reason is aimed.

1. **a.** The Iso-wheel bicycle is comfortable and easy to pedal.

   b. The awesome Iso-wheel bicycle will blow your friends away.

2. **a.** Watch Channel 6 News for the latest high school basketball scores.

   b. Channel 6 News gives the rush hour travel times every 12 minutes.

3. **a.** Chill out in South Carolina on the hottest beaches along the Atlantic coast.

   b. Visit historic South Carolina and experience a taste of the Old South.

4. **a.** HiForce energy bars provide essential vitamins and minerals.

   b. HiForce energy bars give you the power to play like a champion.

5. **a.** The Igloo jacket has cool colors and is maxed out with pockets for all your gear.

   b. The Igloo jacket comes in many colors and has more pockets than any other jacket available.

Read the following persuasive article. Then answer the questions.

On Saturday a group of students and teachers is going to meet in the vacant lot across the street from our schoolyard. Our plan is to pick up the trash that has made the lot an eyesore in the neighborhood. Mrs. Soca and other local residents have complained about the mess. Students from our school have added to the litter there. We helped make the mess, and we should clean it up. The project won't take long if enough students show up. Please come and help beautify the neighborhood on Saturday at 10 a.m.

1. Who is the intended audience for this persuasive article?

2. What is the topic?

3. What is the writer's point of view?

4. What does the writer want the audience to do?

5. What reasons does the writer give to persuade the audience?

6. What facts does the writer give to support the topic?

Writer's Corner

Choose one of the three topics that you wrote about in the Writer's Corner on page 161. Use the Internet and reference books to look for reasons to support your point of view. Write an explanation telling why the topic might be important to someone else.

Fact and Opinion

Both facts and opinions are used as reasons in persuasive writing. A fact is a statement that can be proved. You can check facts on the Internet or at the library. Here is an example of a fact.

> Puerto Rico is a territory of the United States.

An opinion is a statement of a person's judgment, belief, or feeling about a topic. Opinions cannot be proved true or false. Words such as *should*, *could*, *believe*, and *feel* often signal opinions. The opinions in a persuasive article should be supported by facts. Here is an example of an opinion.

> Puerto Rico should be made a state.

The point of view in a persuasive article states the writer's opinion about the topic. A writer should use facts to support that opinion. If a writer uses only opinions to persuade, the argument will be weak and may not convince readers.

Activity A

Tell which sentence in each pair is an opinion.
Tell which sentence is a fact.

1. **a.** I believe that parrots are intelligent birds.
   b. There is a parrot that can say 950 different words.

2. **a.** Maple trees lose their leaves every fall.
   b. Every neighborhood should have maple trees.

3. **a.** I think that Vincent Van Gogh was a great artist.
   b. Vincent Van Gogh sold only one painting in his life.

Activity B

Identify each statement as a fact or an opinion. Explain your answer.

1. Construction workers put up new buildings.
2. Construction is exciting work.
3. Machines called bulldozers dig and dump dirt.
4. All boys want to drive bulldozers.
5. Construction sites are dangerous.
6. Construction workers wear hard hats on the job.
7. Carpenters and plumbers work in construction.
8. Construction workers are paid by the hour.
9. Construction workers like to work overtime.

Activity C

Read each point of view. Write an opinion that supports each one.

1. Young children should eat fruit instead of candy.
2. Theaters should not show ads before the movie.
3. Smoking should be against the law.
4. Everyone should recycle their trash.
5. Girls and boys should be allowed to play on all school teams.

Writer's Corner

Think of an interesting topic and write two or more facts about it. Then write your opinion about the topic. Discuss what you wrote with a partner. How could you prove each fact? What clues show that the other statements are opinions?

Checking Facts

When you write to persuade, make sure that all of your facts are correct. If readers know that one statement is not true, they could decide that your work is not believable. You can check your facts by looking them up in books or on the Internet. You could also talk to an expert.

Activity D

Check each statement in a reference book or on the Internet. Tell which are facts and which are false.

1. The song "Satin Doll" was written by Duke Ellington.
2. The 1996 Olympic Games were held in Berlin, Germany.
3. Parts of Lake Superior are over 1,000 feet deep.
4. Michigan was the 15th state to join the United States.
5. The Everglades are in Arizona.

Activity E

Read each point of view below. Tell whether the sentence that supports it is a fact or an opinion. Discuss how you could check each fact.

1. Students should not have to wear school uniforms. Uniforms are too expensive.

2. Schools should not serve soft drinks in cafeterias. Milk has more vitamins than soft drinks.

3. Classes should start later in the morning. Students will have more time to prepare for school.

4. Schools should be in session throughout the year. I believe that a 3-month summer vacation is too long.

5. Classes should have no more than 25 students. Teachers will have more time for each student.

Activity F

Reread the model on page 159. Find two opinions and two facts. Write them down. Discuss what words signaled opinions. Discuss how you could check each fact.

Activity G

Read the following paragraph from a persuasive article. Answer the questions.

I should receive more allowance. I pay for my own lunch. The cost of lunch has gone up, but my allowance has stayed the same. Now I have less money to spend on things I want. Grownups get raises when prices of things go up. I should get a raise too. It's only fair.

1. What is the writer trying to persuade the reader to do?

2. Which sentences are facts?

3. Which sentences are opinions?

4. Does the writer do a good job of supporting his opinions? Explain your answer.

Writer's Corner

Choose one pair of sentences from Activity E. Use the sentences in a piece of persuasive writing. Add other facts and opinions to support your topic.

Synonyms

Synonyms are words that have the same or almost the same meaning. Here are some pairs of synonyms that you might use when you read or write.

sleepy/tired	price/cost
victory/win	scared/frightened
huge/enormous	right/correct
icy/cold	angry/upset
dull/boring	silly/foolish

Writers sometimes use synonyms to replace words that they use too often. Synonyms can make your writing more interesting or more precise.

● Activity A ●

Some synonyms are more precise than others in certain sentences. Choose the synonym that fits better in each sentence below.

1. The toy (starts, begins) when you push the button.

2. Dogs can be trained to (lead, guide) people who are blind.

3. The cookie jar is (empty, vacant).

4. The pioneers had to cross many (thick, wide) rivers.

5. My watch seems to be running (quickly, fast).

6. The bus was (late, tardy) this morning.

7. We crossed the Illinois (edge, border) and entered Iowa.

8. The pie was baked (new, fresh) this morning.

Activity B

Read the lists of words. Match each word in Column A to its synonym in Column B.

Column A	Column B
1. pretty	**a.** fast
2. angry	**b.** beautiful
3. laugh	**c.** stroll
4. walk	**d.** mad
5. quick	**e.** giggle

Activity C

Tell whether the underlined words in each sentence are synonyms.

1. Diane's grin looked like a clown's smile.

2. The dirt in our yard is good soil for plants.

3. A narrow bridge crossed over the wide river.

4. Jake is pleased with the idea and happy to help.

5. The team wanted to win, but they lost.

6. His pants were dirty, and his shoes were filthy.

7. This is an actual Roman coin, a real treasure.

8. A nice man returned the book I lost.

9. The rain was a refreshing shower on such a hot day.

10. If you scrub the kitchen floor, I'll vacuum the hall carpet.

Writer's Corner

Describe a person or place you saw recently. Then choose five words from your description and replace them with synonyms. How did your synonyms change your description?

Our Wide Wide World

The first battle of the American Revolution took place in 1775 in Lexington, Massachusetts. The British soldiers were regular military. They were paid to fight in the king's army. The Americans were volunteers. They were called "Minutemen" because they could be ready to fight on short notice. The first shot fired at Lexington was called "the shot heard 'round the world." Why do you think it was given this name?

Synonyms can add variety to your writing. A paragraph that has variety does not use the same words over and over again. Read the following paragraph. Does it have variety?

A big dog chased me up a big hill. I was lucky because there was a big tree at the top. I climbed up and sat on a big branch. The dog jumped up and ripped a big piece out of my pant leg. After a while the dog left and I climbed out of the tree.

It is easy to understand what is happening in the paragraph. However, most people would not enjoy reading it. Even though the word *big* is used correctly, it is used too often. The paragraph doesn't have variety. Read the following paragraph with synonyms replacing the word *big*.

A huge dog chased me up a high hill. I was lucky because there was a tall tree at the top. I climbed up and sat on a thick branch. The dog jumped up and ripped a large piece out of my pant leg. After a while the dog left and I climbed out of the tree.

The second paragraph tells the same story as the first. It is more interesting, though, because it has more variety.

Activity D

Write the sentences below. Replace each word in italics with a synonym from the word box. If you need help, use a dictionary to check word meanings.

| quarrel | liberty | tardy | bushes | twine |

1. I tied the sticks together with *string*.

2. Abraham Lincoln gave enslaved people their *freedom*.

3. Let's not *argue* today.

4. Kylie was *late* for class.

5. We lost the ball in the *shrubs*.

Activity E

Think about what you learned about antonyms in Chapter 2.
Draw the following chart on a separate sheet of paper.
Complete the chart by adding antonyms and synonyms.
The first one is done for you.

Word	Antonym	Synonym
tiny	huge	small
1. fix		
2. sadness		
3. good		
4. honest		
5. shack		

Activity F

Rewrite the paragraph. Replace five words with synonyms.
Underline the synonyms you use.

Jerry is afraid that his sister, Sonya, is going to be late for
Marta's surprise party. He is afraid that if Sonya is late, Marta
might come to the party at the same time. Then the surprise
would be ruined. Jerry is also afraid that the guests will be
noisy. If the guests are too noisy, Marta will hear them. That
could also ruin the surprise. We need to help Jerry so he
won't be afraid.

Writer's Corner

Think of a word that has several synonyms, such
as *big, good,* or *happy.* Write down 10 synonyms
for the word. Then write a story that includes the
10 synonyms.

Dictionary

Our Wide Wide World

Today, whale watching is a popular activity in Massachusetts. Long ago, whales were a source of food and fuel. New Bedford, Massachusetts, was once known as the whaling capital of the world. Whaling is also part of the history of the Native Americans who live in southeastern Massachusetts.

Imagine that you read in a book that an army has set up a bivouac outside of town. If you have never seen the word *bivouac* before, you could look it up in a dictionary and learn that a bivouac is a military camp.

You know that you can use a dictionary to find the meanings of words that you do not know. Dictionaries also have other uses.

When you learn a new word, try to use it in your writing. Also use it in your everyday speech whenever you can. However, you want to be sure that when you say the word, you pronounce it correctly. A dictionary shows the correct way to pronounce words. Look at this sample entry for the word *bivouac*.

biv•ou•ac (biv′ o͞o ak′) *n.* a temporary camp set up for soldiers in the field.

Syllables

The dots in the entry word show how the word is divided into syllables. A syllable is a word part that can be pronounced separately. How many syllables are in the word *bivouac*?

Dictionary Respelling

In parentheses right after the entry word is the dictionary respelling. The respelling shows how to pronounce the word. Sometimes you can figure out how a word is pronounced just by looking at the respelling. Other times you may have to check the pronunciation key.

Pronunciation Key

The dictionary respelling for *bivouac* shows that the first syllable is *biv*. You know that *b* and *v* are always pronounced the same, but *i* can be pronounced in different ways. How can you decide the correct way to say *biv*? You can use the pronunciation key. Look at the pronunciation key on the right.

Look for the letter *i* in the key. There are two of them. One is an ordinary *i* and the other is an *i* with a bar over it (ī). The ordinary *i* is next to the word *fit*. That means it is pronounced the same way as the *i* in *fit*. Because the *i* in *biv* is an ordinary *i*, you know that it stands for the sound of *i* in *fit*. Look at the second and third syllables in *bivouac*. How would you pronounce them?

a	cat	u	up
ā	ape	ʉ	fur
ä	cot, car	ch	chin
e	ten	sh	she
ē	me	th	thin
i	fit	*th*	then
ī	ice	zh	measure
ō	go	ŋ	ring
ô	fall, for	ə— a *in* ago
oo	look	— e *in* agent
ōo	tool	— i *in* pencil
oi	oil	— o *in* atom
ou	out	— u *in* circus

Activity A

Tell which two words in each row rhyme. Use dictionary respellings to help you pronounce each word.

1. grown   gown   faun   dawn
2. squall   brawl   fowl   knoll
3. slough   bough   beau   gruff
4. brown   known   hewn   sewn
5. ballet   mallet   wallet   chalet

Writer's Corner

Write about something you did last weekend. Then replace some of the words with dictionary respellings. Trade work with a partner and read your partner's writing aloud.

Accent Marks

A dictionary respelling uses special marks to show how to say a word. There are also marks to show which syllables are pronounced with more stress. Look at the dictionary respelling for *bivouac*.

(biv′ $\overline{oo}$ ak′)

The marks after *biv* and *ak* are called accent marks. They show that these syllables are stressed more than the second syllable. Because the accent mark after *biv* is darker than the one after *ak*, the stress is heavier on the first syllable. Often respellings have only one accent mark. That syllable is given more stress than the others. The other syllables are given equal stress.

Activity B

Say these words softly to yourself. Write them on a sheet of paper. Write how many syllables each word has. Then draw an accent mark after the syllable that you think is stressed the most. Check a dictionary to see if you were correct.

1. generation
2. responsible
3. university
4. electricity
5. refrigerator

6. opportunity
7. manufacture
8. veterinarian
9. magnificent
10. illustration

Activity C

Use a dictionary. Write out the dictionary respellings of these words. Use accent marks.

1. plateau
2. crochet
3. guffaw
4. loquacious
5. sallow

• Activity D •

Find each underlined word in a dictionary and write its dictionary respelling. Be ready to pronounce the word correctly as you read the sentence to the class.

1. We watched the <u>dirigible</u> fly over our heads.

2. The curtain was moved by a warm May <u>zephyr</u>.

3. Aunt Rhoda wears <u>pince-nez</u> glasses when she reads.

4. A lightning storm is a terrifying <u>phenomenon</u> to experience.

5. The woman's <u>chauffeur</u> picks her up every day at four.

• Activity E •

Use a dictionary to find the word in each pair that is pronounced the way that the respelling shows. Then write a sentence using that word. Be ready to read your sentence aloud in class.

1. mə ral'   morale/moral

2. fi nal' ē   finally/finale

3. dē sent'   decent/descent

4. pʉr sə nel'   personal/personnel

5. i ras' ə bəl   erasable/irascible

6. def' ər əns   difference/deference

Writer's Corner

Write five sentences, using words from this lesson that you did not know before. Be ready to read the sentences aloud in class.

Compound Subjects and Predicates

You can make your writing more interesting if you vary the lengths of your sentences. Readers can become bored reading a lot of short, choppy sentences. Often, short sentences can be combined to make longer, more interesting ones.

Compound Subjects

One way to make longer sentences is by using compound subjects. You can make compound subjects when you have two or more subjects doing the same thing.

> Parents support Irma Batz for senator. Teachers are also for Irma Batz.

> Parents and teachers support Irma Batz for senator.

Notice that the ideas in the two sentences are not worded exactly the same way. As long as the action is the same in the sentences, the subjects can be combined.

Subjects can be combined if the sentences have being verbs instead of action verbs.

> My uncle is a veteran. My cousin is also a veteran.

> My uncle and my cousin are veterans.

The conjunction *or* can also be used to make a compound subject.

> Mom or Dad will pick you up at the station.

Questions can have compound subjects too.

> Will Hank and Fiona try out for the band?

Activity A

Tell which sentences contain compound subjects.

1. Tina and her dog are in the backyard.
2. Janine or Frieda will be our next class president.
3. The twins misbehaved all day long.
4. You and I can beat these guys.
5. Mark, Eric, and Laura missed the bus.
6. John and his brother were at the party.
7. Jerzy took Melissa to the doctor.
8. Two runners tied for second place.
9. Do the dog and cat have fresh water?
10. Five people boarded the train.

Activity B

If the two sentences in each item can be combined into one sentence with a compound subject, write the new sentence on a separate sheet of paper. If they can't be combined, write _no_.

1. Bubba plays tennis. Sissy plays the flute.
2. Do you like to watch old movies? Does your sister like them too?
3. I was sick on Monday. My sister was also ill.
4. Tina likes her steak rare. She likes hamburgers well done.
5. Mr. Li is learning English. Mrs. Gomez is learning it too.

Writer's Corner

Describe things in nature, using sentences with compound subjects. Then divide each sentence into two sentences. Do the longer sentences sound better than the short ones?

Compound Predicates

Another way to combine sentences is when the same subject is doing two or more things at the same time. You can write the two actions as a compound predicate.

The old cat sat in the sun. It purred contentedly.

The old cat sat in the sun and purred contentedly.

Just as with compound subjects, the conjunction *or* can be used to make compound predicates.

Terri may sing for us. She may play her flute instead.

Terri may sing or play her flute for us.

Compound predicates can be made with the conjunction *but*.

I pushed hard but couldn't budge the car.

Just as with compound subjects, compound predicates can be used in questions.

Will you help us and vote for clean air?

• Activity C •

Tell which of the following sentences contains a compound predicate.

1. Ernest forgot to wear a hat and caught a cold.
2. The car ran out of gas and sputtered to a stop.
3. Are you cooking tonight or should I?
4. I just started piano lessons, but my brother has played for years.
5. Mom will leave early and get there before noon.
6. Pedro divided the cake between Eric and Missy.
7. Jacques watched two birds circling overhead.
8. Emil lost his bus pass and had to walk home.
9. Who drove the car and didn't fill the tank?
10. Allison found the gloves that she lost yesterday.

Activity D

Decide if the two sentences in each pair can be combined into one sentence with a compound predicate. If they can be combined, write the new sentence on a separate sheet of paper. If they can't be combined, write *no*.

1. Jack fell down. He broke his crown.

2. Merna fell off her horse. She takes riding lessons on Saturdays.

3. Donna took off her shoes. She walked across the waxed floor.

4. The young tree bent. It did not break.

5. She served my pizza piping hot. I'll eat it cold too.

6. Greg opened the refrigerator. He took out a jar of pickles.

7. I could buy new shoes. I could save for a video game.

Activity E

Tell whether the following sentences have a compound subject or a compound predicate.

1. Keesha and Leona got As on the test.

2. Bunny practiced every day and became a good dancer.

3. The flowers wilted and died.

4. I heard my favorite song and started to sing.

5. Squirrels and hamsters are rodents.

Writer's Corner

Write five pairs of sentences, each with one predicate. Trade papers with a partner. Expand your partner's sentences, using compound predicates. Share the expanded sentences with your partner.

Oral Persuasion

Oral persuasion is a common form of communication. You hear it every day when you listen to TV and radio commercials. You probably use it yourself to try to convince people to agree with you. This morning you might have tried to persuade someone to drive you to school. Maybe you asked for some extra spending money for after school.

Choosing a Topic

Give an oral presentation to persuade your audience to buy a product or service. Your audience will be your classmates. Choose a product your audience might be interested in purchasing. You might choose a bike washing service or a video game.

Introduction

Clearly state your point of view in your introduction. Explain why your audience will want to buy the product or service. You might begin your introduction with a catchy sentence. For example, a presentation about a bike-washing service might begin "If your bike could talk, would it say, 'Wash me!'?"

Body

In the body give reasons to support your point of view. Include facts and opinions. A fact about a bike washing service might be, "It costs three dollars." An opinion might be, "People will be dazzled by your clean bike."

Conclusion

For a conclusion restate your point of view clearly and positively. Sum up the reasons for using your product or service. Tell the audience how their lives will be improved. End with a sentence that will leave your audience thinking about your product or service.

Planning Your Presentation

When you have decided what you want to talk about, begin planning your presentation. You can plan by writing keywords and phrases for your introduction, body, and conclusion on separate note cards. Think of visual aids you might use in your presentation, such as the product or a picture of it. For example, if your topic is a new baseball mitt, you might bring to class a baseball mitt and point out its features. You might also draw several pictures detailing your product or service. Plan a time during your presentation to show your visual aids.

• Activity A •

Imagine you are writing a commercial for a product or service. Choose a topic and write an opening statement or question. Write one fact and one opinion about why the audience might buy the product or service. Then write a closing sentence for the commercial that will convince your audience to buy your product.

Speaker's Corner

Work with a partner. Use what you wrote in Activity A to persuade each other to buy the product or service. After your partner has finished, ask questions about the topic. Work together to think of answers that might persuade an audience to buy the product or service.

Practice

Before giving a speech, it is important to practice. The more you practice, the less nervous you will feel when giving your presentation. Practice in front of a mirror, or in front of a friend or family member. Look at your audience as you talk, but refer to your note cards when you need to jog your memory. Use a tone of voice that shows excitement about what you are selling. Practice showing visual aids. Ask for suggestions to improve your speech.

Listening to Persuasive Speeches

You should listen to the speaker with an open mind. When you listen with an open mind, you wait until the speech is over to decide if you agree or disagree. Be ready to think about what are the speaker's opinions and what are the facts. It is up to you to decide what makes sense and what doesn't.

If you have questions about what a speaker has said, raise your hand after the speech. Ask your question politely. If the speaker used facts that you don't think are true, research them later to see if they are correct.

Whether you agree with the speaker's point of view, you should follow the same listening tips that you follow for any presentation.

- Sit still and look at the speaker.
- Pay attention to what the speaker is saying.
- Don't talk to people in the audience.
- Clap when the speaker has finished.

LIBERTY LINE.
NEW ARRANGEMENT---NIGHT AND DAY.

The improved and splendid Locomotives, Clarkson and Lundy, with their trains fitted up in the best style of accommodation for passengers, will run their regular trips during the present season, between the borders of the Patriarchal Dominion and Libertyville, Upper Canada. Gentlemen and Ladies, who may wish to improve their health or circumstances, by a northern tour, are respectfully invited to give us their patronage.
SEATS FREE, irrespective of color.
Necessary Clothing furnished gratuitously to such as have "fallen among thieves."

"Hide the outcasts—let the oppressed go free."—Bible.
☞For seats apply at any of the trap doors, or to the conductor of the train.
J. CROSS, Proprietor.
N. B. For the special benefit of Pro-Slavery Police Officers, an extra heavy wagon for Texas, will be furnished, whenever it may be necessary, in which they will be forwarded as dead freight, to the "Valley of Rascals," always at the risk of the owners.
☞Extra Overcoats provided for such of them as are afflicted with protracted chilly-phobia.

Activity B

Work with a small group. Look through a magazine or think of TV commercials. For each advertisement or commercial, discuss whether it uses any of the following reasons to persuade its audience. Write down any other persuasive reasons. Talk about which reasons were most effective and why.

1. This product is better than the competition.

2. You will have fun using this product.

3. This product is less expensive than the competition.

4. Your life will be improved by using this product.

5. You will be healthier if you use this product.

Activity C

Think of a product or service that you want to persuade your classmates to buy. Write a catchy opening sentence or question for your introduction. Consider reasons that might persuade your audience. You might choose some of the reasons from Activity B to help you think of ideas. Write a memorable conclusion to sum up your presentation. Record keywords and phrases on separate note cards. Choose a visual aid to use in your presentation.

Speaker's Corner

Give your presentation to the class. Make eye contact with your audience and speak in a clear, lively voice. Be sure that any visual aids can be easily seen. Invite questions and comments at the end of your presentation. Ask questions and give feedback on your classmates' presentations.

Persuasive Writing

Prewriting and Drafting

Writing to persuade is an important type of writing. Today you will start writing a leaflet to persuade people to do what you want them to do.

Prewriting

Prewriting is the time you choose a topic and organize ideas. It is the time you decide who your audience will be. You usually have strong feelings about the topic, or you have a personal interest in it.

Choosing a Topic

Simeon wanted to make a citizenship leaflet as part of his leadership challenge for student council. Simeon started by thinking of topic ideas and listing them on a sheet of paper. He considered persuading people to vote in school elections or being nicer in the hallways, but those ideas didn't spark his interest. Then he thought of the yearly bazaar coming up at his school. Simeon decided to make a leaflet persuading parents to attend the bazaar. He knew that the money from the bazaar would help the school buy the video equipment they needed.

Your Turn

Are you trying to earn money for something special? You might want to persuade people to hire you to do chores. Maybe your cat had kittens that you want to give away. Perhaps there is something that you feel strongly about. Brainstorm ideas that you would like to persuade people to act on. Choose one that would be a good topic for your leaflet.

Think of a short statement that tells what you want your audience to do. It should be something that you can support with facts as well as opinions. Write a statement of your point of view.

Organizing Ideas

Last year's bazaar was a big success. People liked the baked goods so much they bought them all. They also bought over 50 pieces of students' art that were on sale. The games were busy all day. Simeon made an idea web to organize his thinking about reasons that people came to the bazaar.

In Simeon's center circle was "Come to the Monroe School Bazaar." He added reasons that people should come. He also added more facts to support the reasons.

Simeon showed his idea web to Mrs. Roth. She said that it was a good beginning, but he had left out the most important reason. He forgot to include making money for Monroe School. Many educational programs were on DVDs, and the school didn't have a DVD player. The school also needed a bigger TV to make sure that all the students could see the educational programs. Simeon added another circle to his idea web.

Your Turn

Read the statement that you wrote in the middle of your paper. Use it as the center circle of an idea web. Write down reasons why readers would want to do as you ask in circles around the statement. The reasons could be facts or opinions.

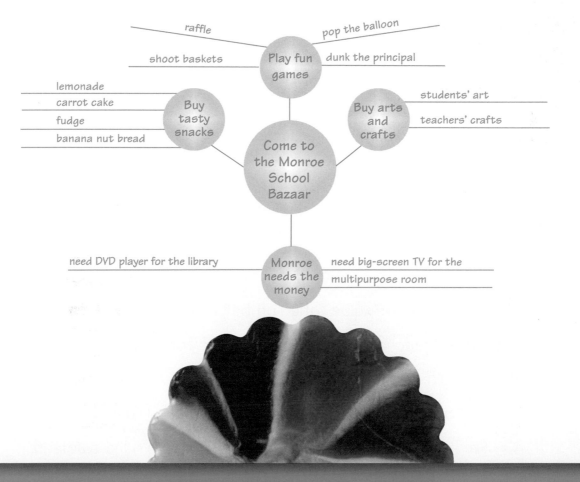

Drafting

Simeon used his idea web to help him as he wrote the first draft of his leaflet. He knew that his final copy would be different from this one. He probably would change words and sentences to improve his draft.

Simeon asked Mrs. Roth to read over his writing. She had reminded him to add making money for the school as a reason for parents to come to the bazaar. She would probably have other good suggestions.

Come to the Monroe School Bazaar!

On May ninth, Monroe School is having its yearly bazaar. Come and spend a little of your money to help our school a lot. Buy delicious fudge, carrot cakes, banana nut bread, and other goodies baked by parents of Monroe Students. How do you know the goodies are delicious? Last year we ran out of them way before the bazaar was over. Now our volunteer bakers have promised to double their batches. There will be plenty of goodies to go around. You can take them home. You can eat them at the bazaar.

Don't forget the artwork and crafts! Beautiful pictures and clay sculptures made by Monroe students will be on sale. There will also be knitted goods made by several teachers. A beautiful quilt will be rafled off before the end of the day. Monroe teachers pitched in to make it. Even Principle Losetsky helped to peice it together.

Last, but not least we garantee that you will have a lot of fun. There will be plenty of loud music to dance to in the cafeteria.

There will be games in the gym. Hit the target and dunk Principle Losetsky in the water tank. Break three out of five balloons with the darts and win a bank. Make 3 out of 5 free throws with the basketballs and win a chance to push a cream pie into Mr. Goetz's face. You know you always wanted to do that to a gym teacher.

The best reason to come to the bazaar is that you will help Monroe School to get a new big-screen TV and a DVD player. The 24-inch TV that we have now is too small for students in the back row to see. Many educational programs now come on DVDs.

Your Turn

Review your idea web before you start writing. Think about your audience and what you want them to do as you write your first draft. State your topic and point of view early in your leaflet. Restate it at the end, using different words.

The reasons that you use to support your point of view should appeal to your audience. Be sure to include facts that support your point of view.

Persuasive Writing

Content Editing

Simeon was happy with his draft. He had chosen an interesting topic and thought of good reasons to support his point of view. He knew, however, that his draft could be improved during content editing.

Simeon used this Content Editor's Checklist for persuasive writing as he read through his leaflet.

Content Editor's Checklist

✓ Do the introduction and conclusion state your topic and point of view?

✓ Are there reasons that will convince readers to do what you want them to do?

✓ Are the reasons aimed at the right audience?

✓ Are facts and opinions given to support the point of view?

✓ Is all important information included?

✓ Is unimportant information left out?

Simeon thought that he should remind his audience at the end to come to the bazaar.

After writing those sentences, Simeon felt good about his leaflet. However, he knew that there were probably other ways to improve it that he had missed. He asked his friend Chris to take a look.

Chris read over Simeon's work several times. She used the checklist to make sure that she didn't miss anything important. She wrote notes about some ways that Simeon could improve his leaflet.

When she finished, Chris pointed out many good things about the draft. She thought that the introduction clearly stated the topic and point of view. She thought his reasons were strong. Chris also did not find any information that was unrelated to the topic.

She thought that adding the two sentences to restate his point of view at the end was a good idea.

Chris also pointed out ways that Simeon might improve his leaflet.

- You should tell why the students' art we are selling at the bazaar is special.

- You need to remember your audience. Most parents will not be interested in dancing to loud music.

- When you say that people will want to push a pie into a gym teacher's face, you are giving your opinion. Maybe you should leave out that sentence.

- Many parents will think that a VCR is fine for showing educational films. Can you give some reasons for buying a DVD player?

Simeon saw how Chris's suggestions would improve his leaflet and decided to follow most of them.

Your Turn

Reread your first draft carefully several times. Check it against the Content Editor's Checklist. Can you answer yes to all of the questions?

Work with a classmate. Use the Content Editor's Checklist as you read your partner's leaflet. Would the leaflet persuade you? Talk with your partner when you have both finished. First, point out the strong parts in your partner's leaflet. Then make suggestions that you think will improve the leaflet.

Persuasive Writing

Revising

Here is how Simeon revised his leaflet.

Come to the Monroe School Bazaar!

On May ninth, Monroe School is having its yearly bazaar. Come and spend a little of your money to help our school a lot. Buy delicious fudge, carrot cakes, banana nut bread, and other goodies baked by parents of Monroe Students. How do you know the goodies are delicious? Last year we ran out of them way before the bazaar was over. Now our volunteer bakers have promised to double their batches. There will be plenty of goodies to go around. You can take them home. You can eat them at the bazaar.

Don't forget the artwork and crafts! ~~Beautiful pictures and~~ Several Monroe students have won prizes locally for their drawings and sculptures. ~~clay sculptures made by Monroe students will be on sale.~~ They have donated some of their best work to be sold. There will also be knitted goods made by several teachers.

A beautiful quilt will be rafled off before the end of the day. Monroe teachers pitched in to make it. Even Principle Losetsky helped to peice it together.

Last, but not least we garantee that you will have a lot of fun. ~~There will be plenty of loud music to dance to in the cafeteria.~~

There will be games in the gym. Hit the target and dunk Principle Losetsky in the water tank. Break three out of five balloons with the darts and win a bank. Make 3 out of 5 free throws with the basketballs and win a chance to push a cream pie into Mr. Goetz's face. You know you always wanted to do that to a gym teacher.

The best reason to come to the bazaar is that you will help Monroe School to get a new big-screen TV and a DVD player. The 24-inch TV that we have now is too small for students in the back row to see. Many educational programs now come on DVDs. It won't be long before taped videos will be hard to find. You should keep May 9 open on your calender for our bazaar. We hope to see you there.

Look at the changes that Simeon made to improve his leaflet.

- He explained that the art that is for sale was done by Monroe students who have won prizes for their work.

- He took out the sentence about dancing to loud music.

- Simeon left in the sentence about the cream pie. He thought that it made the leaflet more fun for the readers.

- He explained why Monroe School needs a DVD player.

Simeon was pleased with his leaflet after making the changes. Still, he wanted his leaflet to be as persuasive as he could make it, so he kept looking for ways to improve it.

Your Turn

Revise your leaflet. Make improvements so that your writing is clearer and more persuasive. Use any of your partner's suggestions that you think will help convince your readers. When you have finished, use the Content Editor's Checklist to check your writing one more time.

Persuasive Writing

Copyediting

Simeon thought his revisions had improved his draft. Next, he started to look more closely at his choice of words and his sentences. He used this Copyeditor's Checklist to help him.

Simeon read his leaflet, using the checklist. He looked for just one item each time he read. He caught some things that he wanted to fix.

The last two sentences in the first paragraph could be combined. Simeon combined them into one sentence with a compound predicate. How would you do this?

Simeon also decided to combine the last two sentences in the second paragraph. He would make these one sentence with a compound subject.

The word *goodies* was used three times in the first paragraph. Simeon replaced two of them with synonyms. He also found two problems with transition words. Can you find them?

Your Turn

Read over your leaflet several times. Use the Copyeditor's Checklist to help you look for ways to vary your sentences. Make sure that you also have variety in the words that you use. Look for prefixes and suffixes that are not used correctly.

Copyeditor's Checklist

- ✓ Are compound sentences used to vary sentence length?
- ✓ Are sentences with compound subjects or compound predicates used for variety?
- ✓ Is there variety in word choice?
- ✓ Are the words the best ones for persuading the audience?
- ✓ Are prefixes and suffixes used correctly?
- ✓ Are transition words used correctly?

Proofreading

Simeon was glad he had found so many ways to improve his draft. He knew his next step would be to proofread his draft for errors. He used this Proofreader's Checklist to help him.

Proofreader's Checklist

✓ Is the first line of each paragraph indented?

✓ Does each sentence and proper noun begin with a capital letter?

✓ Are punctuation marks used correctly?

✓ Is the grammar correct?

✓ Are all the words spelled correctly?

✓ Have all the revisions been checked for new mistakes?

Using the checklist, Simeon found that the word *students* should not have been capitalized in the first paragraph. He also noticed that he had misspelled the words *Principal* and *raffled.*

After Simeon proofread his leaflet, he asked his friend Jules to look it over. Jules used the checklist too, and he found some mistakes that Simeon had missed. First, he noticed that Simeon sometimes spelled out numbers and other times he wrote the numerals. Simeon decided to use numerals every time.

He also found one more misspelled word in the third paragraph and a new one that Simeon made in one of his revisions. Can you find these mistakes?

Your Turn

Proofread your leaflet carefully, using the Proofreader's Checklist. Check it once all the way through for each question on the checklist. This will help you to spot mistakes and to find last-minute improvements. After you have finished using the checklist to proofread your own writing, trade your paper with a partner.

Proofread your partner's writing as closely as you did your own. Mark any mistakes that you find.

Persuasive Writing

Publishing

Simeon felt that he had done well and had given parents good reasons to come to the bazaar. He carefully typed out his final copy. He felt ready to give it to Mrs. Roth. She would make enough copies for every Monroe School student. When the students' families read the leaflet, it would be published. This is how Simeon's finished leaflet looked.

Come to the Monroe School Bazaar!

On May 9, Monroe School is having its yearly bazaar. Come and spend a little of your money to help our school a lot. Buy delicious fudge, carrot cakes, banana nut bread, and other goodies baked by parents of Monroe students. How do you know the sweets are delicious? Last year we ran out of them way before the bazaar was over. This year our volunteer bakers have promised to double their batches. There will be plenty of treats to go around. You can take them home or eat them at the bazaar.

Don't forget the artwork and crafts! Several Monroe students have won prizes locally for their drawings and sculptures. They have donated some of their best work to be sold. There will also be knitted goods made by several teachers. A beautiful quilt will be raffled off before the end of the day. Principal Losetsky and many Monroe teachers pitched in to make it.

We guarantee that you will have a lot of fun. There will be games in the gym. Hit the target and dunk Principal Losetsky in the water tank. Break 3 out of 5 balloons with the darts and win a bank. Make 3 out of 5 free throws with the basketballs and win a chance to push cream pies into Mr. Goetz's face. You know you always wanted to do that to a gym teacher.

The best reason to come to the bazaar is that you will help Monroe School to get a new big-screen TV and a DVD player. The 24-inch TV that we have now is too small for students in the back row to see. Many educational programs now come on DVDs. It won't be long before taped videos will be hard to find. You should keep May 9 open on your calendar for our bazaar. We hope to see you there.

Your Turn

You publish your persuasive leaflet when you share it with your audience. You might do this by making copies to hand out or posting it on local bulletin boards.

Before printing out your finished leaflet, look it over one more time. Be sure you have made all the necessary corrections and that no new errors have been made. If your audience will need specific names, dates, addresses, or phone numbers to do what you have suggested, be sure that you have included them.

Decide with your teacher and classmates how you will share your leaflets. Think about posting them on a class bulletin board. Perhaps some of your classmates made leaflets for a personal purpose, such as advertising to do chores or offering to give away kittens or puppies. If parents agree, your classmates could hand out these leaflets in your neighborhood. Keep track of which leaflets persuaded people to respond.

Our Wide Wide World

Spanish explorers were the first Europeans to travel to what is now Colorado. They noticed that the soil looked red, so they named the area Colorado, which means "colored red." Colorado became a state in 1876. This was 100 years after the United States became a country.

Creative Writing

The Mouse's New Home

A busy mouse was working on his home in a field. He already had a nice cozy home made of twigs and leaves. He wanted an even bigger home where he could relax in the evenings.

A chipmunk who was walking by watched the mouse taking apart the roof of his old home.

"Can I help you with your work?" asked the chipmunk.

"Oh, no," replied the mouse, who never thought he needed help. "I can do it myself."

Soon the mouse had taken apart the roof and walls. He wanted to build the tallest, biggest home in the field. He started new, higher walls.

Next a squirrel came by.

"Can I help you finish up?" the squirrel asked. "It looks like a storm's coming." The mouse didn't pay attention to the squirrel or to the dark clouds in the sky. He just kept working.

Just as he was starting to patch on the roof, it started to rain. He looked around to see if anyone could help him, but everyone was gone.

The rain started pouring into his home. It got so wet that the walls he had built all washed away. He realized, a little too late, that he couldn't do everything himself.

What Makes a Good Fable?

A fable is a story that teaches a lesson. It is not a story about real life. In fact, the main characters in a fable are usually animals who talk and act like people.

In a fable a main character faces a problem. The problem is solved in a way that teaches the reader a lesson about life. Here are some things to keep in mind when writing a fable.

Setting

The setting of a fable is often a place in nature. It should be a place where the characters in the story might be found. A story about a bird might be set at the top of a tree. A story about a mole might be set underground. The setting you choose can help shape the story you will tell in your fable.

Characters

The characters are an important part of a fable. Each character in a fable might be a different kind of animal. Or all the characters might be the same kind of animal.

A good character in a fable is more than just an animal that does something. Good characters do things for a reason. They have personalities that make them act the way they do.

The story told in a fable often takes place because a character thinks and acts a certain way. A character might make a mistake and learn a lesson. He or she might do something wise that teaches the reader a lesson.

Activity A

Think of a good setting for each of the following characters. Explain why each setting is a good choice.

1. an eagle

2. a mountain goat

3. a bear

4. a seahorse

5. a beaver

Activity B

Choose three characters below. Choose a word on the right that might describe each character's personality. Write a sentence about the character and its personality.

1. a horse
2. an ant
3. a cat
4. a beaver
5. a snail
6. a fox

A. cunning
B. friendly
C. eager
D. lazy
E. hard-working
F. curious

Writer's Corner

Think of an animal character that you know from a book or movie. Describe the character and his or her personality. Describe how the character's personality affects what he or she does.

Problem

In almost every fable, a character faces a problem. The story in a fable often tells how (or if) the problem is solved. Sometimes the problem might be a danger that the character faces, such as falling into a well or being chased by a hungry wolf. In other cases the problem might be less serious. A character might just be looking for a tasty snack or a chance to cool off in a stream.

Moral

A moral is a life lesson that a character learns. The whole purpose of a fable is to teach the reader this lesson. The moral is usually told at the end of the story.

The moral is often shown in the way the problem is resolved. The character might make a mistake that he or she will not forget the next time. Or the character might make a wise decision that the reader can learn from.

The moral of the story is often related to the personality of the character. For example, a selfish hedgehog might learn a lesson about sharing. A patient crow might teach a lesson about not acting too quickly.

• Activity C •

Read the fable on page 197 again and answer these questions.

1. What is the setting of this fable?

2. Who is the main character?

3. What words would you use to describe this character?

4. What problem does the main character face?

5. What is the moral of the story?

• Activity D •

Read this fable. Then answer the questions below.

The Ant and the Grasshopper

One summer's day a grasshopper was hopping around in a field, chirping and playing games. Along came a hard-working ant who was struggling to carry an ear of corn into his home.

"Don't work so hard," said the grasshopper. "Come play with me!"

"Winter is coming, and I must store food before it gets cold," the ant said. "You should do the same."

"Why worry about the winter?" the grasshopper said. "Today it is warm, and there is plenty of food to eat."

The ant went on working, and the grasshopper went on playing. Then winter came, and the grasshopper was hungry. He went to the ant begging for food.

"Don't come to me," said the ant, who was munching on a piece of corn. "You should have gathered your food when you had a chance, but instead you decided to play games."

1. What is the problem in this story?

2. What words would you use to describe the characters?

3. Which character learns a lesson?

4. What is the moral of this fable?

Writer's Corner

Imagine another fable that could have the same moral as "The Ant and the Grasshopper." Describe the characters of your fable and the problem they might face.

Beginning, Middle, and Ending

When you write a fable, there are many things to keep in mind. You should write your fable in a natural, lively way. You need a good setting and interesting characters. You need a problem for your characters and a moral. You also need to put all these parts together in the right order, with a clear beginning, middle, and ending.

Beginning

The beginning of a fable should describe the setting of the story. It should also describe the main character or characters. It might describe what the main character is doing at the beginning of the story. It should tell the problem that the characters face in the fable.

Middle

In the middle of the story, the characters try to solve the problem. The way they act should fit their personalities. The middle should include all the important events of the story in time order. It might also include dialog, which is the characters' spoken words.

Ending

At the end of a fable, the problem is resolved. That doesn't mean the ending is always a happy one. Often the story ends badly for the main character.

The end of the story teaches a lesson. Sometimes the main character learns a lesson the hard way. Other times the main character solves the problem, teaching an important lesson to the reader. The writer often states the moral of the story in the last sentence. Sometimes a character might state the moral, using dialog.

Activity A

Decide which of the following would make good beginnings for fables. Tell what changes you might make to the bad beginnings to improve them.

1. There once was an animal who lived somewhere with his friends. He had a problem that he wanted to solve, but he didn't know how.

2. A little owl who lived in the woods wanted to throw a surprise birthday party for his friends.

3. A speedy fish wanted to prove that he was the fastest fish in his school. He challenged the other fish to a race, which he was going to lose. He was going to learn that too much boasting can get you into trouble.

4. A friendly elephant was cooling off by a river when a rabbit came up to him. "Excuse me," the rabbit said. "Can you help me get across?"

5. A lazy turtle was sitting by the side of the road with nothing to do. But he was happy doing nothing, because he was lazy. Everything was fine with him.

Writer's Corner

Choose one of the beginnings from Activity A that you think should be rewritten. Write a better beginning for the fable.

Activity B

Decide whether each of these sentences belongs in the beginning, middle, or ending of a fable.

1. "You silly skunk," the raccoon said. "Don't you know that you should never make a promise you can't keep?"

2. The rabbit cried out for help from his spot in the middle of the river.

3. There once was a lonely bear who lived in the forest.

4. You should never save for tomorrow what you can do today.

5. "Excuse me," the fox said to the wolf. "Can you help me? I seem to be lost."

6. A clever sheep was walking through a meadow on a beautiful spring day.

Activity C

The sentences below are from a fable, but they are all mixed up. Put them in the correct order.

1. A fox once fell into a deep well and could not get out.

2. "Next time," the fox said as he walked away, "remember to look before you leap!"

3. The goat jumped in and began to drink.

4. The goat suddenly realized that he had no way out.

5. As the goat was drinking, the fox climbed on his back and jumped out of the well.

6. Along came a goat who looked in the well, hoping for a drink.

7. "The water is delicious. Jump in with me," the fox said.

Activity D

Choose one of these ideas for a fable. Write the beginning of this fable. Include words that describe the character and the setting.

A. An ant tries to carry a giant pea back to his hill.

B. A horse wants to go for a run outside the gates of the farm.

C. A cardinal wants to relax instead of fixing his nest, which has come apart in a storm.

D. A squirrel wants to take all the nuts on the ground for himself.

Activity E

Write an ending for this fable. In your ending, show how the problem is resolved. Include a moral.

The Fox and the Crow

A crow was perched at the top of a tree in the woods. She was holding a piece of cheese in her beak. A hungry fox came by and saw the crow. He wanted the cheese for himself.

"That crow is so lovely," the fox called out loudly. "Her black feathers are so beautiful. I wonder if her voice is as fine as her feathers."

The crow was very vain. She wanted the fox to think her voice was beautiful too. She let out a loud caw, and the cheese fell out of her mouth.

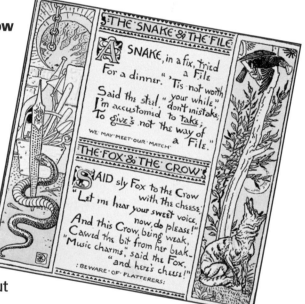

Writer's Corner

Look at the fable you began in Activity D. Write what might happen in the middle of this fable.

Homophones

Homophones are words that sound the same but have different spellings and meanings. Writers often misspell a word by writing its homophone. Here are a few common homophones.

Homophones	Examples
there	I left my shoes over there.
they're	They're leaving without me.
their	Mark and Peter put their hands in the air.
to	Alberto went to the supermarket.
too	The summer is too far away.
two	Two birds were chirping in the tree.
your	Don't count your chickens before they hatch.
you're	Are you sure you're ready?

The best way to avoid using the wrong homophone is to think of the meaning of the word you are using. If you are unsure of which spelling to use, check a dictionary.

Activity A

Choose the homophone that completes each sentence below.

1. The fans were glad to see (there their they're) team win.

2. If you ask me to come, I'll be (there their they're).

3. It's raining (to too two) hard to play today.

4. The show will be starting in (to too two) minutes.

5. I don't have money (to too two) pay for the movie.

6. Be sure to pack extra socks for (your you're) trip.

7. (Your You're) not wearing that, are you?

Activity B

Complete the paragraph below by choosing the correct homophones from the list. Use each homophone only once.

their	**they're**	**there**
to	**too**	**two**
your	**you're**	

One day a ladybug came to a river that was _____ wide to cross. Near the river _____ was a scorpion, and the _____ creatures began talking. The scorpion offered _____ take the ladybug across on his back. "Promise that _____ not going to sting me," the ladybug said, and the scorpion promised. Once they had made _____ way across the river, the scorpion stung the ladybug. "Why did you break _____ promise?" the ladybug asked. "Ladybugs should know that _____ not supposed to trust scorpions," the scorpion said. "Stinging is in our nature."

Writer's Corner

Describe a character and setting for a fable, using homophones from these pages. Trade descriptions with a partner. Check that your partner used the correct homophones.

More Common Homophones

The English language is filled with homophones. Because they sound alike, they are often confused in writing. Here are some other homophones to keep in mind when you are writing.

Homophones	Example
knew, new	We knew from the leaky roof that the house wasn't new.
threw, through	I threw the ball through the hoop.
hole, whole	Mandy ate the whole box of donut holes.
buy, by	I want to buy a book written by Dr. Seuss.
wear, where	Do you know where I can find a nice dress to wear?
peace, piece	The old enemies made peace and shared a piece of cake.
hour, our	We set our alarms to go off in an hour.
hear, here	Come over here so I can hear you.

Activity C

Choose the homophone that correctly completes each sentence.

1. (knew new) Nobody ———— that climbing the mountain would be so hard.

2. (peace piece) After a long battle, the two armies finally made ————.

3. (hour our) The television program lasts more than an ————.

4. (wear where) I didn't know ———— I'd put my shoes.

5. (hole whole) The rain was leaking through a ———— in the roof.

6. (hear here) I could ———— the sound of the train in the distance.

Activity D

Complete the paragraph below, using the homophones from the word bank. Use each homophone only once.

knew	our	hear	wear
new	hour	here	where

The Tortoise and the Hare

Once there was a hare who ———— she could beat anyone in a race. One day a ———— animal came to town, a slow tortoise. The hare challenged the tortoise to a race, and he agreed.

The hare sprinted out far ahead. After an ———— of running, the hare came to a tree ———— she sat down to rest her legs. "I think I'll stop ———— for a while," the hare said. "The tortoise will never catch up, and besides, all this running can ———— you out." The hare fell into a long sleep and didn't ———— the tortoise walking slowly by.

The hare finally woke up just as the tortoise was crossing the finish line. "I guess ———— speed isn't what matters in the end," the tortoise said. "Sometimes slow and steady wins the race."

Writer's Corner

Choose at least three pairs of homophones below. Look up the meaning of each word in a dictionary. Write a sentence using each word you chose.

ore, oar	bough, bow
root, route	patience, patients
some, sum	male, mail
threw, through	soar, sore

Expanding Sentences

A sentence can tell you a little or a lot. Sometimes adding words to a sentence can paint a clearer picture. Adjectives and adverbs are two kinds of words that can add meaning to a sentence. They can make a sentence more detailed and interesting.

Adding Adjectives

Adjectives tell more about a noun in a sentence. Some adjectives describe how something looks, sounds, feels, smells, or tastes. Other adjectives show other qualities; for example, *quick*, *brave*, and *hungry*. Notice how adjectives add meaning to each sentence below.

> The wolf howled from the mountaintop.
> The old gray wolf howled from the snowy
>   mountaintop.
>
> A boy rode his bicycle across the field.
> A teenage boy rode his shiny new bicycle across
>   the grassy field.
>
> The turtle looked across the river.
> The clever turtle looked across the raging river.

Adding adjectives helps you give a clearer idea of what is happening in the sentence.

Activity A

Add adjectives to these sentences to make them clearer.

1. Atop the ————— hill stood a ————— dog.
2. The ————— lady wore a ————— hat.
3. A ————— ship sailed through the ————— sea.
4. The ————— basket was filled with ————— apples.
5. Under the ————— rock I found a group of ————— snakes.

Activity B

Add adjectives to this paragraph to create a clearer picture.

I wrapped myself in a ————— coat and pulled a ————— hat over my head. Then I stepped out the ————— door. The ————— breeze smacked my face. As I walked down the ————— pathway in front of the house, I saw a ————— squirrel scurry up the ————— tree in the yard. A ————— bird looked down at me from a ————— branch. Unlike these animals, I was glad I could go back into my ————— house whenever I felt too ————— .

Activity C

Write sentences that use each of these adjectives.
Look in a dictionary if you are unsure what a word means.

1. clever
2. impatient
3. refreshing
4. spectacular

Writer's Corner

Rewrite the sentences from Activity B in different ways, using different adjectives each time. Describe how the adjectives changed the meaning of the sentences.

Adding Adverbs

Adverbs can give a clearer picture of the way people, animals, or things act. Adverbs describe how, when, where, or why something happens.

Some adverbs describe things you see or hear. For example, you can see or hear something happening quickly, quietly, or gracefully. Other adverbs, such as *honestly*, *kindly*, or *politely*, describe ideas that cannot be seen.

See how adding adverbs changes the sentences below. In each sentence, the adverbs give a clearer picture of how, when, where, or why the action takes place.

I rubbed my eyes and walked down the stairs.

I rubbed my eyes sleepily and walked slowly down the stairs.

"How can you do that?" my sister asked.

"How can you do that?" my sister asked angrily.

The frog gazed at the fly resting on the log.

The frog gazed hungrily at the fly resting lazily on the log.

Activity D

Add adverbs to the paragraph below to show how, when, where, or why the action takes place.

Paul and I looked up _____ at the sky. The clouds were coming _____. "We should get going," Paul said _____. We hopped on our bicycles and started pedaling _____ down the street. When we got to the house, I _____ realized I had left my umbrella outside. "Better wait for this storm to let up before going back out there," Paul said _____.

Activity E

Add adverbs to these sentences.

1. Myra smiled ———— when we asked where she had been.

2. The wolf growled ———— at the intruder.

3. When I did not come ————, my mother called to me ————.

4. Peter ———— displayed the prize he had won.

5. The children watched ———— for the bus to arrive.

6. "Summer's finally here!" Tina called ————.

7. The dancers drifted ———— across the stage.

8. When questioned by the teacher, Nina looked away ————.

9. The dog ———— appeared when its master called.

10. Nobody doubted that the soldier had fought ————.

Activity F

Rewrite each sentence by adding both an adjective and an adverb.

1. The boat sailed out to sea.

2. A snake slithered through the grass.

3. The witch cackled as she flew through the air.

4. The horse galloped across the field.

5. The music filled the room as the people danced.

Writer's Corner

Look through a book for five sentences with at least one adjective or adverb. Rewrite the sentences, using different adjectives and adverbs. How did the new words change the meaning of each sentence?

Haiku

Haiku is a Japanese form of poetry. A haiku is short. It is just three lines long and contains seventeen syllables. There are five syllables in the first line, seven syllables in the second line, and five syllables in the third line. (A syllable is a word or part of a word that has a vowel sound. *Snow* has one syllable. *Snowboard* has two syllables. *Snowboarding* has three syllables.)

A haiku does not tell a story. It describes one idea, moment, or feeling. Often it creates a peaceful image of nature. It might describe a quiet spot in the woods or a bird chirping in a tree. It could also describe any other memorable moment, such as the end of a school day, nighttime in a city, or waking up on Christmas morning.

Look at this haiku. The syllables are marked.

A giant firefly:

that way, this way, that way, this—

and it passes by.

—*Issa*

Issa, the author of this haiku, does not try to tell a whole story in his poem. Instead, he describes one brief moment in nature when a firefly flits past him. What feeling do you get when you read this haiku?

Activity A

Which of these might be easy to write a haiku about? Which ones might be hard? Explain your answers.

1. a trip to the moon and back
2. sitting by a stream
3. waking up in the morning
4. a movie that you saw recently
5. laughing with a friend
6. what happened on summer vacation
7. a grasshopper sitting on a leaf

Activity B

Write each haiku on a separate sheet of paper. Make a mark above each syllable.

1. Walking into class
   I see my best friend smiling.
   This year could be fun.

2. Sitting in the sun,
   The waves lulling me to sleep—
   I love summertime.

3. Rex sits at my feet
   Hoping for a scrap of food.
   Don't dogs ever learn?

Writer's Corner

Choose one season to write a haiku about—spring, summer, fall, or winter. Write a list of ideas, moments, or feelings that could be part of your haiku.

Writing a Haiku

Haiku can be easy and fun to write. They can be the perfect way to show something you saw or imagined. Here are some tips for writing a haiku of your own.

1. Think of an idea. You might close your eyes and let your mind drift. Write down the ideas on a sheet of paper. Then choose an idea that would make a good haiku.

2. Make a list of words related to your idea. Think of words that use your senses. What do you see? What do you hear or smell? How does this idea make you feel?

3. Begin writing your haiku. Write a line that is five syllables long. Use words from your list.

4. Write a second line that is seven syllables long and a third line that is five syllables long. Try to make the second line connect to the first or last line. Often in a haiku, the first two lines form one idea. The third line shows a new idea.

5. Look at the lines you have written. Is there one line you really like? Are there other lines you might change? Try changing your haiku, keeping the lines you like. You might change just one word in a line. Keep working on your haiku until it is just right.

Activity C

Match the first two lines of the haiku on the left with the final lines on the right.

1. Jolted from behind
   I see my brother laughing—

2. A tiny kitten
   Curls up in a sunny spot.

3. Out my bus window
   I see a world waking up;

4. A small voice cries out
   from the bundle in Mom's arms.

a. I love bumper cars.

b. My sister is home.

c. A new day dawning.

d. What a life she has!

Activity D

Choose three haiku beginnings below. Write a final line for each poem.

A. Red and yellow leaves
  Scatter across the backyard

B. Cup of hot cocoa
  Defrosts my shivering bones

C. Dusty spider webs
  Line the slanted attic walls

D. Windowpane rattles,
  Raindrops patter on
    the roof

E. My best friend Lucy
  Whispers secrets in
    my ear

F. Saturday in bed—
  The sun peeks through
    my window

G. Squirrel on a branch
  Looks up, then darts
    through the air

Activity E

Choose a phrase below. Write a haiku using the phrase as the first or last line.

A. vacation's coming

B. a fly buzzes by

C. waiting for the bus

D. running through a field

E. crickets chirp at night

Writer's Corner

Write your own haiku following the steps from this lesson. Use your idea from the Writer's Corner on page 215 or think of a new idea. When you have written a first draft, see if there are any words or lines that you can revise. Keep revising until you are happy with your haiku. Share your haiku with the class.

Telling a Fable

A fable can be a fun kind of story to tell. Lively, memorable characters do interesting things and can teach your audience an important lesson about life. Here are some tips for telling a good fable.

Audience

Think of your listeners when you choose your fable. Choose a fable they might not have heard. Be sure the fable has a moral that your audience can understand.

Characters and Setting

Think of where your fable takes place. Imagine this setting in detail. Use your mental picture when telling your fable.

Think about the characters. What in the characters' personalities leads them to act the way they do? As you prepare, write a list of words that describes each character.

Beginning, Middle, and Ending

Your fable should have a clear beginning, middle, and ending. The beginning should mention the setting, the characters, and the problem they face. In the middle a character might try to solve the problem.

The ending should tell how the problem is solved or whether it is solved at all. You should also state the moral at the end of the fable.

Make a Chart

As you prepare your fable, you can make a graphic organizer to organize your ideas. Here is an example of a chart you might make.

The Scared Cat

Setting: on a branch of an oak tree

Characters: a scared but cute cat, a clever crow

Main events:

1. The cat asks the crow to help him get down.
2. The crow tells the cat he can get down himself, but the cat says he is too scared.
3. The crow laughs at the cat and starts shaking the branch.
4. The cat gets even more scared and runs down the tree, safe and sound.

Moral: Sometimes you have to do something unpleasant in order to help someone.

Activity A

Look at the chart for the fable "The Scared Cat." Think of what each character might say. Then write it down. Which character do you think would tell the moral?

Speaker's Corner

Tell the fable "The Scared Cat" to a partner. Describe the setting and characters in the beginning. Tell the main events in your own words. Use the dialog you wrote in Activity A. Compare your fable with your partner's.

Using Your Voice

Using your voice well is one of the keys to telling a good fable. You might have an interesting fable with original characters and a good moral. However, if you don't use your voice well, your audience may lose interest. Here are some speaking tips to keep in mind.

- Change your pace for different parts of your story. You might speak slowly at the beginning and ending. Speak more quickly when the fastest action happens.
- Use a different tone of voice for each character. Be sure your tone of voice fits the character. This will help your listeners tell who is speaking. It will also make your characters more interesting.
- Use your voice or an object to make sound effects. You might make a whooshing sound to show the blowing breeze. A ticking noise can remind your audience of a clock.

Practice

It is important to practice telling your fable before you tell it to an audience. Begin by writing down on note cards the information about the setting, the characters, the main events, and the moral. Look at the note cards as you practice telling the story to a friend or in front of a mirror.

Try changing your pace as you practice. Use different voices and sound effects. Keep practicing until you feel comfortable telling your fable.

Listening Tips

When you listen to someone else tell a fable, use these tips to help you be a good listener.

- When the setting and characters are described, try to picture them in your mind.

- Listen carefully for what each character says and how they say it. How they speak may tell you something about their personalities.

- Listen for any sound effects that can help you imagine the scene.

- Pay attention to the moral of the story at the end. Think of how the moral is shown by the fable.

Give feedback to the speaker at the end of the story. You might say something you liked about the story or ask any questions you have.

Activity B

Think of a fable you would like to tell. You may choose a fable you know or make up one yourself. Make a chart like the one on page 219 that lists the setting, characters, main events, and moral. Then copy the information onto note cards. Practice telling your fable with a partner. Vary the tone of your voice to show different characters. Change your pace to fit the story.

Speaker's Corner

Tell your fable to the class. You might refer to your note cards, but try to speak in your own words. When you have finished, invite your classmates to ask questions or give feedback. When you listen to your classmates' fables, use the listening tips to help you be a good listener.

Creative Writing
Prewriting and Drafting

What fables do you know? Do you remember the story of the tortoise and the hare, the fox and the crow, or the ant and the grasshopper? Each is a simple story that teaches a lesson.

Prewriting

For a fourth-grade creative writing project, Tony decided to write a fable. He began by prewriting. First he brainstormed a moral. Then he used a graphic organizer to plan his story.

Brainstorming

Tony began prewriting by brainstorming lessons that he had learned in his life. He made this list of morals he could use in his fable.

The first moral didn't seem very interesting. The second one reminded him of the time he kept his Halloween candy for later. When he finally went back to it, the candy was stale. Tony liked this moral better than any of the others.

Your Turn

Begin prewriting by brainstorming one part of your fable. You might brainstorm a list of morals, like Tony did, or you might brainstorm a list of characters or settings. When you have completed your list, choose your favorite one to help you start your fable.

Always try hard at things.

Don't wait too long for something or in the end it may be too late.

If at first you don't succeed, try again.

Be nice to people and they will be nice to you.

Sometimes it's better to be smart than to be strong.

Planning a Story

When he was finished brainstorming, Tony began planning his fable. He made a chart to keep track of his ideas. He made spaces for his characters, setting, main events, and moral of the story.

First Tony thought of different animals that might be characters. He decided a squirrel would be an interesting character. Tony thought that the squirrel might be friends with a bird.

Then Tony thought of the setting. A squirrel and a bird might live in the woods. Since there are lots of nuts, fruits, and berries in the woods, it would be a good place to find food.

Next he thought about his story. Maybe his characters could find some food but then lose it because they waited too long, just as Tony had done with his Halloween candy. He decided that the squirrel would find some food but not take it home because he was lazy. Tony wrote down all the important events for his story in his chart.

As he planned his story, Tony added to his character and setting sections. He added words to describe the personalities of his characters.

He added an apple tree to the setting because it was an important part of the story. Here is the chart Tony made.

Characters: a squirrel who is hungry, friendly, and lazy; a bird who is helpful and smart

Setting: in the woods, near an apple tree

Main events:

1. A group of squirrels go looking for food.

2. A bird leads one squirrel to an apple tree.

3. The bird says that the squirrel should take some apples home.

4. The squirrel eats a bunch of apples and falls asleep.

5. Other squirrels find the tree and take the apples while he's asleep.

Moral: Don't wait too long for something, or in the end it may be too late.

Your Turn

Make a chart for your fable. Include the characters and setting. Add words to describe the characters' personalities. Include all the main events in the fable in time order. Write the moral that you want your readers to learn.

Drafting

Tony used his chart to help him write his fable. Here is the draft he wrote.

Ricky and the Blue Jay

One day a squirrel named Ricky was searching for food with his friends. They each went in there own direction. Ricky went down a path with his friend Jay, who was a blue jay.

Jay told Ricky about a tree he had found that had lots of apples under it. Soon they came to the tree. They had hit the jackpot! Ricky was so hungry. He ate as many apples as he could.

"Let's take some of these back home," Jay said.

"We can do that later. Let's eat some more!" Ricky said. He kept on eating, and soon he was very full. He lay down and fell asleep under the tree.

A few hours later Ricky woke up with a stomachache. He felt sick because he had eaten so many apples. He looked around he found that all the apples were gone! Ricky asked Jay what had happened.

"While you were asleep, you're friends came and took all the apples away," Jay said.

Tony wrote his fable using lively, natural language that would keep his readers interested. He wrote a beginning that introduced his characters, Ricky and Jay. He also mentioned the problem they faced: searching for food.

In the middle, he told what happened in time order. The events in his story showed what Ricky and Jay did to solve their problem.

In the ending, he showed how the problem was solved. Jay's words at the end hint at the moral of the story.

Your Turn

Use the chart you made in prewriting to write your fable. Write in a lively voice to keep your audience interested. Start with a beginning that tells about the characters, the setting, and the problem.

Next tell what the characters do to try to solve the problem. Include all the events you need to tell a good story. Write the events in time order.

At the end of the fable, if the problem was solved, tell how. The ending should show who learned a lesson. Be sure to clearly tell the moral of the fable in the ending.

Writing Dialog

Dialog is the words that your characters speak. Any words that are spoken should begin and end with quotation marks. Be sure to tell who is speaking after each line of dialog.

Dialog can give important information and move the story along. In Tony's story, Jay's final line of dialog tells the reader what happened to the apples.

Using dialog in a fable can also help you show the characters and their personalities. For example, Jay's dialog showed how he liked to plan ahead. Ricky's dialog showed how impatient he was.

One way to show a character's feelings or personality in dialog is to add an adverb. When Ricky said, "Let's eat!" in Tony's fable, Tony could have added that he spoke "greedily" or "excitedly." Use adverbs that show how your characters speak or act.

Creative Writing

Content Editing

Tony had enjoyed writing his first draft. He liked his characters and thought his fable had a good moral. He knew that he could make his fable better by editing. He read his draft again. He wanted to make sure it made sense and that there was nothing important missing. He wanted to make sure the story was clear and complete. As he edited, he used this Content Editor's Checklist.

After editing his draft, Tony gave his fable to his classmate Carl. He thought Carl would enjoy reading his fable. Tony hoped Carl would find some ways to improve his draft.

Carl read Tony's fable once for fun. Then he read it again more carefully, using the Content Editor's Checklist. He tried to think of ways to improve Tony's fable. Carl listed his ideas and shared them with Tony.

Content Editor's Checklist

✓ Are the setting and characters introduced in the beginning?

✓ Does each character have a special personality?

✓ Is there a problem that the characters face?

✓ Does the fable have a moral?

✓ Are all the important events included?

✓ Have any unnecessary details been deleted?

Carl began by telling Tony what he liked about the fable. He really liked Ricky's personality, and he thought the problem was a good one. He thought that Ricky had done something many people might do and that he had learned an important lesson. Carl also made these suggestions:

- Where is the setting of this fable? It's probably in the woods, but you should tell that somewhere.

- You should probably add a sentence telling that other squirrels came to take the apples.

- I think the reader can guess why Ricky had a stomachache, so you probably don't need that sentence.

- I think I know what the moral of the story is, but you don't really tell it. Can you add that to the ending?

Tony thanked Carl for his comments. Tony liked many of his classmate's ideas. Tony decided to use most of Carl's suggestions as he revised his draft.

Your Turn

Read over your draft, using the Content Editor's Checklist. Make sure you have included a setting, characters, a problem, and a moral. Look for any places where you are missing important events and add them. Look for any unnecessary details and delete them.

Trade your draft with a partner. Use the checklist to make suggestions for your partner's draft. Share your suggestions with your partner. Remember to tell your partner what you liked about the draft.

Listen carefully to your partner's suggestions. Thank your partner for his or her comments. Make any changes that you think will make your fable better.

Revising

Tony made several changes after reading his draft again and going over it with Carl. Here are the changes that he made.

Ricky and the ~~Blue Jay~~ Apple Tree

One day a squirrel named Ricky was searching for food ∧with in the woods his friends. They each went in there own direction. Ricky went down a path with his friend Jay, who was a blue jay.

Jay told Ricky about a tree he had found that had lots of apples under it. Soon they came to the tree. They had hit the jackpot! Ricky was so hungry. He ate as many apples as he could.

"Let's take some of these back home," Jay said.

"We can do that later. Let's eat some more!" Ricky said. He kept on eating, and soon he was very full. He lay down and fell asleep under the tree.

A few hours later Ricky woke up with a stomachache. ~~He felt sick because he had eaten so many apples.~~ He looked around he found that all the apples were gone! Ricky asked Jay what had happened.

"While you were asleep, you're friends came and took all the apples away," Jay said. "Sometimes if you wait too long to do something, you lose your chance!"

Look at some of the changes Tony made to his draft. He used his own ideas and some of Carl's suggestions to improve his fable.

- Tony realized he had forgotten to include the setting of his fable, so he added that it was in the woods.

- He decided not to add another sentence about what happened while Ricky was asleep. He thought that Jay's dialog explained it well enough. Besides, he thought that by waiting to tell what happened, he made the ending more interesting.

- Tony agreed that he didn't need to say why Ricky had a stomachache. It wasn't that important. He thought that the readers would probably guess anyway.

- He was surprised that he had forgotten to include the moral. He decided to make it part of Jay's dialog in the ending.

After making some of the changes Carl had suggested, Tony decided to change the title. He didn't think the blue jay was important enough to the story. He wrote a new title that included the apples.

Your Turn

Look at the changes your partner suggested and the ideas you had. Make any changes you think will make your draft better. When you have finished, go over the Content Editor's Checklist again. Be sure you can answer yes to each question.

Creative Writing

Copyediting and Proofreading

Copyediting

After revising, Tony was ready to copyedit his draft. He wanted to make sure that he had chosen the right words and written each sentence correctly. He used this Copyeditor's Checklist to help him.

Copyeditor's Checklist

✓ Are the sentences complete?

✓ Are there any run-on sentences?

✓ Are any sentences too choppy?

✓ Do all the words have the right meaning?

✓ Are any words repeated too often?

✓ Are there places where adjectives or adverbs could be added to make the story clearer?

After looking over his draft, Tony found a few places where he could make changes. First he realized that there were several short sentences in the second paragraph. This made his paragraph seem choppy. He combined two sentences to help the paragraph flow better.

Next, Tony decided to add a few adjectives to paint a clearer picture. He added the adjective *friendly* to describe Ricky's personality. He added the adverb *excitedly* to show how Ricky spoke.

Finally, Tony found a run-on sentence in the paragraph about Ricky waking up. He changed the word *he* to *and* to make the sentence correct.

Your Turn

Read your fable again and copyedit it, using the Copyeditor's Checklist. Be sure that you have used complete sentences and avoided run-on sentences. Check that you have chosen the right words to make your fable clear and interesting.

Proofreading

Tony thought his fable was coming along nicely. He hoped that by proofreading his draft, he could catch any mistakes that he had missed. Tony asked his sister Maria to proofread his draft because she was good with details. She used this Proofreader's Checklist.

Proofreader's Checklist

✓ Are the paragraphs indented?

✓ Have all the words, including homophones, been spelled correctly?

✓ Is the grammar correct?

✓ Are capitalization and punctuation correct?

✓ Were any new mistakes made during editing?

Maria liked Tony's fable, though she was surprised that Ricky would be eating apples instead of nuts. She thought he was a very foolish squirrel. She also found a few mistakes to correct.

First, she noticed that several words were misspelled because Tony had used their homophones instead. In the second sentence, he should have used the word *their* instead of *there*. In the last paragraph, he should have used the word *your* instead of *you're*.

Next, Maria found that Tony had forgotten to indent the last paragraph, so she reminded him to do that.

Finally, she noticed a mistake in the last sentence he had added. She reminded him that every line of dialog should begin and end with quotation marks. He had forgotten the quotation marks at the end of the sentence.

Tony thanked his sister for her help and agreed that all of her corrections should be made.

Your Turn

Ask a partner to proofread your draft, using the Proofreader's Checklist. Use the checklist to proofread your partner's draft. Then explain your suggestions politely. Listen to your partner's suggestions. Make the changes that you think will improve your draft.

Creative Writing

Publishing

Tony's fable was almost complete. He looked it over one more time to make sure that all the changes had been made correctly. He typed his fable on his computer. He made sure to include a title and his name. Then he printed out his fable.

Ricky and the Apple Tree

By Tony Stephani

One day a friendly squirrel named Ricky was searching for food in the woods with his friends. They each went in their own direction. Ricky went down a path with his friend Jay, who was a blue jay.

Jay told Ricky about a tree he had found that had lots of apples under it. Soon they came to the tree. They had hit the jackpot! Ricky was so hungry, he ate as many apples as he could.

"Let's take some of these back home," Jay said.

"We can do that later. Let's eat some more!" Ricky said excitedly. He kept on eating, and soon he was very full. He lay down and fell asleep under the tree.

A few hours later Ricky woke up with a stomachache. He looked around and found that all the apples were gone! Ricky asked Jay what had happened.

"While you were asleep, your friends came and took all the apples away," Jay said. "Sometimes if you wait too long to do something, you lose your chance!"

Your Turn

Read over your draft one more time. Make sure that all the changes have been made correctly. If you have typed your fable on a computer, you might use the computer's spell checker to double-check the spelling. But remember that a computer will not find incorrect homophones!

If you did not type your fable on a computer, print it neatly by hand. Be sure to include a title and your name at the top. If the fable is more than one page long, number the second page.

You might present your fable to an audience by reading it aloud. Younger students might enjoy hearing your fable. Use the speaking and listening tips from Lesson 6 when you read your fable.

Post your fable in a place where other students can read it. Read some of your classmates' fables too. See if you can find any other fables that have the same moral as yours!

CHAPTER 7

Pennsylvania is named after William Penn, an English settler who arrived in 1682. He was different from most settlers because he paid the local native people, the Lenape, for the land he wanted. Penn hoped that people from different backgrounds could live together peacefully. What do you think Philadelphia, the city he founded, was like when Penn was alive?

Expository Writing

How Do You Spell Winner?

Spelling Bee

Seventh grader Josh Franzen may not have taken home a trophy from the National Spelling Bee last week, but his strong showing made his friends proud back at Melrose Middle School.

Josh was the first Melrose student ever to reach the national competition in Washington, D.C. He was eliminated in the fourth round, misspelling *inchoate*, but he was not disappointed.

"It was amazing just to get here," Josh said. "It was an experience I'll never forget."

Getting there certainly was not easy. First, he had to win the local and state spelling bees. He spent hours every night studying words, including many that he had never even heard of.

"There were lots of late nights with the spelling books. He really drove us crazy sometimes," said his mother, Marie Franzen.

As a result of his hard studying, he got to spend four days in the nation's capital. He made friends with some of the best young spellers in the country.

"These people are so smart," Josh said. "I was proud to have gotten as far as I did."

Expository Writing

What Makes a Good Expository Article?

Expository writing tells a reader about a real-life topic. It uses facts to describe real people, places, things, or events. Book reports and textbooks are examples of expository writing. Another example is an article in a newspaper. Here are some tips for writing a good expository article.

Introduction

The introduction of an expository article tells what the article is about. Sometimes the article might start with a catchy sentence to grab the reader's attention. In a news article, this sentence is called a "lead." The introduction should also include a topic sentence that states the most important facts about the topic. In the introduction below, the third sentence is the topic sentence.

> Have you ever wondered how the school's tasty peach crisp dessert is made? Just ask Fran Steele. As the head cook of the cafeteria, she's been cooking delicious meals for students for more than 15 years.

Body

In the body of an expository article, the writer gives information that supports the topic sentence. The body answers the questions *who, what, when, where, why* and *how*. In a news article, the most important information is told first.

Conclusion

The conclusion of an expository article sums up the article. A good conclusion will leave the reader thinking about the topic. It might end with a quotation or an interesting statement. In a news article, the conclusion is called a "wrap-up."

Activity A

Which of the following makes a good topic for an expository article? Why do you think so?

1. new animals at the zoo

2. how to recognize beings from other planets

3. a brief history of my school

4. how snow forms

5. what I'll do when I become president

Activity B

Decide whether each sentence below fits best in the introduction, the body, or the conclusion of an expository article about a class field trip.

1. This was the second field trip this year for Mrs. Parker's class.

2. "The class really enjoyed it," teacher Mrs. Parker said. "It felt as if an ancient culture were suddenly brought to life."

3. A busload of fourth graders saw the wonders of ancient Egypt on Friday on a field trip to the Caldwell Museum.

4. Marcos Johnson said his favorite part of the trip was seeing a mummy up close.

Writer's Corner

Think of a game that you've seen people play at recess or after school. Write the introduction for an expository article about that topic.

Order of Importance

In news articles, facts are given in order of importance. This is because people often do not read the whole article. They might read just the first few sentences. Therefore, the most important information is given first.

The school newspaper article below is organized in order of importance.

Carlos Gonzales was elected class president Monday, defeating Courtney Halm by 11 votes.

Tina Bremer was elected vice president. Misha Jacobs won the vote for secretary, and Pauline Paulson was voted treasurer.

Friends of Carlos cheered when the announcement was made over the loudspeaker. Even many of the students who voted for the other candidate said Carlos would be a good president.

"He's really smart, and he's a good speaker," said student Maria Higgins.

More than 200 students voted in this year's election.

The news that Carlos was elected president is more important than who won the other offices. The number of students who voted is less important than the students' reaction.

Activity C

Imagine you are going to write an article about a band that is planning to perform in your community. Which facts would be the most important? Which facts are the least important?

1. Many people are excited about the concert, and tickets are selling fast.

2. The concert is sponsored by the local PTA.

3. The band will be performing on Saturday at 8:00 p.m.

4. The band is touring all across the country.

5. The name of the band is "The Crushed Peanuts."

Activity D

Arrange each of these sets of sentences from a news article in order of importance. Explain your choices.

1. **A.** Marsha Haywood was the highest scorer for the Rockets, scoring 10 points.

   B. The Reading Rockets beat the Newton Nuggets 32–28 for their first win of the basketball season Tuesday night.

   C. The Rockets' next game will be on Wednesday against the Waltham Wildebeests.

2. **A.** The old building will be torn down next May.

   B. Students are excited about the new school. "Everything looks so fresh and clean. It might actually be fun to go to school!" said Mark O'Shea.

   C. The brand-new Marshall Elementary School opened yesterday, as students and teachers carried their books across the street from the old school.

3. **A.** The student council decided to make the eagle the new school mascot Wednesday, replacing the aardvark.

   B. This was the third time in the history of the school that the mascot has been changed.

   C. The decision was made to change the mascot because the eagle is a more exciting animal than the aardvark.

Our Wide Wide World

When the Lenape people met the first English settlers of Pennsylvania, they probably gave the settlers wampum. Wampum are tiny beads carved from shells. Many Native Americans who lived on the Atlantic Coast carved wampum to use as money, decoration, and gifts. Sometimes beads were woven into wampum belts, which might be used in ceremonies.

Writer's Corner

Find an article in your local newspaper and list at least three ideas from the article, in the order that they appear. Work with a partner to decide why the writer placed the ideas in that order. Share what you found with the class.

Gathering Information

Rachel Carson was a writer and scientist who helped Americans understand the dangers of pollution. She was born in 1907 in Springdale, Pennsylvania, near Pittsburgh. Rachel grew up to love writing and nature. She published her first work in a magazine at age 10. Her book *Silent Spring* is her most famous.

Before you write an expository article, you must gather information about your topic. Anywhere you look for information is called a source. For news articles, a reporter often goes to an event, such as a baseball game or a town meeting, to get information. Other sources of information include books, Web sites, and newspapers. An interview with someone connected to the topic can also be an effective source.

Interviewing

Often the best information comes from people who are connected to an event. If your school is buying new computers, your principal can probably tell you why they are needed. If there was a heavy snowstorm, a snowplow driver would know which streets are blocked. Always bring a parent or teacher if you are interviewing someone you don't know.

Deciding What Is Important

Part of good note-taking is deciding which facts are important and which ones aren't. Important facts have an effect after the event is over. If a baseball player drops a ball, but no one scores, the fact is not important. If the home team loses the championship because a player drops a ball, the fact is important.

Choose one person to interview for an article about each topic. Explain why you would choose that person.

1. a fire at the local skating rink

   the rink's owner   a firefighter   a skater

2. a teacher who is retiring

   the retiring teacher   another teacher   a student

3. a traffic jam caused by a school bus breaking down

   a student   a police officer   the bus driver

● Activity B ●

Read the following newspaper story. Decide which of the facts are not important enough to include in the story.

The Rosa Parks School custodian was bitten while protecting a student from a dog. John Mayer ran out to the schoolyard when he heard screaming. He had been replacing batteries in the school's smoke alarms. A small poodle had cornered Alicia Tomarz against the playground fence. It may have smelled Alicia's cat on her clothes. Mayer stepped between the poodle and Alicia, and the dog bit him. When the custodian shouted, the dog ran off.

The dog's owner was located and said that the dog had been given all of its shots. The poodle's name is Snowball. Mr. Mayer was taken to the hospital. He didn't want to go, but Principal Wicki insisted. A doctor gave him three stitches. Mr. Mayer will be back in school tomorrow.

Writer's Corner

Imagine you are going to interview someone who works in your school. Write a list of questions that you might ask to find out what that person's job is like from day to day.

The Five *W*s

The most important facts in a news article should be included near the beginning. The most important facts are told in the topic sentence in the introduction, while the rest are told in the body. These facts should answer questions known as "the five *W*s." These questions are *who*, *what*, *when*, *where*, and *why*. The facts might also answer the question of how something happened.

Sometimes one of these questions may not be answered in an article. Or it might be answered in a different way than you expect. For example, an article about a tornado may not have a *why*.

Activity C

Look back at "How Do You Spell *Winner*?" on page 235. Answer these questions.

1. Who is Josh Franzen?

2. What did he do?

3. Where did this event take place?

4. When did this event take place?

5. Why was the person not disappointed?

6. How did the person get to this event?

Activity D

Use three facts from the following information to write the introduction to an expository article.

Who?   fourth graders Maria Jones and Britney LaPierre
What?   formed a new gardening club
When?   last Friday
Where?   in the garden behind Jefferson School
Why?   to share their love of gardening
How?   by asking classmates to sign a petition and presenting it to Principal McLaughlin

Activity E

Read each introduction to an expository article. Write down two questions that need to be answered in the article. Begin each question with *who, what, when, where, why* or *how*.

1. A moose escaped from the Stafford County Zoo and has been sighted walking behind people's houses along Main Street.

2. A group of fourth-grade students decided to spread holiday cheer by making box lunches for a shelter in the area.

3. A powerful snowstorm hit the area Monday, knocking out power in some places and forcing some schools to close.

4. One of the teachers in Markham Elementary School announced that she will retire.

5. A student has created a new kind of ball game that many kids around school have started to play.

6. Students performed the play *Stone Soup* in the school auditorium, and those who attended said they enjoyed the performance.

7. A new study showed that smoking can be especially harmful to those who start when they are young.

8. A local author has written a book about the history of the town. The book will be in bookstores on Tuesday.

Writer's Corner

Think of an event that happened in the past year, such as a birthday, a wedding, or a vacation. Imagine you are a reporter covering the event. Write a short article about the event, answering the questions *who, what, when, where, why* and *how*.

Negatives

A word that means "no" is called a negative. Writers use negatives to express the opposite of something in a sentence. For example, if a writer wanted to say the opposite of Everyone was at the park, he or she might write, No one was at the park. The following are typical negatives used in writing:

no	not	none	nothing
nobody	no one	never	nowhere

Contractions with *Not*

Contractions with *not* (*n't*) can also be used to express *no*. *Did not* becomes *didn't*. You can give a sentence the opposite meaning by adding a *not* contraction.

> The children couldn't believe their eyes. (could + not)
>
> Christina hasn't visited Paris. (has + not)
>
> I don't have a ride to baseball practice. (do + not)

You might have heard the contraction *ain't*. It is sometimes used informally to express *am not*, *isn't* or *aren't*. However, *ain't* is a slang term and is not proper English.

Negative Adverbs

Words like *hardly*, *scarcely*, *rarely*, and *barely* are negative adverbs. When used with *ever* or *any*, these words express a negative idea.

> I hardly ever go to the theater.
>
> We have barely any money.

Activity A

Choose a word from the box to fill in the blank. Write each new sentence.

nobody	never	none	nothing	nowhere	not

1. Ann is _____ on time.

2. The driver did _____ know where he was going.

3. _____ wanted to help clean up after the party.

4. I was hoping to see paintings by Picasso at the museum, but there were _____.

5. Jason has _____ to do.

6. The monkey was _____ to be found.

Activity B

Rewrite the following sentences using *hardly, scarcely, barely,* or *rarely* with *any* or *ever* instead of *no* or *never.*

1. I never eat junk food.

2. Carrie never goes on vacation.

3. They have no time to go to the store.

4. We never ice skate in the winter.

5. I was expecting a blizzard, but there was no snow.

Writer's Corner

Choose a topic and write a description using five or more negatives.

Double Negatives

You may have heard that two wrongs don't make a right. In a sentence, however, two negatives often do make a positive. When two negative words are put together in a sentence, they cancel each other out. This is called a double negative.

In most cases it is incorrect to write a double negative. Often, people who use them end up saying the opposite of what they mean. For example:

> There wasn't no cake left.

This sentence actually means "There was some cake left." To fix this sentence, you might change wasn't to was or no to any. Either of these revised sentences are correct:

> There wasn't any cake left.
>
> There was no cake left.

When using negative adverbs such as *hardly*, *scarcely*, *rarely*, and *barely*, you should also avoid double negatives. Avoid phrases such as *barely never* or *hardly none*. Instead, use *barely ever* or *hardly any*.

In some cases, two negative words do not create a double negative. If two negatives are in different parts of a compound sentence, they do not make a double negative. Adding the introductory word *no* at the beginning of a sentence also does not create a double negative. For example:

> Tommy isn't going, so I'm not going either.
>
> No, we aren't going to the amusement park.

When you write, keep an eye out for sentences with more than one negative. Check to make sure that you have not written a double negative.

Activity C

**Choose the word that best completes each sentence.
Avoid double negatives.**

1. Marcos didn't invite (anyone, no one) to the birthday party.

2. I have (anything, nothing) to wear to the dance.

3. We've hardly (ever, never) seen a tomato like that.

Activity D

**Find the sentences that contain double negatives.
If a sentence contains a double negative, rewrite it.**

1. I'd never want to live nowhere but here.

2. If Tina can't stay up late, then you can't either.

3. No, I haven't been to Peru.

4. Paulette couldn't scarcely believe what had happened.

Activity E

**Revise the following paragraph by removing the double
negatives.**

    It wasn't nothing that Detective Hopkins had ever seen
before. The money wasn't in the safe, but he didn't know
what had happened. He couldn't find nobody who knew the
combination. There weren't no fingerprints on the safe, either.
"Don't you have no ideas, Detective Hopkins?" his assistant
asked. "No, I don't," the detective replied.

Writer's Corner

**Write a story, using negatives. Avoid double negatives.
Trade papers with a partner. Check your partner's story
to be sure your partner avoided double negatives.**

Rambling Sentences

Have you ever read a very long sentence? When you got to the end, did you wonder what the sentence was about? Sentences that go on too long are rambling sentences.

A rambling sentence contains too many thoughts or ideas. You can often spot a rambling sentence because it contains several conjunctions such as *and*, *or*, or *but*.

Read this rambling sentence.

> Students in the fourth grade said art was their favorite subject, mainly because they enjoy painting, and their next favorites were gym, music, and science, and their favorite part of the day was recess because they got to play with their friends.

Look at all the ideas in the sentence. The writer first names the students' favorite subject, art, and explains why it was chosen. Next the writer lists students' other favorite subjects. Finally the writer names students' favorite part of the day and explains why they enjoy it.

The best way to fix a rambling sentence is to break it into separate sentences. You can break it in places where conjunctions are used. Read these revised sentences. Which version is easier to understand?

> Students in the fourth grade said art was their favorite subject, mainly because they enjoy painting. Their next favorites were gym, music, and science. Their favorite part of the day was recess because they got to play with their friends.

Revise each rambling sentence to make it into two or more shorter, clearer sentences.

1. One day I went skateboarding in my cousin's neighborhood, but I forgot to look where I was going, and some sticks were in my way and I fell.

2. Our class learned how to use a computer the first month of school, and then we learned how to write a computer program, and one group even created a math game.

3. Jeremy built a model of the space shuttle for the science fair, and he was excited when he won first prize, and he received a trophy.

4. The artist unwrapped the wet ball of clay, and she molded it in her hands, and then she used the potter's wheel to make a vase.

5. George picked blueberries on the farm, but he was in a hurry, and he didn't pick them carefully, and he got stains on his shirt.

6. Dogs are one of the most popular pets because they are loving animals, and they are fun to play with, and they can protect your home by scaring away any strangers.

7. Students in Mrs. Pekin's class are happy to be taking part in a book-reading contest, and they said the contest would give them a chance to win some great prizes or at least allow them to read some new books.

Writer's Corner

Write five or more sentences about things you like to do, using at least two conjunctions. Revise the sentences by dividing them into more than one sentence. Do the revised sentences sound better?

Revising Sentences

Often there is more than one way to revise a rambling sentence. A rambling sentence with four ideas could be broken into four short sentences. It could be broken into two sentences, or two short sentences and one longer sentence. Read the sentence below.

> Hundreds of people attended the game, and they enjoyed the songs played by the marching band, and the crowd cheered hard for the football team but the team lost in overtime.

Here are two ways this sentence could be revised.

> Hundreds of people attended the game. They enjoyed the songs played by the marching band. The crowd cheered hard for the football team. The team lost in overtime.

> Hundreds of people attended the game, and they enjoyed the songs played by the marching band. The crowd cheered hard for the football team, but the team lost in overtime.

In the first revision, each idea is given its own sentence. In the second revision, two related ideas are included in each sentence. How else could this sentence be revised?

• Activity B •

Revise one of these paragraphs. Turn the rambling sentences into shorter, clearer sentences.

A. Jenny brushed Pegasus down and threw a saddle blanket and pad over his back before she went to get his saddle from the tack room, but by the time she returned, he had reached around and pulled the pad and blanket off and dropped them on the sawdust-covered floor. "Oh, you're going to be like that," she scolded as she picked them up and brushed them off, but Pegasus wasn't done, and he kicked over the trash can that was directly behind him.

B. Quilts are beautiful bedspreads, and they are made by sewing together many types of cloth patches. Old shirts and dresses and other scraps of colorful clothing are good material for patches, and some people even go to used-clothing stores to buy the fabric for these patches. In the past, neighbors, friends, and relatives gave one another scraps of clothing to make the quilts, and so for each scrap there was an interesting story to tell about its owner.

Our Wide Wide World

Activity C

Revise each rambling sentence in a way that makes it clearer and easier to read.

1. The motorcyclist stopped at the top of the hill and looked down the hill, and he saw a quiet little village below that he could visit and he headed down the hill.

2. Mrs. Powell said she loves her job as a librarian and she enjoys reading to the students or helping the children find books, but as a child she wanted to be a television star.

3. The town of Williamsville was founded in 1823 and had 200 people by 1840, but a great fire caused many people to move away in 1852.

4. Doctors say that people should eat a balanced diet in order to get all the vitamins they need, and some people take additional vitamins, but it is important to check with a doctor to make sure they're the right vitamins.

Writer's Corner

Make a list of things you like to do with your friends. Write them as sentences, using conjunctions to combine some of your ideas. Then break your ideas into more sentences by removing the conjunctions. Which sentences do you think are more effective?

Library Catalogs

How quickly can you find information in the library? Do you just go to the shelves and start looking for a good book? Or do you search the library catalog to help you look? Here are some tips for finding what you want at the library.

Card Catalogs

Many libraries have a card catalog that helps people find books. The cards are in alphabetical order, using the title, author, or subject of the book.

Title Card

On a title card, the title of the book is at the top of the card. Look for this card if you know only the title of the book. This card can be found in alphabetical order by the first word of the title. If the title begins with *The*, *A*, or *An*, skip to the second word.

Author Card

An author card shows the author's name at the top. Author cards are arranged alphabetically by the author's last name. Look for this card if you know only the author of a book or if you want to find several books by one author.

Subject Card

A subject card lists the main topic of the book at the top of the card. Use these cards to help you look for information on a certain subject.

Catalog Information

Besides a book's title and author, a card catalog tells the number of pages, whether it is illustrated, and what it is about.

For nonfiction books, the card provides the books' call numbers. The call numbers tell you where to find nonfiction books on the shelves. Fiction books are arranged alphabetically on the shelves by the authors' names. Here is an example of a card from a card catalog.

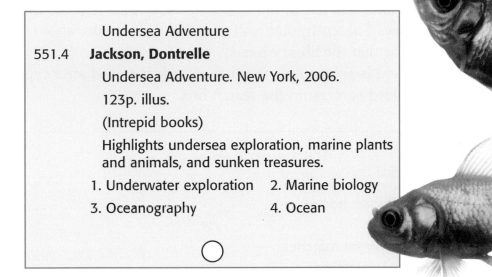

> Undersea Adventure
>
> 551.4 **Jackson, Dontrelle**
>
> Undersea Adventure. New York, 2006.
>
> 123p. illus.
>
> (Intrepid books)
>
> Highlights undersea exploration, marine plants and animals, and sunken treasures.
>
> 1. Underwater exploration   2. Marine biology
>
> 3. Oceanography   4. Ocean

Activity A

Find this information on the example card above.

1. Is this a title card, an author card, or a subject card?

2. What is this book's call number?

3. What subjects might this book be listed under in the card catalog?

Writer's Corner

Choose a topic and write questions that you would like to answer about the topic. Look up books about the topic in the card catalog.

Electronic Catalogs

Most libraries now have their catalogs on computer. These electronic catalogs are similar to card catalogs. Like card catalogs, electronic catalogs include entries listed by title, author, and subject.

Electronic catalogs are often easier to search than card catalogs. All you have to do is type the word into the search box and the computer will give you a choice of entries.

When you type in an author's name, for example, the computer will list all the books by the author that are in the library. The computer will also list any books about the author that the library owns.

Here is an example of what a student found after typing the word *horses* into the search box.

Barrie Park Library System

Search was: horses

232 keyword matches
2 author matches
38 subject matches

Browse titles beginning with *horses*
Browse authors beginning with *horses*
Browse subjects beginning with *horses*

Enter terms: | horses | (Search) (Clear)

When the student clicked on *Browse subjects beginning with horses*, she found a list of books on that subject. When she clicked on one of the books, she saw the following screen:

Barrie Park Library System
Search was: horses
Title: Galloping Through History
Author: Johnson, Rose
Call No: 575.84
Publisher: Freestyle Books: Newark, NJ, 2004
197p. illus.
Summary: A survey of the evolution of the horse through history and its domestication by humans.
Subjects: Horses, evolution, mammals, natural selection, domestication

Where to find it:	Copies:	Available:
North Branch Library	2	1

Activity B

Use the example electronic catalog entry above to answer the following questions.

1. What is this book about?

2. What is the call number for this book?

3. At what library can this book be found?

4. How many copies are available?

5. What other words might a person use to search for similar books on this subject?

Writer's Corner

Find a nonfiction book in the library and write a summary of what it is about. Look up the book in a library catalog and compare your summary to the one in the catalog.

News Reports

Have you ever watched the news on television? When you do, you are watching an oral news report. News reports are much like expository articles. News reports tell the audience about a topic, offering important information that focuses on the topic. In this lesson you will present your own news report as part of a class news show.

Choose a Topic

For your news report, think of a topic that will interest your classmates, who will be your audience. You might report on an interesting person at school, an activity students enjoy, or some other topic related to school.

Gather Information

When you have chosen your topic, list several sources you could use in your news report. Then write questions your report should answer, such as *who, what, when, where, why,* and *how.* Interview the people who are sources for your report. Use the library or the Internet to find information. Take notes and write the name of your source below each note.

Organize Your Notes

When you have finished your notes, arrange them in order of importance. Begin your news report with an introduction that includes a topic sentence stating the most important facts about the topic. End with a conclusion that sums up your report.

Tone of Voice

Reporters who deliver news reports usually use a serious tone of voice. They speak clearly and slowly, stating the facts without showing their feelings. If the story is about a lighthearted topic, they might use a cheerful, lively voice.

Activity A

Choose one topic below. Write three questions that a news report about the topic should answer.

A. an author who is planning to visit the school

B. the problem of messy desks

C. the new fad of wearing suspenders to school

Activity B

Use the information gathered below to write an introduction for a news article about the topic. Write at least two sentences. Practice delivering the introduction.

- The music teacher is leading a school musical.

- Mr. Ramirez is the music teacher.

- Fourth graders and fifth graders will be in the musical.

- The musical will be *Peter Pan*.

- The musical will take place April 29 in the auditorium.

- Students are excited about being in the musical.

Speaker's Corner

Interview a partner about a topic that he or she is familiar with. It might be a hobby, a school activity, or a sport your partner plays. Take notes. Get answers to the questions *who, what, when, where, why,* and *how.* Ask any other questions that would help make a complete news report. Organize your notes.

Create Your News Show

In the news you see on TV, a team of reporters works together to present a news show. The reporters take turns delivering their reports. They use visual aids such as photographs, film clips, or maps. Sometimes the reporters interview people. The show takes place in a newsroom, with a news desk, microphones, and a sign with the name of the show.

You can create a news show in your classroom. Begin by meeting with a group of four classmates. Work together to decide the order of the reports.

Next turn your class into a newsroom. Set up a news desk. You could use a toy microphone. You could make a sign that displays the name of your news show.

Finally make any visual aids that go with your report. You might show an object or a photograph that relates to the report. You might even interview a classmate during the show.

Practice

Before presenting your news show, you need to practice. It will be helpful to practice a few times so you can give a good presentation.

Use a clear, serious voice. Speak directly to your audience instead of reading from your notes. You might make cue cards by writing your notes in large print on poster board. Ask a classmate to sit in front of the audience with the cue cards and flip them as you speak.

Practice presenting any visual aids that go with your report. If you plan to interview someone from class, introduce the person before the interview. Go over the questions you will ask and practice the interview a few times.

The first speaker should introduce the name of the show, saying something like "Welcome to Grade 4 Action News. Here is our top story of the day."

When each speaker finishes, he or she should introduce the next speaker. A speaker might say, "And now here's Paul Lewis, who will tell us about our school's new holiday food drive." End your news show by thanking the audience.

Listening to News Reports

When you watch another group present its news show, listen to the reports carefully. Think of any questions you have that were not answered in the report. Give feedback to the group, saying what you liked and asking any questions you have.

Activity C

Work in a group of four to create a news show. Prepare the report you began in the Speaker's Corner on page 257. Prepare any visuals for the report. If you plan to use cue cards, create them with poster board.

Activity D

Set up your newsroom, using the tips from this lesson. Decide the order of the reports. Then practice presenting your news show. Practice speaking in a clear voice. If you use cue cards, ask another student to hold them during your report.

Speaker's Corner

Present your news show to the class. Set up everything carefully before the show. Speak loudly and clearly, talking directly to the audience. Use your notes or cue cards to help you remember what to say. When you watch your classmates' news shows, listen carefully and give feedback at the end.

Chapter 7 Writer's Workshop

Expository Writing

Prewriting and Drafting

What interesting people do you know? What new things are happening in your town or school? Are your friends enjoying any new games, hobbies, or fads? Any of these topics can be fun to explore in an expository article.

Prewriting

André's fourth-grade class was making a class newspaper, and the students were the reporters. Each student was asked to think of a topic for an article. André began by brainstorming ideas for articles. Next, he thought of questions he wanted to ask and gathered information for his article.

Choosing a Topic

André's teacher, Miss Mangus, suggested that each student write a feature article. A feature article is a fun article about a topic that is not too serious. She gave her students these topic suggestions:

- an interesting teacher or someone who has done something unusual

- some part of school life, such as a new club or a favorite class

- a special event at school or in the community

- a new trend, such as a clothing style or kind of music

- a favorite game or activity that students enjoy

Miss Mangus encouraged students to choose a topic for which they could interview at least a few students.

André used his teacher's ideas to help him think of a topic. He made a list of topics that fit each suggestion. Then he chose his favorite topic. André decided to write an article about the touch football games that the fourth and fifth graders played before school. He could describe the games and interview some of the students who played.

Your Turn

Use Miss Mangus's suggestions to help you choose a topic for your article. Write down at least one idea for each suggestion. Then choose the idea you think will be the most interesting for your audience.

Gathering Information

After choosing his topic, André thought about the sources he could use to gather his information. He knew he could use his own personal experience because he played in the games himself.

He could interview other people who played in the games. He could also interview Mr. Nelson, the school gym teacher, since he was an expert on football and exercise. André could look on the Internet for articles about touch football.

Next, André wrote down questions he wanted to answer in his article. He wrote down these questions:

Who plays in the games?

What happens when they play?

Where and when do they play?

Why did they start playing?

How do the kids like playing?

Is it a good game for kids our age?

Is playing touch football good for you?

André wrote down everything he knew about the topic. Then he interviewed some students who played and Mr. Nelson. He asked them some of the questions he had written. He also looked on the Internet for facts about touch football.

Your Turn

Think about sources you could use for your article. Can you use your own experience? Are there students or adults you could interview? Are there any books, magazines, or Web sites you could use? Try to think of at least two different sources other than yourself.

Make a list of questions you would like to answer in your article. Then gather your information, using the sources you thought of. Write down anything you know about the topic, but leave out your own opinion. Interview the people on your list and use any other sources.

Drafting

André used the information he had gathered to write his article. He stated the topic of the article in the introduction. He organized the article in order of importance, and ended his article with a quotation.

Football in the Morning

Have you seen the kids playing football every morning in the back field of Twin Meadows Elementary School? They're the fourth and fifth graders. They have been playing this fun game before school since the beginning of the year.

It started when fifth graders Joey Padrone and Sanjay Kumar started playing catch after the bus dropped them off before school. They come on the first bus, so they have extra time before the bell rings. Soon other fourth and fifth graders started playing. When they had enough players, they decided to play a real game.

Touch football is a good game for kids. It's also good exercise, said Mr. Nelson, the gym teacher.

"Any time kids are being active and playing together, I'm happy," Mr. Nelson said.

The games are'nt as long as real football games, and usually about 10 kids play. So far, the teams have been the fifth graders against the fourth graders.

"They usually win, because they're better," said Peter Cardillo. "But we won the last game. John Walsh got this great touchdown at the last minute."

Sanjay Kumar said "he started playing just because he was bored, but now he's always excited to play," and other students said playing football before school is much more fun than just standing around and talking.

Your Turn

Use the information you gathered to write your article. Start with an interesting introduction that tells what the article is about. Include a topic sentence that states the most important facts about the article.

Write the body of the article, using information that supports the topic sentence. Begin with the most important facts. Answer questions such as *who*, *what*, *when*, *where*, *why*, and *how* in your article.

End your article with a conclusion that sums up your information. You might end with a quotation that leaves your readers thinking about the topic.

Using Sources

There are many ways to use your sources in an article. Here are some suggestions.

Personal Knowledge: You do not need to name the source if the fact is something you saw or already knew. Just state what you know as fact.

People: If a fact comes from a person you interviewed, name the person in the sentence. You could use a quotation, which should include the person's exact words.

You could also use your own words to explain what a source said. If you do this, do not use quotation marks. However, be sure to name the source.

Written sources: If you use a written source, such as a book, article, or Web site, name the source after you state the fact. You do not need to name the source if the fact is something you could find in lots of places.

Expository Writing

Content Editing

André's expository article was full of information from different sources, and it gave the most important information about the topic. He knew that he could make it even better, however, by content editing it.

First, he read his draft again to make sure it made sense. He checked his notes to make sure he had the important information connected with the right sources. André also made sure his quotations were right. He used this Content Editor's Checklist.

After reading his draft, André asked his classmate Laura to read it. He thought she might notice if anything was unclear or missing.

Content Editor's Checklist

✓ Does the introduction state the topic of the article?

✓ Does the body give all the important information in order of importance?

✓ Does the information include sources when necessary?

✓ Have the writer's opinions been left out?

✓ Do quotations use the source's exact words?

✓ Have unimportant details been left out?

Laura read André's article twice and checked it, using the Content Editor's Checklist. She started by telling him what she liked. She thought the quotations were good and the article's topic was clearly stated. Next, she gave these suggestions:

- In the first paragraph, you call touch football a "fun game." Do you have a source for that, or is it just your opinion?

- Since this article is for the school paper, your audience will know which school you're talking about, so you don't have to say it.

- The sentence about why Joey and Sanjay come early doesn't seem very important.

- Some people might get confused when Peter Cardillo says that "they usually win." Maybe you should say what team he's on.

- The quotation from Mr. Nelson is good, but it doesn't seem as important as the other information. Maybe it would fit better at the end.

André thanked Laura for her suggestions. He liked her ideas and decided to use all of them when he revised his draft.

Your Turn

Read your draft, using the Content Editor's Checklist. Check that you have included all the important information in order of importance. Make sure you have named your sources and quoted them correctly. See if any facts should be added or any opinions taken out.

Trade your draft with a partner. Use the checklist to take notes on your partner's draft. Tell your partner what you liked about his or her draft. Then suggest changes your partner could make.

Be open to your partner's ideas for your draft. Thank your partner for his or her comments. Think about making any changes that could improve your draft.

Expository Writing

Revising

This is how André revised his draft after listening to Laura's suggestions and using his own ideas.

Football in the Morning

Have you seen the kids playing football every morning in the back field of ~~Twin Meadows Elementary School~~ the school? They're the fourth and fifth graders. They have been playing ~~this fun game~~ before school since the beginning of the year.

It started when fifth graders Joey Padrone and Sanjay Kumar started playing catch after the bus dropped them off before school. ~~They come on the first bus, so they have extra time before the bell rings.~~ Soon other fourth and fifth graders started playing. When they had enough players, they decided to play a real game.

Touch football is a good game for kids. It's also good exercise, said Mr. Nelson, the gym teacher.

"Any time kids are being active and playing together. I'm happy," Mr. Nelson said.

The games are'nt as long as real football games, and usually about 10 kids play. So far, the teams have been the fifth graders against the fourth graders.

> older
> "They usually win, because they're ~~better~~." said Peter
> , a fourth grader
> Cardillo. "But we won the last game. John Walsh got this
>
> great touchdown at the last minute."
>
> Sanjay Kumar said "he started playing just because he
>
> was bored, but now he's always excited to play." and other
>
> students said playing football before school is much more fun
>
> than just standing around and talking.

Notice the changes André made to improve his draft.

- André realized that since he couldn't prove that football was a "fun game," it was not a fact. He took out the words.

- He agreed that the name of the school was not necessary, so he took it out.

- He also took out the sentence about why Sanjay and Joey get to school early.

- André agreed that some readers might not know which team Peter Cardillo was on. He wrote that Peter was a fourth grader to make it clearer.

- André moved the quotation from Mr. Nelson to the end. André thought that Mr. Nelson's statement would make a good conclusion for the article.

André made one other change to his article. When he looked over his notes, he realized he had used the wrong word in his quotation from Peter Cardillo. Peter had said that the fifth graders usually won because they were older, not because they were better.

Look over the changes André made to his draft. Would you have made any other changes?

Your Turn

Revise your draft, using your own ideas and your partner's suggestions. When you have finished, go over the Content Editor's Checklist again. Be sure that you can answer yes to every question.

Expository Writing
Copyediting and Proofreading

Copyediting

After revising his draft, André needed to copyedit. He wanted to make sure that his sentences all made sense and that he had used the right words. He used this Copyeditor's Checklist.

Copyeditor's Checklist

✓ Are all the sentences complete?

✓ Are there any rambling or run-on sentences?

✓ Are any sentences choppy?

✓ Are there any double negatives?

✓ Do all the words have the right meaning?

✓ Are any words repeated too often?

After going over his draft, André decided to make a few changes. The first thing he noticed was a rambling sentence. The sentence that started with "Sanjay Kumar" was too long and had too many ideas. He decided to put Sanjay's reason in one sentence and the other students' reasons in another sentence.

Next, he saw that the first part of Mr. Nelson's quotation was not a complete sentence. He corrected it by making the whole quotation into one complete sentence.

Finally, André realized that calling touch football a "good" game for kids did not use the best word. He was trying to say that lots of kids liked it, a fact that he had learned from the Internet. He changed the word *good* to *popular*.

Your Turn

Copyedit your draft, using the Copyeditor's Checklist. Make any changes that will improve your draft.

Proofreading

After copyediting, André's draft still needed to be proofread. He asked his classmate Isabel to proofread it. She would check the article for mistakes in spelling, grammar, and punctuation. She used this Proofreader's Checklist.

Proofreader's Checklist

✓ Are the paragraphs indented?

✓ Have any words been misspelled?

✓ Is the grammar correct?

✓ Are capitalization and punctuation correct?

✓ Have quotations been written correctly?

✓ Were any new mistakes added during editing?

Isabel enjoyed reading André's article. She had wondered how the kids started playing football in the back field. She also pointed out a few mistakes in André's draft.

Isabel found a place where the punctuation for a quotation was written incorrectly. She saw that André had used his own words to write what Sanjay had said. For that reason, André did not need quotation marks in the sentence.

Next, Isabel saw that a contraction had been spelled incorrectly. The word *aren't* was misspelled as *are'nt*. She reminded André that the apostrophe should be placed where the letter *o* is taken out of the word *not*. Finally, she noticed that his first paragraph was not indented.

André thanked Isabel for proofreading his draft and made the corrections she suggested.

Your Turn

Read over your article, using the Proofreader's Checklist. Make sure you have used correct spelling, grammar, and punctuation. Look for any new mistakes you might have made when you revised.

Trade drafts with a partner and proofread your partner's draft. Share your suggestions. Make any corrections that will improve your draft.

Expository Writing
Publishing

André checked over his draft once more and then typed it on a computer. He put a title and his name at the top and printed out his article. Then he combined it with other students' expository articles to create a school newspaper.

Football in the Morning
André Andrews

Have you seen the kids playing football every morning in the back field of the school? They're the fourth and fifth graders. They have been playing before school since the beginning of the year.

It started when fifth graders Joey Padrone and Sanjay Kumar started playing catch after the bus dropped them off before school. Soon other fourth and fifth graders started playing. When they had enough players, they decided to play a real game.

The games aren't as long as real football games, and usually about 10 kids play. So far, the teams have been the fifth graders against the fourth graders.

"They usually win, because they're older," said Peter Cardillo, a fourth grader. "But we won the last game. John Walsh got this great touchdown at the last minute."

Sanjay Kumar said he started playing just because he was bored, but now he's always excited to play. Other students said playing football before school is much more fun than just standing around and talking.

Touch football is a popular game for kids. It's also good exercise, said Mr. Nelson, the gym teacher.

"Any time kids are being active and playing together, I'm happy," Mr. Nelson said.

Your Turn

Read over your draft once more to make sure that everything is correct. Be especially careful that the names of people in your article are spelled correctly and that the quotations are correct.

Work together with your class to turn the articles into a school newspaper. You might print them out in narrow columns, as a newspaper does.

Put the name of your newspaper in large type at the top. Glue a few important articles on the front page. Then add the other articles on other pages. Make copies of your newspaper so that other people can read all about what's happening in your school and community.

•IN THE NEWS•

4th Edition

Spri

Football in the Morning
André Andrews

Have you seen the kids playing football every morning in the back field at the school? They're the fourth and fifth graders. They have been playing before school since the beginning of the year.

It started when fifth graders Joey Padrone and Sanjay Kumar started playing catch after the bus dropped them off before school. Soon other fourth and fifth graders started playing. When they had enough players, they decided to play a real game.

The games aren't as long as real football games, and usually about 10 kids play. So far, the teams have been the fifth graders against the fourth graders.

"They usually win, because they're older," said Peter Cardillo, a fourth grader. "But we won the last game. John Walsh got this great touchdown at the last minute."

Sanjay Kumar said he started playing just because he was bored, but now he's always excited to play. Other students said playing football before school is much more fun than just standing around and talking.

Touch football is a popular game for kids. It's also good exercise, said Mr. Nelson, the gym teacher.

"Any time kids are being active and playing together, I'm happy," Mr. Nelson said.

CHAPTER

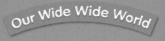

Washington was made a state in 1889 and remains the only U.S. state to be named after a president. Explorers from Spain were probably the first Europeans to visit the area that would become Washington. Early settlers included English, American, Chinese, Russian, and Swedish people. The port city of Olympia is the capital of the state. How might Olympia be different if it were not a port city?

Research Reports

A Note from the Nurse's Office at McAuliffe Elementary School

More than one quarter of school-age children in America do not have healthy eating habits. Many health workers put much of the blame on TV. Others say parents and children are responsible for their own diets. Experts agree, however, that children should ignore their TV sets and change their eating habits in order to live healthy lives.

According to Marlene Most and John Windhauser of Louisiana State University, on Saturday mornings there are almost as many commercials for fast-food restaurants as there are for breakfast cereals. The target audiences of these commercials are children. Not only that, the focus of the advertising for fast-food restaurants has changed from the food itself to the size of the portions. With most Americans already eating more than they should, Dr. Most warns that increasing portion sizes could be dangerous.

Healthy eating should not be your parents' concern alone. You should take an active role in choosing healthy foods and reasonable portion sizes. However, don't expect that just by making the right meal choices you will be able to keep your weight at a healthy level. You also need to watch the way that you eat. It takes about 15 to 20 minutes for your stomach to tell your brain that you are full. If you gobble down a lot of food quickly, you are more likely to overeat. When your stomach says, "I've had enough," stop eating.

Remember that TV commercials are trying to sell products, not keep you healthy. If you ignore them and follow these healthy eating tips, you will be healthier and happier.

What Makes a Good Research Report?

A research report gives information. The writer chooses a topic and finds facts about it in different sources. Then he or she writes this information in a way that gives readers a new understanding of the topic.

A research report is a formal paper. There are rules that you must follow. Do not use contractions or abbreviations. Always give credit to the sources of your information.

Choosing a Topic

When you choose a topic, pick one that interests you and the audience that you are writing for. Choose a topic that is broad enough to find information to write about, but narrow enough to cover in two or three pages.

For example, you might be interested in the Old West. You can find millions of facts about the Old West. You could not write about the Old West in only a few pages. You must think of a narrower topic. You could write about the Pony Express, cattle drives, or train robberies in the Old West.

When you have chosen a topic, think of things that you would like to know about it. Ask questions that you would like to have answered. Use the questions to help you decide what information to look for in your research.

Researching Your Topic

When you look for information about your topic, use more than one source for a variety of ideas. Use different types of sources, such as magazine articles, encyclopedias, nonfiction books, and Web sites. Write down each source in which you find information.

Refer to your questions as you research. Don't read an entire book. Use the contents page or pages or use the index to find the answers to your questions. If your research brings up new questions, write them down and research those answers too.

Be sure to use your own words to rewrite the information you find. Doing that will help you understand what you have read.

Activity A

Read each pair of topics. Tell which one would be better for a research report. Explain your choice.

1. a. Charles Lindbergh   **b.** the history of flight

2. a. golden retrievers   **b.** hunting dogs

3. a. the U.S. Space Program   **b.** the first person on the moon

4. a. electric trains   **b.** toys

5. a. American railroads   **b.** the first tracks across America

Writer's Corner

Look through a nonfiction book from the library. Make a list of narrow topics the book covers. Choose one topic and write five questions you might want to answer if you researched the topic.

The Yakama people have lived in and around what is now the state of Washington for thousands of years. For generations they had a ready source of food from the salmon, which regularly crowded the Columbia River. When Lewis and Clark reached the end of their journey west, the Yakama welcomed them and shared their food. Today the Yakama people live on the Yakama Nation Reservation. At 1,300,000 acres, it is twice the size of Rhode Island.

Organizing Your Research Report

When you have finished doing your research, you will have many notes from several sources. You need to organize all of this information into writing that flows from one idea to the next.

Introduction

The introduction should tell what the report is about. State the topic in a topic sentence. Try to catch your audience's interest early. Make your readers curious about your topic with an unusual fact or an interesting question.

Body

The body of your research report is where you include the facts that you found in your research. All of the information should be important to your topic. Leave out anything that is not important. Give each main idea its own paragraph.

Answer the questions that you asked yourself before you began researching your topic. If some of the facts raise new questions, find answers to those questions. Your audience will probably wonder about them too.

Organize the information so that similar facts are grouped together. If you are writing about peregrine falcons, finish the section about what they look like before you write about where they live.

Conclusion

The conclusion should sum up your report. The end of your report might repeat the most important information or leave readers with an interesting thought. Do not introduce new information in the conclusion. A good research report will make readers want to find out more about the topic.

Read over page 273 and answer the following questions.

1. What is the topic of this report?

2. Which sentence is the topic sentence?

3. What is the main idea of the second paragraph?

4. What is the main idea of the third paragraph?

5. Does the conclusion fit the guidelines from this lesson?

● Activity C ●

Read each group of sentences. Tell which sentence would belong in the introduction, which would belong in the body, and which would belong in the conclusion.

1. **a.** Bull riding is the most dangerous event in a rodeo.

   b. Rodeos are hard to beat for bone-jarring excitement.

   c. Do you like to watch contests between people and animals?

2. **a.** Your parents can probably remember when there were no remote controls.

   b. Garage doors had remote controls before televisions did.

   c. The problem now is remembering where the remote control is.

Writer's Corner

Think of a topic that might make a good research report. Write a statement for the introduction that catches the audience's attention. Write the types of information you might include in the body of the research report.

Researching

A big part of writing a research report is finding information. You can look in books, magazines, and on the Internet. Before you begin your research, look at your questions to help you get started. When you do research using books, go to the sections that are likely to answer your questions. When you use the Internet, use keywords from your questions in your searches.

The wood that is used in making any stringed instrument affects how it sounds when played.

Guitar Maker's Guide

by Matt Beanworth, p. 102

Taking Notes

When you take notes, don't just write down facts on a sheet of paper. Be organized. One good way is to use note cards. Write one fact on each card, using your own words. This will help you make certain that you understand the ideas.

Look at the bottom of this note card. Whenever you take notes, include where you found the information and who wrote it. That way you can find the information again if you need to.

After you have taken your notes, arrange them into groups of similar facts. The facts in each group should be about one main idea, such as "what guitars are made of." Each group will become a paragraph in the body of your report. The facts will be details that support the paragraph's main idea. If you have facts that don't fit under any main idea, leave them out.

Activity A

The following groups of facts are on note cards. Find the fact that does not belong in each group.

Group A

1. Koalas have thick, gray coats of fur.
2. They have pouches where they raise their babies.
3. The forests where many koalas live are disappearing.
4. Their paws are adapted for gripping tree branches.

Group B

1. Confucius was born in China in 551 BC.
2. Confucius believed in doing what is right and loving others.
3. He thought people should rule by example, not by force.
4. He hoped his ideas would help people rule themselves.

Activity B

The following facts are not organized. Organize them into two groups. Tell what the main idea of each group might be.

1. About 10 percent of the earth is covered with glaciers.
2. Glaciers move slowly over hundreds of years.
3. Most of the world's fresh water is stored in glaciers.
4. Glaciers moved somewhat south between the 17th and 19th centuries because of the cool climate.
5. Glaciers advance to the south and retreat to the north depending on climate change.
6. Almost 90 percent of a glacier is below water.

Writer's Corner

Find five facts in a nonfiction book. Write down the facts in your own words.

Listing Sources

At the end of a research report, it is important to tell your audience where you found the information. Listing your sources will also tell them where to look if they want to find out more about the topic. Here are the main ways of listing books, encyclopedia entries, articles, and Web sites.

Books

When listing a book, list the author first, starting with the last name. Then write the name of the book and underline it.

> Haywood, Elijah. <u>Galileo's Mystery</u>.

Encyclopedia

For an encyclopedia entry, write the name of the entry in quotation marks, then name the encyclopedia and underline it.

> "Industrial Revolution." <u>The New World Encyclopedia</u>.

Newspaper and Magazine Articles

For a newspaper or a magazine article, list the author's name, the title of the article, the underlined name of the newspaper or magazine, and the publication date.

> Previn, Hae Jung. "Whatever Happened to Slide Projectors?" <u>Progress Weekly</u>, December 15, 2005.

Web Sites

When listing an article from a Web site, list the author's name and the article title, and write the Web address in angle brackets (< >). If you cannot find the author's name, begin with the article title.

> McCarthy, Lauren. "Life of a Ballerina." <www.ballet41.org>

Our Wide Wide World

Olympic National Park is in the northwest corner of Washington. This wilderness area, named for the Olympic Mountains, boasts hot springs, glaciers, waterfalls, coastline, and rain forests. As many as 14 feet of rain fall annually in these forests. All that rain helps the growth of giant ferns and trees, including the world's largest Sitka spruce.

Activity C

Use the guidelines on page 280 to list the following sources as they would appear at the end of a research report.

1. The book Bronze Age, which was written by Julio Alvarez.

2. The article "Russia Says Goodbye to a Favorite Son" by Natasha Harding, which appeared in the October 7, 2005, Dallas Morning News.

3. Nancy Cleary's Web page titled "Bats," which can be found at www.pageturner.net/cleary021.htm.

4. The November 2004 issue of Reader's Monthly, where the article "Voyager from the Deep" by Tino Sanchez was found.

5. Carson Peterson's biography of Abraham Lincoln, which is titled Presidential Timber.

6. The Web page titled "Kinds of Mica," which can be found at www.stonecenter.edu/mica.htm. The Web site does not say who wrote the page.

7. The entry for "Meerkat" from Encyclopaedia Britannica.

Writer's Corner

Find two sources for a topic, such as a book, an encyclopedia, an article, or a Web site. Write down one thing you learned from each source. Then list the source, using the guidelines from page 280.

Reference Sources

Today people can find information about almost anything in the world. There are so many sources of information that you can do research on just about any topic that you choose. In order to do thorough research, be sure to use different sources.

The Library

Libraries are an excellent resource when researching information for a report. Most libraries have a section just for reference books such as encyclopedias, atlases, and almanacs. These books contain information about many different topics. When you use any reference source, write down where your information came from.

Always use the most recent reference book that you can find. Check the publication date, which can usually be found on the page right after book's title page.

A good resource in any library is the librarian. If you are unable to find the information that you need, ask a librarian. He or she will help you find the best sources for the information.

Encyclopedias

An encyclopedia is a reference source that contains general information about people, places, things, and events. An encyclopedia may be only one book or it may be a set of many books. Encyclopedia articles are listed in alphabetical order by the topic.

Almanacs

Almanacs are printed every year. They contain very recent facts. They can tell you the population of Brazil, the winner of the 1996 World Series, or last year's total rainfall in South Dakota. Always use the most recent almanac that you can find. Almanacs organize information by type. Use the index to find the information that you need.

Atlases

Atlases are books of maps. They show geographical features such as rivers, lakes, and mountains. They also show political or human-made features, such as roads, cities, and borders. Atlases may also tell the climates and populations of countries. Atlases often organize their maps by region. Look in the index for the locations you are researching.

Activity A

Tell if you would use an encyclopedia, an almanac, or an atlas to find information about these topics. What word would you look under to find the topic in the source?

1. how diamonds are formed

2. the largest lake in Minnesota

3. the discovery of oil in Pennsylvania

4. the coldest location in America last year

5. all the states that border Iowa

Writer's Corner

Use a reference source in the library to find five facts about a country you would like to visit. Write down what you find.

The Internet

The Internet contains more information than any other reference source. This information is often more recent than other sources. It can be posted immediately without waiting for books or magazines to be printed.

Search Engines

Search engines can help you find information on the Internet. To use a search engine, first type a keyword or words into the search box. Use exact words that will help you find only sites about your topic. Leave out the articles *a*, *an*, or *the*. Then click on the word *Search*. The search engine will look through the Internet for Web sites that contain the keyword and list those sites for you. If you do not know how to use a search engine, ask a librarian for help.

Web Sites

When you use information from the Internet you must consider the site to decide if the information is accurate.

To decide whether a Web site is reliable, check the letters at the end of the address. Here is what a few of them mean.

.com	commercial sites
.org	sites created by organizations
.edu	sites created by schools
.gov	government sites

Sites developed by organizations or the government are usually accurate. Be careful, however, when using a .com site. People who create these sites are sometimes more interested in selling a product than in giving correct information. A site ending in .edu might be a good source if created by professors or a university. If created by a student, however, the information might not be reliable.

Our Wide Wide World

Beginning in 1841, pioneers traveled to the Pacific Northwest in wagon trains, following the Oregon Trail. The route started in Missouri and ended along the Columbia River in Oregon. The trail crossed the southeast part of the state of Washington. Miles of ruts made by the wagon wheels are still etched in the ground.

Always try to find out about the author of a Web site. An expert on the subject is more reliable than someone who is not an expert. Also check when the site was last updated. If it was updated recently, the information might be more current.

Activity B

Write the keywords that would be most useful for an Internet search on each of the following topics.

1. the early life of Harry Truman, the 33rd president of the United States

2. how to make chocolate truffles

3. the number of women in the U.S. Senate

4. how Beatrix Potter got the idea to write *Peter Rabbit*

Activity C

Use the Internet to answer the following questions.

1. How did the town of Truth or Consequences get its name?

2. When did the last dodo bird die?

3. What is Virginia Dare's claim to fame in American history?

4. What name do the French give to the English Channel?

5. Who made the first nonstop flight across the Atlantic?

Writer's Corner

Search the Internet for facts about the Oregon Trail. Write at least five things that you learned.

Word Study

Compound Words

Compound words are single words that are made by joining two or more words together. Often the new word makes sense as soon as you read it. For example, a fireplace is a place for fire, and the backyard is the yard in back of a house. Sometimes the two words don't seem to add up to the longer word. The word *understand* doesn't mean to stand under something. A holdup is either a robbery or a delay, not a support. Make certain that you know what a compound word means before you use it in your writing. If you are not sure, check a dictionary.

What two words make up each of these compound words? Can you use each compound word in a sentence?

sidekick	background	faraway
daydream	anybody	troublemaker

• Activity A •

Match each word in Column A with a word in Column B to make a compound word.

Column A	Column B
1. hand	**a.** cut
2. some	**b.** plane
3. hair	**c.** weight
4. air	**d.** where
5. light	**e.** made
6. blue	**f.** berry

Activity B

Complete the compound word in each sentence.

1. I wear _____ glasses to protect my eyes in bright light.

2. We packed our winter clothes in card_____ boxes.

3. I hate when it rains on the week_____.

4. Nicky looked for _____ shells along the beach.

5. The farmer used a pitch_____ to toss hay to his horses.

6. The company's _____ quarters are in Dallas, Texas.

7. I do my _____ work on the desk in my bed_____.

8. Does _____ body want to play _____ ball?

9. The car's _____ lights lit up the high_____.

10. Pinecones come from _____ green trees.

Activity C

Tell what compound words these clues are describing.

1. A jacket that is not very heavy is _____.

2. When you want to walk quietly, you walk on _____.

3. If you wake up before dawn, you might see the _____.

4. The room where your teacher teaches you is a _____.

5. If you are climbing up steps, you are going _____.

Writer's Corner

The words *out, under, sun,* and *up* are often used in compound words. Write as many compound words as you can containing these words. Then write a short poem, using some of the words you thought of.

Research Reports • **287**

Our Wide Wide World

Mount St. Helens is a volcano that is about 100 miles south of Seattle, Washington's largest city. In 1980 the volcano sent hot ash and rocks flying. The ash, fires, and flooding caused by the eruption in 1980 killed 57 people and countless animals. Mount St. Helens is still active.

Spelling Compound Words

Most compound words are easy to spell. You simply write two words as one word. However, some compound words are not as easy to spell.

Some compound words need a hyphen between the two words.

> bull's-eye   chin-up   hand-me-down

Some compound words need a space between the two words.

> leap year   Stone Age   blue jay

There is no rule that tells when you should use a hyphen or a space. If you are not sure how to spell a compound word, look it up in a dictionary.

• Activity D •

Use a dictionary to see how to join the words that are used to make these compound words. Write the words.

1. When my sister got married, I became a (brother + in + law).

2. It seems like everyone has a (cell + phone).

3. I ate the last (grape + fruit) for breakfast.

4. Dad and I both wanted the (left + over) pizza.

5. Barb is sick, but (never + the + less) she mowed the lawn.

6. Since my (hair + cut) it's easier to (blow + dry) my hair.

7. Franklin forgot to dial the (area + code) and got a wrong number.

8. The (jack + in + the + box) scared my baby sister.

9. Mandy did 25 (sit + ups) in gym class.

10. What is the (list + price) of your (lap + top) computer?

Activity E

Rewrite each of the following sentences, using a compound word to replace two words.

1. The knob on the door was sticky.

2. I put on a coat over my clothes.

3. The light of the moon was bright enough for us to play.

4. I have a lot of work to do around the house.

5. Sometimes during the day I just like to sit and dream.

6. The case of books collapsed under the weight.

7. Our teacher often gives us work to do at home.

8. Everyone huddled around the fire in camp.

Activity F

Rewrite each of the following sentences, using two or more words to replace a compound word.

1. I like applesauce.

2. We rested on the hillside.

3. The skyrocket exploded above us.

4. A few raindrops won't stop us.

5. Mom likes to shop in bookstores.

6. The kids made a snowman.

7. The shovel hit an underground pipe.

Writer's Corner

Look in a book and locate several compound words. Use the words that you find to write sentences of your own.

Writing Skills

Outlines

When you have gathered your facts for a research report, it is important to organize them in a logical order. One way to do this is to create an outline.

To begin an outline, write your topic at the top of a sheet of paper. Then list the main ideas about your topic. Each main idea will sum up the facts in one of your groups of note cards. Put a Roman numeral (I, II, III) and a period in front of each main idea.

Under each main idea list the facts from that group of note cards. These are the details that support your main idea. Put a capital letter and a period before each detail.

Here is an outline that Patrick, a fourth grader, made for a report about the inside of the earth.

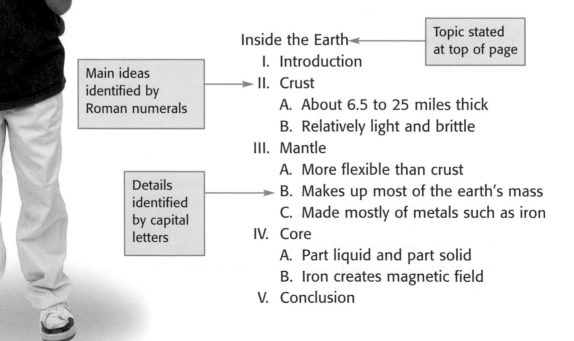

Inside the Earth ← Topic stated at top of page

I. Introduction

Main ideas identified by Roman numerals →

II. Crust
    A. About 6.5 to 25 miles thick
    B. Relatively light and brittle

III. Mantle
    A. More flexible than crust

Details identified by capital letters →

    B. Makes up most of the earth's mass
    C. Made mostly of metals such as iron

IV. Core
    A. Part liquid and part solid
    B. Iron creates magnetic field

V. Conclusion

Look at Patrick's outline. He capitalized the main ideas and details in the same way. He lined up the main ideas along the left side. He lined up the details under the main ideas. Be sure to set up your outline in the same way.

Patrick's first main idea had no details. His second main idea had two details, while his third main idea had three. It is not necessary to have the same number of details for every main idea. Just be sure that if a main idea has details, it has more than one.

All of Patrick's details were written as words and phrases. You should be consistent with your details too. You might use words and phrases, or you might use sentences.

Activity A

Read the following mixed-up main ideas and details. Organize them and use them to make an outline. The topic is "Dogs that help people."

- Sheepdogs help herd livestock.
- Pointers locate birds for hunters.
- Dog guides help people who are blind.
- How dogs help people work
- Sled dogs pull sleds in races.
- How dogs help people play
- Watchdogs help protect property.
- Many dogs catch Frisbees.

Writer's Corner

Create an outline about a part of your school day. Make the different subjects your main ideas. Make the things you learn in each subject your details.

Writing from Outlines

Once you have created your outline, you can begin to write. First check over your outline. If you find a detail that does not belong with the main idea it is written under, leave it out of the paragraph. See if it fits under any other main ideas. If not, leave it out of your research report.

Next begin to write from your outline. If you wrote your outline in words and phrases, expand them into sentences. Write a paragraph about each main idea. State the main idea in the paragraph's first sentence.

Activity B

Look at the following outline for a research report about the invention of chewing gum. Move any details that belong under a different main idea. Take out any details that do not fit under any main ideas. Write a revised outline.

The Invention of Chewing Gum

I. Chicle comes to America.
   A. General Santa Anna brought chicle from Mexico.
   B. Santa Anna fought at the Alamo.
   C. He gave it to New York inventor Thomas Adams.
   D. Adams's gum went on sale in 1871.

II. Adams creates chewing gum.
   A. Adams tried and failed to create rubber from chicle.
   B. He remembered that Santa Anna used to chew chicle.
   C. The Aztecs called chicle "chicti."
   D. He tried chewing it himself and liked it.
   E. He decided to sell it as chewing gum.

III. Chewing gum hits the market.
   A. Adams's gumballs were tasteless.
   B. Adams added licorice flavoring and sales shot up.
   C. Chicle came from the sapodilla, a tree from Mexico.

Activity C

Choose one outline section below and write the ideas in paragraph form. State the main idea in your first sentence.

1. Animals at War

II. Pigeons were used for many things.

    A. They carried messages from the frontlines.

    B. They carried news about airplanes that crashed at sea.

    C. They carried photos of enemy positions.

2. Rock 'n' Roll

I. Rock 'n' roll is born.

    A. It grew from a 1950s music style called rockabilly that combined country music with rhythm and blues.

    B. The term rock 'n' roll was first used in 1951 by Alan Freed, a Cleveland disk jockey.

    C. It was made popular by Elvis Presley.

3. Animation

II. There are many types of animation.

    A. For most of the 20th century, most animation was a series of hand-drawn pictures.

    B. Clay animation is as old as hand-drawn animation, but for a long time it wasn't popular.

    C. Today most animation is done by computers.

Writer's Corner

Choose one of the main ideas from the revised outline in Activity B. Write a paragraph that includes all the details that belong under the main idea.

Oral History Report

Have you ever wondered how gold was first discovered in California? Would you like to find out how the Panama Canal changed the world? In an oral history report, you can research interesting events and share them with your class.

Think of a topic that is interesting to you. Ask questions that you would like answered about the topic. Keep these questions in mind as you prepare your oral history report.

Research

Researching for an oral report is like researching for a written report. Remember to write questions that can help guide your research.

Search for answers to your questions. If your research raises new questions, write them down and look for answers to them too. Use note cards to record and organize your information. Write the information from the sources in your own words. Keep track of which facts came from which source.

As you research, look for pictures, maps, or any other visual aids that might be useful when you speak. Make sure that they are big enough for your audience to see.

Organize

Grab your audience's attention in the introduction of your report. Try to start with an interesting fact or question to make listeners want to pay attention. Be sure to state the topic in the introduction.

Use time order to organize the body of a report about a historical event. First tell what happened right before the event you are talking about. Then describe the event itself. Finally tell what happened as a result of the event. Keep in mind the questions you had when you chose your topic. Answer them in the body of your report. Arrange your note cards so that you can present your ideas smoothly.

The conclusion should sum up your report. It should also leave your audience with the feeling that they have learned something interesting or important.

Activity A

Imagine you are writing oral history reports for the topics below. Write two questions that you think should be answered in a report on each topic.

1. Lindbergh's solo flight across the Atlantic Ocean

2. the assassination of President James Garfield

3. the Louisiana Purchase

4. the making of Mount Rushmore

5. Neil Armstrong's first walk on the moon

Activity B

Choose an event for an oral history report. You may use a topic from Activity A or you may choose any other topic that interests you. Write additional questions to help guide your research.

Speaker's Corner

Gather information about your topic from different sources. Use note cards to write down and organize your facts.

Prepare and Practice

After you have organized your facts, prepare your report. Begin by writing your facts on new note cards. Write a few notes on each card, using keywords and phrases to remind you of what to say. If you plan to use quotations or statistics, write them down exactly. Prepare your visual aid and think of the best way to display it.

Practice presenting your report several times. Try giving the information in your own words without looking down at your notes too often. Remember to speak in a clear voice that shows your interest in the topic.

Speaking Tips

Keep these things in mind when you give your report:

- Speak loudly and clearly so that listeners in the back can understand what you are saying.

- Don't stare straight ahead. Look at people in different parts of the room as you talk.

- Stand naturally and don't be afraid to gesture as you speak. Raising your hand or pointing your finger at the proper moment can hold your audience's attention.

- Make your listeners believe that you are an expert about your topic. Try to make them as interested in your topic as you are.

When you have finished your presentation, ask if there are any questions. If people ask questions that you cannot answer, don't make up answers. Instead, provide the resources that you used and suggest that your classmates try to find the answers for themselves.

Thousands of grizzly bears once roamed across the Pacific Northwest, but their population in Washington is almost gone. Grizzlies can grow to be eight feet tall and weigh more than 600 pounds. Even though they are very big, grizzlies can run up to 35 miles per hour for short distances.

Listening Tips

Show each speaker the same courtesy that you want when you present your speech. Use these tips to help you be a good listener.

- Look at the speaker while he or she is talking. Don't glance around the room or read books or papers at your desk.

- If the topic interests you, take notes about facts that you would like to research on your own.

- Write down any questions that you have as you listen to the report. Wait for the speaker to finish the presentation. Then raise your hand to ask your questions.

• Activity C •

Work with a partner. Look through any sources you have available for visual aids. Talk about ways to display them. Think of other places you could find visual aids for your presentations, such as in an atlas or on the Internet.

• Activity D •

Practice presenting your report to a partner. Give your notes to your partner so that he or she can tell if you forgot any important ideas. Practice your report at least three times so that you feel comfortable as you speak.

Speaker's Corner

Present your history report to the class. Remember to make eye contact with your audience and to speak in a clear voice. When you have finished, invite questions and answer them if you can. Share a list of your resources with anybody who wants to learn more about your topic.

Prewriting and Drafting

Are you interested in a graceful animal or a strange plant? Would you like to know more about an important person or event in history? You can learn all about an interesting topic and share what you learned in a research report.

Prewriting

Maren, a fourth grader, was assigned to write a science report. Before she could write it, however, she would have to choose a topic. Then she would research her topic and organize her information.

Choosing a Topic

Maren had lots of ideas for science topics. She collected insects and enjoyed learning about them. She also thought volcanoes were interesting. Finally she decided to write about her favorite animal, the frog.

Maren soon realized that her topic was too broad. She could write books on the general topic of frogs. She tried to choose one interesting thing about frogs. She decided to focus on the way frogs grow from tadpoles, which she thought was amazing.

Your Turn

Think of a topic that interests you. Be sure that your topic is narrow enough to cover in a report. It should also be something that you could research in the library and on the Internet.

Researching

Maren thought about what she wanted to find out about her topic. Here are a few of the questions she hoped to answer.

What happens to a frog egg?
What does a tadpole look like?
How long does it stay a tadpole?

Next Maren started her research. She looked in an encyclopedia under "Frogs." She did a subject search in her library computer catalog, using "frogs" as a subject, and found two books. Finally she did a Web search, using keywords such as "frog," "life cycle," and "tadpole," and found a few Web sites.

As Maren researched, she took notes on note cards. She wrote one fact on each card and listed the source of each fact. Here are a few notes she took.

Clumps of eggs are laid in the water. Sometimes there are more than a thousand.

Life Cycle of a Frog.
<www.kidslearn.org/frogcycle>

The eggs hatch after one to three weeks.

Frogs, Kim Golparvar, p. 29

Organizing Information

Maren began to organize her information. She looked at all of her notes and put them into piles. She wanted each pile of notes to be about one main idea. If a note did not fit into any pile, she left it out.

Next Maren created an outline. She lined up all her main ideas along the left side. Under each main idea, she wrote the details from that pile of notes. Here is the first part of the outline she made.

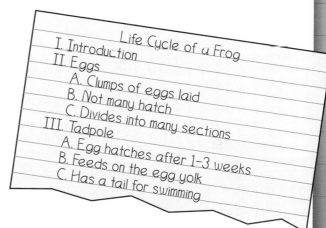

Life Cycle of a Frog
I. Introduction
II. Eggs
   A. Clumps of eggs laid
   B. Not many hatch
   C. Divides into many sections
III. Tadpole
   A. Egg hatches after 1–3 weeks
   B. Feeds on the egg yolk
   C. Has a tail for swimming

Your Turn

Gather your facts for your topic. Begin by making a list of questions you would like to answer in your research. Then search for books, articles, Web sites, and other sources.

Take notes on note cards, writing one fact on each card. Remember to use your own words and list the source on the card.

Your Turn

Organize your note cards into piles. Make sure that the notes in each pile are about one main idea. Then write an outline from your notes. Refer to pages 290 and 291 if you need help creating your outline.

Drafting

Maren used her notes and her outline to write her first draft. She double-spaced her draft so that she would have room to make changes later.

Maren made sure to answer each of the questions she had asked about her topic. She wrote one paragraph for each main idea. She included an introduction that stated the topic and a conclusion that summed it up.

The Life Cycle of a Frog

A frog is an interesting animal. I love to look for them in the stream near my house. It starts out as an egg and begins to grow. The egg hatches into a tadpole that swims and grows for weeks. finally the tadpole turns into a frog. The many changes a frog goes through are kind of amazing.

A frog starts out as an egg. The egg starts out in a big clump, sometimes with thousands of other eggs. Most eggs are laid in calm water to keep them from being moved around. Only a few survive. First the yolk in the egg splits in two. It then splits into more and more parts. It looks almost like a rasberry at this stage. As it grows inside the egg, it starts to look more like a tadpole.

After it hatches, the animal begins its life as a tadpole. The egg hatches after about one to three weeks. It still feeds on its yolk. It lives in the water. It has a long tail for swimming. When it first hatches, a tadpole sometimes attaches itself to floating grass. After about a week, it starts to swim and eat algea.

Then it slowly starts to turn into a frog. Skin starts to grow over the gills. Tiny legs sprout out, and the tail starts to shrink. It starts living on land instead of under-water. When it grows up, an adult frog may lay eggs and start the cycle all over again.

A frog goes through many changes as it grows up. It starts as an egg and then turns into a tadpole. Then it turns into a frog. This is why the frog is one of nature's coolest creations.

Your Turn

Use your notes and outline to write your draft. Your introduction should state the topic in a topic sentence. It should also get the audience's attention.

Begin each body paragraph with a sentence that states the main idea of the paragraph. Make sure that each fact in the paragraph is related to the main idea. If you find a fact that does not fit, move it to a paragraph where it fits better or take it out. Write so your readers think you are an expert on the topic.

Your conclusion should sum up the information. End with an interesting statement that leaves your readers thinking about the topic.

Setting Expectations

A good introduction gives readers an idea of what to expect in the rest of the report. It can be like a guide to the report, previewing all the main ideas that will be discussed in more detail later on.

Look at Maren's introduction. She wrote a sentence about each main idea of the report. Then she wrote a topic sentence that summed up all the main ideas. By doing this, she let her readers know what would be coming in each paragraph of her report.

Research Reports

Content Editing

Maren thought she had done a good job of explaining the life cycle of a frog. Her draft was full of facts from different sources. She knew that by content editing, however, she could make it better.

Maren read her draft over to make sure that it made sense. She checked her facts to make sure they were correct. She looked for any facts that did not fit.

Next Maren asked her friend Evan to content edit her draft. He looked it over to make sure that all the ideas were in the right places and that everything was included. He used this Content Editor's Checklist.

Content Editor's Checklist

- ✓ Does the introduction grab the reader's attention and include a topic sentence?
- ✓ Does each main idea support the topic sentence?
- ✓ Does each detail support the main idea of the paragraph?
- ✓ Is all the important information included?
- ✓ Has unnecessary information been left out?
- ✓ Does the conclusion summarize the report?
- ✓ Does the report use a confident tone?

Evan read through Maren's draft once to get an idea of what it was about. Then he read it more carefully, checking each item on the checklist as he read.

Evan told Maren that he had enjoyed her report. He found that the introduction stated the topic and that the main ideas all supported the topic sentence. He thought the conclusion summed up the report nicely and the whole report was written with confidence. Then he made these suggestions.

- Maybe you could change your introduction so it grabs the reader's attention more.

- The sentence about looking for frogs behind your house seems unnecessary. Also, you shouldn't talk about yourself in a formal report.

- I think the sentence about the egg hatching fits better in the section about the egg.

- How does the tadpole feed on the yolk? Does the tadpole eat it?

- When does the frog have gills? You say that skin grows over them, but you never say how they got there.

Maren thanked Evan for content editing her draft. He had found many ways to improve her draft. Maren decided to use all of them when she revised.

Your Turn

Read over your draft and content edit it, using the Content Editor's Checklist. Look for any ideas that should be added, taken out, or moved. Mark on your draft any changes you plan to make.

Trade drafts with a partner. Read your partner's draft with the help of the Content Editor's Checklist. Make suggestions that you think would improve your partner's draft. Be positive and supportive with your comments.

Listen to your partner's suggestions with an open mind. Use only the suggestions that you think will improve your draft.

Revising

This is how Maren revised her draft after listening to Evan's suggestions.

Amazing
The ∧ Life Cycle of a Frog

One of the strangest animals in nature a frog.
~~A frog is an interesting animal. I love to look for them in the stream~~ ~~near my house.~~ It starts out as an egg and begins to grow. The egg hatches into a tadpole that swims and grows for weeks. finally the tadpole turns into a frog. The many changes a frog goes through are kind of amazing.

A frog starts out as an egg. The egg starts out in a big clump, sometimes with thousands of other eggs. Most eggs are laid in calm water to keep them from being moved around. Only a few survive. First the yolk in the egg splits in two. It then splits into more and more parts. It looks almost like a rasberry at this stage. As it grows inside the egg, it starts to look more like a tadpole. ∧

After it hatches, the animal begins its life as a tadpole.

The egg hatches after about one to three weeks. It still feeds on
, which is inside its belly.   and breathes through gills.
its yolk∧ It lives in the water∧ It has a long tail for swimming. When it first hatches, a tadpole sometimes attaches itself to floating grass. After about a week, it starts to swim and eat algea.

Then it slowly starts to turn into a frog. Skin starts to grow over the gills. Tiny legs sprout out, and the tail starts to shrink. It starts living on land instead of under-water. This whole process is called metamorphosis. When it grows up, an adult frog may lay eggs and start the cycle all over again.

A frog goes through many changes as it grows up. It starts as an egg and then turns into a tadpole. Then it turns into a frog. This is why the frog is one of nature's coolest creations.

Notice the changes Maren made to improve her draft.

- She changed the first sentence so that it would grab the reader's attention.

- She took out the sentence about looking for frogs, which did not fit in her report.

- She moved the sentence about eggs hatching to the previous paragraph, where it fit better.

- She added more information about how the tadpole feeds on the yolk.

- She explained that gills grow in tadpoles to help them breathe.

Maren made a few other changes to her draft. She wanted to make her title more interesting, so she added the word *amazing* to grab the reader's attention. She also wanted to add another cool new word she had learned in her research. She explained in the fourth paragraph that the process of a frog's development is called *metamorphosis.*

Your Turn

Use your partner's suggestions and your own ideas to revise your draft. When you have finished, go over the Content Editor's Checklist again to make sure that you can answer yes to all the questions.

Copyediting and Proofreading

Copyediting

After she had revised her draft, Maren was ready to begin copyediting. By copyediting, she would make certain that her sentences were clear and logical. She would also check that she had used the best words. She used this Copyeditor's Checklist to copyedit her draft.

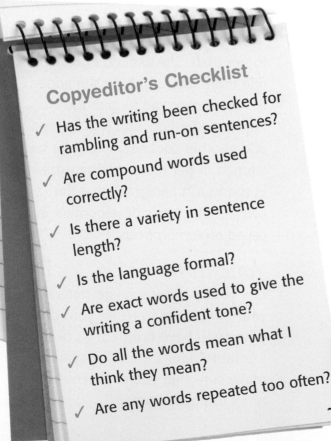

Copyeditor's Checklist

✓ Has the writing been checked for rambling and run-on sentences?

✓ Are compound words used correctly?

✓ Is there a variety in sentence length?

✓ Is the language formal?

✓ Are exact words used to give the writing a confident tone?

✓ Do all the words mean what I think they mean?

✓ Are any words repeated too often?

Maren found a few ways to improve her draft. First she changed the words *kind of* in the first paragraph because they didn't seem confident enough. Using the word *truly* gave her report a more confident tone.

Next she saw that she had used the phrase *starts out* twice in the second paragraph. For variety she changed the phrase to *begins* in the second sentence.

Finally Maren changed the word *coolest* in her last sentence. She knew that slang words did not belong in a formal report. She changed the word to *greatest*.

Your Turn

Copyedit your research report, using the Copyeditor's Checklist. Look for only one kind of mistake at a time. Make sure that each sentence is clear and correct. Check that your words mean what you think they mean, especially compound words.

Proofreading

Maren wanted someone to proofread her draft to make sure that there were no mistakes. She knew that she had read her draft so many times that her eyes might just skip over an obvious mistake. She asked her friend Eric to proofread because she knew Eric was a good speller. Here is the checklist that Eric used.

Proofreader's Checklist

✓ Are all the paragraphs indented?

✓ Have all the words been checked for spelling, especially compound words?

✓ Is the grammar correct?

✓ Are the beginnings of sentences and proper nouns capitalized?

✓ Has the writing been checked to make certain that no new mistakes have been made?

Eric read Maren's draft once for fun. He told Maren that he really enjoyed reading it. Then Eric read it more carefully, checking each item on the checklist.

First Eric noticed that the word *finally* needed to be capitalized in the first paragraph.

Eric found three misspelled words. He saw that Maren had misspelled the compound word *underwater*. The word did not need a hyphen. He also noticed that the words *raspberry* and *algae* were misspelled.

Finally Eric saw that the opening sentence Maren added was not a complete sentence. It needed the word *is* to make it complete.

Maren thanked Eric for finding those mistakes. Maren would make all the corrections Eric suggested before publishing the finished report.

Your Turn

Read through your draft again, using the Proofreader's Checklist. Look for misspelled words and mistakes in capitalization, punctuation, and grammar. Make sure that no new mistakes have been made.

Exchange your draft with a partner. Read your partner's draft carefully with the help of the Proofreader's Checklist. Look for any mistakes that your partner may have missed. Then return your partner's draft and explain what you found.

Publishing

After making her corrections, Maren was almost ready to share her research report with her audience. At the end of her report, she listed her sources. This would tell her readers where she got her facts and where they could look for more information.

Maren looked over her report one more time and printed it out. She created a title page with a picture of a frog she had made in art class. She pinned her report on the class bulletin board where other students could read it.

The Amazing Life Cycle of a Frog
By Maren Ediza

One of the strangest animals in nature is a frog. It starts out as an egg and begins to grow. The egg hatches into a tadpole that swims and grows for weeks. Finally the tadpole turns into a frog. The many changes a frog goes through are truly amazing.

A frog starts out as an egg. The egg begins in a big clump, sometimes with thousands of other eggs. Most eggs are laid in calm water to keep them from being moved around. Only a few survive. First the yolk in the egg splits in two. It then splits into more and more parts. It looks almost like a raspberry at this stage. As it grows inside the egg, it starts to look more like a tadpole. The egg hatches after about one to three weeks.

After it hatches, the animal begins its life as a tadpole. It still feeds on its yolk, which is inside its belly. It lives in the water and breathes through gills. It has a long tail for swimming. When it first hatches, a tadpole sometimes attaches itself to floating grass. After about a week, it starts to swim and eat algae.

Then it slowly starts to turn into a frog. Skin starts to grow over the gills. Tiny legs sprout out, and the tail starts to shrink. It starts living on land instead of underwater. This whole process is called metamorphosis. When it grows up, an adult frog may lay eggs and start the cycle all over again.

A frog goes through many changes as it grows up. It starts as an egg and then turns into a tadpole. Then it turns into a frog. This is why the frog is one of nature's greatest creations.

Sources:
"Frogs," Jaye's Science Encyclopedia for Children
Golparvar, Kim. Frogs.
"Life Cycle of a Frog." <www.kidslearn.org/frogcycle>
Vrabel, Monica. Nature's Wonders.

Your Turn

Look over your draft one more time for any mistakes. Then copy it in your neatest handwriting or use a computer and print out your report. Include a list of your sources at the bottom of the last page. Use the examples on pages 280 and 281 to help you write your sources. List the sources in alphabetical order.

Talk with your class about ways to publish your reports. You might post them on a class bulletin board. If you do, make an eye-catching title page that includes the title of your report, your name, and a picture or photograph of your topic.

When everyone has posted their reports, spend some time browsing the reports. You might learn something you never knew about a topic. If you want to know more about a topic, use the list of sources to help you find more information.

Grammar

Sentences

Sentences: Part I

A **sentence** is a group of words that expresses a complete thought. Every sentence begins with a capital letter. Most sentences end with periods. Every sentence begins with a capital letter.

A sentence has a subject and a predicate. The **subject** tells who or what the sentence is about. The **predicate** tells what the subject is or does. It expresses an action or a state of being.

Complete Subject	Complete Predicate
Eric	played cymbals.
The cymbals	were gold and shiny.
The crowd	enjoyed the concert.
All the children	were happy.

Which of these word groups are sentences?

A. The drums are loud
B. A brass tuba
C. Maggie likes the trumpet
D. Listens to the music

You are right if you said that A and C are sentences. Each one expresses a complete thought. Each one has a subject and a predicate, and each should have a period at the end.

B and D are not sentences. They do not express complete thoughts. B doesn't have a predicate, and D doesn't have a subject.

Exercise 1

Tell which of these word groups are sentences. Tell which are not sentences.

1. The band marched in the parade
2. The band members have nice uniforms
3. Marching to the music
4. The drumsticks
5. The drum major leads the band
6. The tuba looks heavy
7. Carrying their instruments
8. We clapped for the band
9. The music was very loud
10. A group of tumbling clowns

Exercise 2

Match a group of words in Column A with a group of words in Column B to make a sentence. Add a period to the end of each sentence.

Column A	Column B
1. During the parade, bands	a. sounded their sirens
2. The floats	b. played music
3. Clowns	c. made the crowd laugh
4. Fire engines	d. moved down the street

Practice Power

Choose four of these topics. Write a sentence about each.

A. parade   C. marching band   E. clowns

B. floats   D. horses   F. fire truck

Sentences: Part II

A **declarative sentence** makes a statement. It ends with a period.

> There are many creatures in the sea.
> Ocean water is salty.

An **interrogative sentence** asks a question. It begins with a question word or with a verb. It ends with a question mark.

> What kind of fish is it?
> Is that fresh water?
> How can I conserve water?

Which of these sentences is declarative?

A. How can I protect the oceans?
B. What happens when the oceans are polluted?
C. Trash can hurt sea animals.

You are right if you said sentence C. It makes a statement and ends with a period. A and B are interrogative sentences. They ask questions and end with question marks.

Exercise 1

Rewrite these sentences. Add periods at the end of declarative sentences. Add question marks at the end of interrogative sentences.

1. How much of the earth's water is salty

2. Is lake water salty or fresh

3. Only 3 percent of the earth's water is fresh

4. Water is found in oceans, lakes, and rivers

5. Where else is water found

6. Some water is frozen as ice caps and glaciers

7. All of us can conserve water

8. Do you always turn the faucet completely off

9. You can save water when you brush your teeth

10. You should not let the water run

11. Does a bath or a shower use more water

12. Can you water your garden less often

Exercise 2

Make statements and questions by matching the words in Column A with the words in Column B.

Column A	Column B
1. Do people	a. often dumped into oceans?
2. Oil tankers	b. cross the oceans.
3. Sometimes oil	c. concerned about the oceans?
4. Is garbage from cities	d. spills from tankers.
5. Are you	e. care about pollution?

Practice Power

Write a question for each of these topics: recycling, saving water, and pollution. Then interview a classmate. Write his or her answers.

Example: What do you recycle?
I recycle plastic.

Sentences: Part III

An **imperative sentence** gives a command or makes a request. It usually ends with a period. The subject of an imperative sentence is generally *you*, which is often not stated.

> Tell me about spiders.
> Please handle the spider with care.

An **exclamatory sentence** expresses strong or sudden emotion. It ends with an exclamation point.

> That is one ugly spider!
> That spider web is beautiful!

Which of these sentences are imperatives?

> **A.** That spider is gross!
> **B.** Stay calm.
> **C.** Don't harm the spider, please.
> **D.** Do you see the spider web?

You are right if you said that B and C are imperative sentences. They give commands. Each ends with a period.

Sentence A is an exclamatory sentence. It expresses strong or sudden emotion and ends with an exclamation point. Sentence D is an interrogative sentence. It asks a question and ends with a question mark.

Exercise 1

Rewrite the sentences. Add periods at the end of imperative sentences. Add exclamation points at the end of exclamatory sentences.

1. Oh, that's a big spider

2. Look at its web

3. Gross, that spider has eight eyes

4. Hold out your hand

5. Please be gentle with the baby spider

6. Watch it closely

7. Oh, it is tickling my hand

8. Oh, no, it's running away

9. Don't step on it

10. Pick up the spider carefully

Exercise 2

Imagine you are an actor. Read each sentence aloud twice. Follow the two stage directions.

1. What a big spider this is!
   a. You are amazed by the spider's size.
   b. You are frightened by the spider's size.

2. Oh, the web is in the doorway!
   a. You think the spider web is disgusting.
   b. You think the spider web is beautiful.

Practice Power

What would you say to a friend who was afraid when a spider was nearby? Write three imperative sentences.

Example: Don't be afraid.

Subjects and Predicates: Part I

Every sentence must have a **subject** and a **predicate.** The subject names the person, place, or thing talked about in a sentence. A **complete subject** includes the specific person, place, or thing and all the words that go with it. A **complete predicate** is the verb and the words relating to it. It describes the action or state of being of the subject

Complete Subject	Complete Predicate
The class	studies geography.
All of the students	like to learn new things.
Jamie and Marie	are excited about the class.

What is the complete subject of the following sentence? What is its complete predicate?

The teacher listed the Seven Wonders of the World.

If you said the complete subject is *The teacher,* you are right. *The teacher* names the person the sentence is about. The complete predicate is *listed the Seven Wonders of the World.* It tells what the teacher did.

Exercise 1
Find the complete subject in each sentence.

1. An ancient Greek writer listed several amazing monuments.

2. The name of the list is the Seven Wonders of the World.

3. A 40-foot statue of Zeus appears on the list.

Exercise 2

Find the complete predicate in each sentence.

1. The Egyptians built the Great Pyramid at Giza for the pharaoh Khufu.

2. An earthquake toppled the Mausoleum at Halicarnassus.

3. An ancient colossal statue on the island of Rhodes looked somewhat like the Statue of Liberty.

4. The Pharos of Alexandria guided sailors.

5. The word *pharos* was the Greek word for "lighthouse."

Exercise 3

Finish each sentence with a complete subject or a complete predicate. Choose from the list below.

The Great Pyramid	are triangles
The Mayan people	built a model pyramid
The Egyptians	is 449 feet high

1. _____ is the only ancient wonder that still stands.

2. The Great Pyramid _____ .

3. _____ used two million blocks of stone for it.

4. The class _____ .

5. _____ also built pyramids.

6. The sides of pyramids _____ .

Practice Power

Write four sentences about wonderful things or places you would like to see. Put one line under the complete subject. Put two lines under the complete predicate.

Example: <u>The Sears Tower</u> <u>is a tall building</u>.

Subjects and Predicates: Part II

The subject names the person, place, or thing talked about. The most important word in the subject is usually a noun. The noun is the **simple subject.** Asking *who* or *what* before the predicate reveals the subject.

The predicate describes what the subject is or does and contains a verb. The verb is called the **simple predicate.**

	Simple Subject	Simple Predicate	
The	flag	waved	in the wind.

	Simple Subject	Simple Predicate	
The	principal	raised	the flag.

What are the simple subject and the simple predicate in this sentence?

> Every new country needs a flag.

If you named *country* as the simple subject, you are correct. *Country* is the noun. It is the most important part of the subject. If you named *needs* as the simple predicate, you are correct. *Needs* is the verb. It is the most important part of the predicate.

Exercise 1

Find the simple subject and the simple predicate in each sentence.

1. The United States declared independence from Britain.
2. The original colonies used many different flags.
3. Some flags resembled the British flag.
4. The country's leaders wanted a different flag.
5. Betsy Ross tailored clothes for George Washington.
6. Washington recognized Betsy's remarkable sewing skills.
7. Washington requested her help.
8. This talented tailor produced the first American flag.

Exercise 2

Complete each sentence with a simple subject or a simple predicate from this list.

calls	citizens	stands	stars	says

1. Many _____ decorate the U.S. flag.
2. U.S. _____ respect the American flag.
3. The American flag _____ in the corner of the room.
4. My grandfather _____ the flag *Old Glory.*
5. The class _____ the Pledge of Allegiance.

Practice Power

If you were to make a flag, what would it look like? Write four sentences about your flag. Draw one line under the simple subject. Draw two lines under the simple predicate.

Example: My <u>flag</u> <u><u>is</u></u> purple.

Compound Subjects

Every sentence has a subject. The subject is who or what the sentence is about. Usually the simple subject is a noun. A **compound subject** has two or more simple subjects connected by *and* or *or*.

Simple Subject

Cats	are curious.

Compound Subject

Cats and kittens	are curious.
Cats or kittens	make good pets.

Notice that the compound subjects include two simple subjects: *cats* and *kittens*.

Which of these sentences have compound subjects?

A. Katie helps at an animal shelter.
B. Max and Mandy do volunteer work there too.
C. The animals are happy in their new homes.
D. Veterinarians or volunteers play with the animals every day.

You are right if you said that sentences B and D have compound subjects. *Max* and *Mandy* are two simple subjects joined by the word *and*. *Veterinarians* and *volunteers* are two simple subjects joined by the word *or*.

Exercise 1

Tell whether each sentence has a simple or a compound subject. Name the subject.

1. Many animals need a good home.
2. Amy and Ryan wanted a dog.
3. Riley and Bogie are two Labradors.
4. A car hit Riley.
5. Riley's leg was broken.
6. A cast and medicine helped Riley.
7. The children's family adopted him.
8. Bones and rawhide treats are Riley's favorite rewards.

Exercise 2

Rewrite the sentences. Use a compound subject to complete each sentence. Remember to use *and* or *or.*

1. _____ are small dogs.
2. _____ are bigger dogs.
3. _____ make strange pets.
4. _____ are good names for pets.
5. _____ are not good pets.
6. _____ are my favorite breeds.
7. _____ are popular breeds.

Practice Power

Write four sentences about a pet or pets that you have or a friend has. Use a compound subject in at least two sentences.

Example: A dog and two cats live in my grandmother's house.

Compound Predicates

Every sentence has a predicate. The simple predicate is the verb that tells what the subject is or does. A **compound predicate** has two or more simple predicates connected with *and, but,* or *or.*

	Simple Predicate	
Tourists	visit	different cities.

	Compound Predicate
Tourists	sightsee and shop.
Tourists	get tired but feel happy.

Sightsee and *shop* are simple predicates joined by *and* to make a compound predicate. *Get* and *feel* are simple predicates joined by *but* to make a compound predicate.

Which of these sentences have compound predicates?

A. Janine walks to the museum.
B. Candace drives a red car.
C. Jeff takes the bus or rides the subway.
D. Tito visits the aquarium and watches the fish.

You are right if you said sentences C and D have compound predicates. *Takes* and *rides* are two simple predicates joined by the word *or.* *Visits* and *watches* are two simple predicates joined by the word *and.*

Exercise 1

Tell whether each sentence has a simple or a compound predicate. Name the verbs in the predicate.

1. My family hiked last weekend.

2. We climbed and scrambled up the steep mountain.

3. It rained and snowed on the same day.

4. The hikers shivered and shook in the rain.

5. I found my rain poncho and put it around me.

6. The rain stopped.

7. The afternoon was bright and sunny.

8. The sun turned orange and set behind the mountain.

Exercise 2

Combine each pair of sentences into one sentence with a compound predicate.

Example: May *washes* dishes. May *makes* her bed.
May *washes* dishes and *makes* her bed.

1. The friends play hopscotch. The friends skip rope.

2. My sisters go to school together. My sisters come home together.

3. Lou phones Roberto. Lou talks to him every day.

4. Lee and I go to the movies. Lee and I buy popcorn.

5. I read a book. I studied for the test.

Practice Power

Write four sentences about something you have done with family or friends. Use a compound predicate in at least two of the sentences.

Example: My family water-skied and swam.

Direct Objects

The **direct object** is the noun or pronoun that receives the action of the verb. Many sentences need a direct object to complete their meaning.

To find the direct object of a sentence, ask *whom* or *what* after the verb.

	Direct Object
The Mississippi River divides the	country.

The Mississippi River divides *what. Country* is the direct object. It tells what the Mississippi River divides.

	Direct Object	
The river provides a	route	for transportation.

The river provides *what. Route* is the direct object. It tells what the river provides.

What is the direct object in this sentence?

> The Ojibwa Indians named the river.

The direct object in this sentence is *river.* The Ojibwa Indians named *what.* The answer is *river.*

This sentence has a compound direct object.

> A shipping channel moves goods and people up and down the river.

The compound direct object in the sentence is *goods and people. Goods* and *people* are two simple direct objects joined by the word *and.*

Exercise 1

Find the direct object in each sentence. Read carefully. Some sentences have compound direct objects.

1. The ice age changed the earth.

2. Melting water from glaciers formed valleys.

3. The flowing water carved the Mississippi River and the Grand Canyon.

4. Europeans like Louis Joliet led voyages of exploration.

5. Henry Schoolcraft discovered the river's source.

6. Boats on the Mississippi provide transportation and entertainment.

7. Barges on the river still carry many products.

Exercise 2

Complete each sentence with a direct object from the list.

boundaries	color	Gulf of Mexico	soil	water

1. The Mississippi River carries _____ from the area between the Rocky Mountains and the Appalachians.

2. The Mississippi forms the _____ of several states.

3. The southern part of the river has a muddy _____.

4. There the Mississippi leaves _____ along its banks.

5. The river enters the _____ in small channels.

Practice Power

Write four sentences about a river you have seen either in person or in a photograph. Use a direct object in each sentence. Underline the direct object.

Example: I crossed the <u>Mississippi River</u> on a ferry.

Subject Complements

A **subject complement** follows a linking verb. It is usually a noun or an adjective that tells more about the subject. The most common linking verb is *be* and its various forms (*am, are, is, was, were*).

Subject	Linking Verb	Subject Complement
The storm	was	a tornado.
The winds	are	strong.

Tornado and *strong* are subject complements. Each follows a form of the linking verb *be*. Each tells more about the subject of the sentence. *Tornado* is a noun that renames the subject, *storm. Strong* is an adjective that describes *winds*.

What is the subject complement in this sentence?

The storm was fierce.

The subject complement is *fierce*. It is an adjective that follows the linking verb *was*. It tells more about the subject *storm*.

This sentence has a compound subject complement.

She was surprised but happy.

The compound subject complement is *surprised but happy. Surprised* and *happy* are two simple subject complements joined by the word *but*.

Exercise 1

Find the simple or compound subject complement in each sentence.

1. Powerful storms in the Atlantic are hurricanes.

2. Similar storms in the Pacific are typhoons.

3. Another type of storm in the Pacific is a tropical cyclone.

4. Some hurricanes are strong and destructive.

5. Hurricane Andrew in 1992, for example, was extremely powerful.

6. Its winds were fierce and violent.

7. Flooding from hurricanes is also the cause of damage.

Exercise 2

Complete each sentence with a subject complement. Use the nouns and adjectives on the list.

calm	common	Florida	month	straight

1. Hurricanes in the Atlantic are most _____ in the fall.

2. September is the usual _____ for these storms.

3. A state with many hurricanes is _____.

4. The eye of a storm is _____.

5. The path of a hurricane is not _____.

Practice Power

Pretend you are a weather forecaster. Write four sentences about weather. Use a noun or adjective as a subject complement in each sentence. Underline each subject complement.

Example: Today's weather is <u>sunny</u>.

Compound Sentences

When two short sentences are related to each other, they can be combined into a **compound sentence.** To combine two short sentences into one longer sentence, add a comma followed by *and, but,* or *or.* The first word in the second part of the compound does not start with a capital letter unless it is *I* or the name of a person or place.

Two sentences that are related:
  Lightning flashed. Thunder boomed.
Compound sentence:
  Lightning flashed, and thunder boomed.

Two sentences that are related:
  The lights flickered. They did not go out.
Compound sentence:
  The lights flickered, but they did not go out.

Two sentences that are related:
  We will play a game. We will watch TV.
Compound sentence:
  We will play a game, or we will watch TV.

What two sentences were combined to make this compound sentence?
  The sun came out, and it was warm.
You were right if you said these sentences.
  The sun came out. It was warm.

Exercise 1

Match each sentence in Column A with a related sentence in Column B to make a compound sentence.

Column A

1. The snow fell all night, but
2. Mom made breakfast, and
3. We can go sledding, or
4. Mom made a snowman, and
5. We were tired and cold, and

Column B

a. I put a hat on him.
b. we can build a snow fort.
c. it had stopped by morning.
d. we went back in the house.
e. we ate in a hurry.

Exercise 2

Combine each pair of short sentences into a compound sentence. Use a comma and *and, but,* or *or.*

1. Winter in Wisconsin is cold. It snows a lot.
2. Ice fishing is popular. Jean doesn't like to sit out in the cold.
3. Danny likes to ski. He doesn't know how to ice skate.
4. He wants to learn. His brother will give him lessons.
5. We went to the rink. We watched his brother do tricks.
6. Danny put on his skates. He wobbled onto the ice.
7. He tried to stay on his feet. He kept falling down.
8. He'll keep trying. I know he will succeed.

Practice Power

Write at least five compound sentences about sports that you and your friends like to do. Each sentence should have a comma and *and, but,* or *or.*

Run-on Sentences

A **run-on sentence** results when two sentences are combined but not connected properly. A run-on sentence occurs when two sentences are separated by only a comma or by no connectors at all.

A run-on is easily fixed by making a compound sentence with a comma and the word *and* or *but*. Another way to fix a run-on, particularly a long run-on, is to divide it into two or more separate sentences.

Run-on sentence:	I went to the store, I bought milk.
Correction:	I went to the store, and I bought milk.
Run-on sentence:	I needed milk the store did not have any.
Correction:	I needed milk, but the store did not have any.

Which of these sentences is a run-on?

- **A.** Sam drank the milk. It tasted good.
- **B.** My friend lives on a farm, and I went to visit her.
- **C.** Cows produce milk, many people drink it.

You are right if you said C. C has two sentences run together with only a comma—without the word *and*.

A is correct because there are two separate sentences that have proper punctuation at the end of each. B is a correctly combined sentence. It links two sentences with a comma and the word *and*.

Exercise 1

Tell whether each sentence is a run-on or a correct compound sentence.

1. Jeff likes cows, he wants to live on a farm.

2. Farmer Frank owns a farm, and he has many cows.

3. Jeff visits the farm, he helps Farmer Frank.

4. Frank knows about cows, and he teaches Jeff.

5. Holsteins have black spots, the spot pattern on each cow is different.

6. Holsteins are good dairy cows, they can each produce about 21,000 pounds of milk a year.

7. Jersey cows produce less milk, but it is richer.

8. Cows have one stomach, it has four compartments.

Exercise 2

Rewrite these run-on sentences as compound sentences.

1. A cow can give about 8 gallons of milk each day, it drinks 16 gallons of water.

2. A one-year-old female cow is a heifer, it weighs between 450 and 500 pounds.

3. Cows produce milk every day farmers need to milk them every day.

4. Calcium is found in milk people need calcium in order to be healthy.

5. Calcium can also be found in broccoli, I don't like broccoli.

Practice Power

Find some facts about cows or another animal. Write four compound sentences. Be sure to use correct punctuation.

Sentence Challenge

Read the paragraph and answer the questions.

1. Do you like pandas? 2. Pandas are endangered. 3. That means there aren't many of them left. 4. That's a shame! 5. Giant pandas are fussy eaters. 6. Pandas eat only bamboo. 7. There is not enough bamboo anymore. 8. People cleared land and eliminated bamboo plants. 9. China has created refuges for pandas. 10. Scientists and other people help pandas stay alive.

1. What kind of sentence is sentence 1?

2. In sentence 1 what word is the direct object?

3. In sentence 2 what is the complete predicate?

4. Is sentence 4 a declarative sentence or an exclamatory sentence? How do you know?

5. In sentence 5 what is the complete subject?

6. In sentence 5 what is the subject complement?

7. In sentence 6 what is the simple subject?

8. In sentence 6 what is the verb?

9. In sentence 9 what part of the sentence is *refuges*?

10. In sentence 10 what is the complete subject? What is the complete predicate?

11. Which sentence has a compound predicate?

12. Which sentence has a compound subject?

Nouns

Nouns

A **noun** names a person, a place, or a thing.

If you are in a city, you can see many different persons, places, and things.

Persons	Places	Things
cab drivers	restaurants	buildings
Mayor Barak	gas stations	tickets
shopper	cathedral	pigeon
pedestrians	bank	traffic lights

Which noun names a person in this sentence?

A police officer stood near an intersection and blew a whistle.

A. police officer
B. whistle
C. intersection

You are right if you said A. A *police officer* is a person who protects other people.

A *whistle* is a thing that makes noise. An *intersection* is the place where two streets meet.

Can you name other people, places, and things in a city? The words you name are probably nouns.

Exercise 1

Find the nouns in each sentence. The number of nouns in each sentence is shown in parentheses.

1. Capitals are special cities. (2)

2. Capitals have offices for the government. (3)

3. The governor works in the capital of a state. (3)

4. The president of the United States lives in Washington. (3)

5. That city is the capital of the country. (3)

6. Senators and representatives make laws. (3)

7. The lawmakers work in a building called the Capitol. (3)

8. Capitols are often large buildings with domes. (3)

9. The area beneath the dome is called the rotunda. (3)

10. Millions of people have visited the Capitol. (3)

Exercise 2

Complete each sentence with a noun or nouns.

1. The _____ visited Washington, D.C.

2. They made a list of _____ to see.

3. _____ asked to see the White House.

4. The _____ suggested the Air and Space Museum.

5. The family saw the _____ on the trip.

6. Everyone's _____ hurt at the end of the day.

Practice Power

Write five sentences about a trip you took. Where did you go? Who went with you? What did you see? Underline the nouns.

Common Nouns and Proper Nouns

A **proper noun** begins with a capital letter and names a particular person, place, or thing. A **common noun** names any one member of a group of persons, places, or things.

PROPER NOUNS	COMMON NOUNS
Person	
Javier Mendez	teacher
Abraham Lincoln	president
Place	
San Francisco	city
Delaware	state
Thing	
Atlantic Ocean	ocean
Sirius	star

Which of the following is a proper noun?

A. street

B. road

C. Madison Avenue

You are right if you said C. *Madison Avenue* is a proper noun. It names a specific street. Both parts of the noun begin with a capital letter.

Exercise 1

Find the nouns in each sentence. The number of nouns is shown in parentheses. Tell whether each is a proper or a common noun.

1. Emma Lazarus was a poet. (2)

2. Emma lived in New York City. (2)

3. The young woman started to help people. (2)

4. People had come to the United States from Europe. (3)

5. These new Americans needed jobs and homes. (3)

6. Lazarus wrote a poem on the subject. (3)

7. The poem was put on the base of a statue. (3)

8. The statue is known as the Statue of Liberty. (2)

Exercise 2

Tell whether each noun is a proper noun or a common noun. Write a common noun for each proper noun and a proper noun for each common noun.

1. athlete
2. Canada
3. holiday
4. *Ella Enchanted*
5. river

6. TV show
7. Vermont
8. song
9. Thomas Edison
10. poet

Practice Power

Answer each of the following with a complete sentence. Underline all proper nouns.

1. What is your name? Tell one interesting fact about yourself.

2. Tell something interesting about your town.

Singular Nouns and Plural Nouns

A **singular noun** names one person, place, or thing. A **plural noun** names more than one person, place, or thing.

The plural of most nouns is formed by adding -*s* to the singular.

Singular	Plural
map	maps
house	houses

The plural of a noun ending in *s, x, z, ch,* or *sh* is formed by adding -*es* to the singular.

Singular	Plural
guess	guesses
fox	foxes
buzz	buzzes
beach	beaches
dish	dishes

The plural of a noun ending in *y* after a consonant is formed by changing the *y* to *i* and adding -*es.*

Singular	Plural
city	cities
baby	babies

If a noun ends in *y* after a vowel, simply add -*s.*

Singular	Plural
day	days

Exercise 1

Find the nouns in each sentence. Tell whether each is singular or plural. The number of nouns in each sentence is in parentheses.

1. Susan attended two parties recently. (2)

2. One celebration was for her own birthday. (2)

3. Many wrapped boxes were on the table. (2)

4. The guests ate all the cookies. (2)

5. The girl made a wish and blew out the candles. (3)

6. Two puppies were sitting in a box outside the door! (3)

7. Then the guests played games and watched videos. (3)

8. The only problem was that the party seemed too short! (2)

Exercise 2

Write the plural for each singular noun.

1. inch
2. cup
3. country
4. play
5. glass

6. hobby
7. ax
8. mitten
9. dash
10. star

11. rose
12. wagon
13. story
14. fox
15. patch

Practice Power

Choose one of these lists of nouns. Write a story using the words, making them plural when necessary.

A	B	C
clown	watermelon	spaceship
monkey	garden	galaxy
elephant	daisy	orbit
tent	shovel	experiment

Irregular Plural Nouns

The plurals of some nouns are not formed by adding -s or -es to the singular. These are called **irregular plurals.**

You need to learn these irregular plurals. If you forget how to spell an irregular plural, you can look it up in a dictionary.

Singular	Plural
ox	oxen
child	children
tooth	teeth
foot	feet
mouse	mice
woman	women
goose	geese
wolf	wolves
knife	knives

Some nouns have the same form in the plural as in the singular.

Singular	Plural
sheep	sheep
deer	deer
fish	fish
series	series

Exercise 1

Write the plural of each irregular noun.

1. goose
2. foot
3. child
4. man
5. deer

6. ox
7. woman
8. tooth
9. person
10. leaf

Exercise 2

Complete each sentence. Use the correct form of the irregular noun in parentheses. Tell whether it is singular or plural.

1. A _____ with a toothache went to the dentist. (man)

2. Three _____ ran through the waiting room. (mouse)

3. Two _____ in the waiting room dropped their toys. (child)

4. A _____ told them to remain calm. (woman)

5. The dentist told the man that three of his _____ had to be pulled. (tooth)

6. A team of _____ couldn't have budged one of them. (ox)

7. Two _____, who were dental assistants, assisted the dentist. (woman)

8. The dentist gave the man medicine, and the man counted _____ as he fell asleep in the dentist's chair. (sheep)

Practice Power

Choose four words from the list of irregular nouns in Exercise 1. Write four sentences, using one of the words in each sentence. Make the nouns plural when necessary.

Singular Possessive Nouns

A **possessive noun** shows possession, or ownership. A **singular possessive** shows that one person or thing owns something.

Catherine's shopping bag is filled with food.
The *market's* food is fancy.

Catherine's shopping bag means that the shopping bag belongs to Catherine. *Market's food* means the food that the market has for sale.

To form the singular possessive, add an apostrophe and the letter *s* (-'s) to a singular noun.

Singular	Singular Possessive	Possessive Phrase
Richard	Richard's	Richard's chore
cow	cow's	cow's milk

What is the correct way to show that each of the following belongs to Bruce?

car   bicycle   wagon

You are right if you said *Bruce's car, Bruce's bicycle,* and *Bruce's wagon.* By adding an -'s to *Bruce,* you show that the car, the bicycle, and the wagon belong to him.

What if you wanted to say that the items belonged to *the boy?* You are right if you said *the boy's car, the boy's bicycle,* and *the boy's wagon.*

Exercise 1

Rewrite each sentence, using the possessive form of each singular noun in parentheses.

1. The _____ job is to run the city. (mayor)

2. _____ office is in City Hall. (Mr. Conlon)

3. The _____ job is to deliver mail. (mail carrier)

4. Our _____ mailperson is Mrs. Alvarez. (neighborhood)

5. The _____ job is to help us cross the street. (patrol officer)

6. A _____ job is to remove garbage. (garbage collector)

7. My _____ garbage is placed outside for pickup on Tuesday mornings. (family)

Exercise 2

Rewrite each sentence as a singular possessive phrase.

Example: The judge has a gavel.
        the judge's gavel

1. A police officer has a badge.

2. Michelle has neighbors.

3. The principal has a secretary.

4. Elio lives in a house.

5. The street cleaner has a broom.

6. My sister owns a DVD player.

Practice Power

Think about things that people in your own neighborhood own and the jobs they do. Write five sentences that show possession.

Example: Our crossing guard's name is Ms. Jones.

Plural Possessive Nouns

A **plural possessive** shows that more than one person or thing owns something.

boys' games   *babies'* toes   *wolves'* teeth

To form the plural possessive of regular nouns, add an apostrophe (') after the -*s* of the plural form. Remember to form the plural of a regular noun before adding the apostrophe.

Singular	Plural	Plural Possessive
boy	boys	boys'
baby	babies	babies'

To form the plural possessive of irregular nouns, add -*'s*.

Singular	Plural	Plural Possessive
man	men	men's
ox	oxen	oxen's

What is the plural possessive for this sentence?

The _____ apples are red.

A. lady
B. lady's
C. ladies'

You are right if you said that C is the plural possessive. When an apostrophe is added to the word *ladies,* it means the apples belong to more than one lady.

Exercise 1

Complete this chart with the plural form and the plural possessive form for each noun.

Singular	Plural	Plural Possessive
1. rabbit	_____	_____ ears
2. child	_____	_____ chores
3. settler	_____	_____ homes
4. Spaniard	_____	_____ horses
5. leader	_____	_____ decisions
6. family	_____	_____ homes

Exercise 2

Write the possessive form of the plural noun in italics.

1. The Plains *Indians* home was in central North America.

2. These Native *Americans* source of food was the buffalo.

3. *Men* tasks included hunting the buffalo.

4. Their *horses* speed allowed them to chase buffalo.

5. Buffalo were important, and the *animals* skins were used for clothing, bedding, and tepees.

6. *Women* tasks were to cook, make cloth, and farm.

7. *Warriors* deeds were praised.

8. The destruction of the buffalo herds changed various Indian *nations* lifestyles.

Practice Power

Think about a group of people in your community, such as teachers, sales clerks, doctors, taxi drivers, or bakers. Write four sentences about their way of life. Use plural possessives.

Collective Nouns

Nouns that name a group of things or people are called **collective nouns.**

The *orchestra* plays at many all-school meetings.

The collective noun *orchestra* names a group of musicians considered together as a unit.

Collective Nouns

army	company	herd	pair
audience	crew	litter	police
band	family	majority	swarm
class	flock	minority	team
club	group	pack	tribe

A singular collective noun usually uses a singular verb. Note that singular verbs in the present tense end in *-s.*

The quartet plays.
The duo dances.

Which sentences include collective nouns?

A. A ballerina twirls.
B. The singer hums.
C. The crowd applauds.

You are right if you said that only C includes a collective noun. *Crowd* names a group. *Ballerina* and *singer* each name one person.

Exercise 1
Find the collective noun in each sentence.

1. The class wanted to help clean up the old park.

2. A group of students wrote a letter.

3. The children wrote to the city council.

4. A committee considered the issue.

5. A team of city workers cleaned the park.

6. Now families go to the park to play and relax.

7. Bands play there during the summer.

8. Flocks of geese stop at the park's newly cleaned pond during the spring and fall.

Exercise 2
Complete each sentence with a collective noun. Use words from the list on page 350.

1. My family chose a puppy from the _____.

2. All the players on the _____ can run well.

3. The _____ decided to do a recycling project.

4. My friend plays a tuba in the _____.

5. We gave bread to a _____ of pigeons.

6. We saw a _____ of bees near the hive.

7. The _____ cheered at the end of the concert.

8. The _____ arrived at the scene of the accident.

Practice Power

Choose three collective nouns and write a sentence for each.

Example: The audience applauded my magic tricks.

Count Nouns and Noncount Nouns

Count nouns name things that exist as individual units. You can count them. A count noun has a singular and a plural form.

COUNT NOUNS

Singular	Plural
chair	chairs
flower	flowers
cat	cats

Noncount nouns name things that can't be counted. A noncount noun has only a singular form.

NONCOUNT NOUNS

salt	love	rain	cotton	air

Which sentence includes a noncount noun?

  A. Alyssa used flour.
  B. She sets the timer.
  C. The cake bakes in the oven.

You are right if you said A. *Flour* is a noncount noun. *Timer, cake,* and *oven* are count nouns.

Some nouns can be count nouns or noncount nouns, depending on how they are used.

  My dad's favorite dessert is pie.
  Mom often makes three pies at a time.

Exercise 1
Tell whether each word is a count noun or a noncount noun.

1. warmth
2. picture
3. prize
4. weather
5. clock
6. boy
7. education

8. ring
9. lamp
10. laughter
11. word
12. puddle
13. sunshine
14. tree

Exercise 2
Find all the nouns in each sentence. Tell which are noncount nouns.

1. The visitors to the fair really had fun.
2. Some pies won awards.
3. Knowledge and practice are needed to make pies.
4. A good crust requires patience.
5. A beautiful spotted cow won a blue ribbon.
6. The animal ate a lot of grass.
7. The cow gave rich milk.
8. Applause rang out for all the winners.
9. The weather was sunny and warm.
10. Several prizes were awarded.

Practice Power

Think of three more noncount nouns. Write a sentence with each.

Example: Courage helps win the race.

Nouns as Subjects

A noun may be used as the **simple subject** of a sentence. The subject tells what the sentence is about. It tells who or what is or does something.

> *Boats* sail.
> The *sea* can·be rough.

Boats is a noun that tells what sails. *Sea* is a noun that tells what can be rough.

To find a subject, ask *who* or *what* before the predicate.

> *Travel* on the sea can be dangerous.

To find the subject, ask *what* can be dangerous? The answer is the subject, *travel*.

Which noun is the subject in this sentence?

> Joanne learned about a sailing expedition.

You are right if you said *Joanne. Joanne,* the subject, tells who learned about the sailing expedition. *Expedition* is also a noun, but it is not the subject. It did not learn anything.

> England once had the most powerful navy in the world.

Ask *who* had the most powerful navy in the world? The answer, *England,* is the subject of the sentence. *Navy* and *world* are also nouns, but they are not the subject of the sentence.

Exercise 1

Find the simple subject in each sentence. To find the simple subject, ask *who* or *what*.

1. Ernest Shackleton wanted to cross Antarctica.

2. *Endurance* was the name of his ship.

3. The expedition started out in 1914.

4. The ship became trapped in pack ice.

5. The crew was stranded there for many months.

6. Some men set out with Shackleton for help.

7. Shackleton crossed wild seas in a small boat.

8. The group arrived on an island.

9. Help arrived in time to rescue the stranded crew.

10. This story is told in Shackleton's book *South.*

Exercise 2

Complete each sentence with a subject noun.

1. _____ sail on the seas.

2. The _____ tossed the ship.

3. The _____ blew.

4. _____ felt seasick.

5. The _____ calmed.

6. The _____ were safe.

7. The _____ ordered the crew to raise the sail.

Practice Power

Tell about an adventure you have read about or have experienced. Write five sentences. Underline the simple subject of each sentence.

Nouns as Direct Objects

A noun may be used as the **direct object** of a sentence. The direct object tells who or what receives the action of the verb.

The Egyptians built *pyramids.*

The Egyptians built *what?* The noun *pyramids* is the direct object of the sentence. It tells what the Egyptians built.

To find the direct object in a sentence, ask *who* or *what* after the verb.

Pyramids contain *tombs.*

Pyramids contain *what?* The answer is *tombs.* It is the direct object.

What is the direct object in this sentence?

Workers carried stones.

If you said the direct object in this sentence is the noun *stones,* you are correct. *Stones* tells what the workers carried.

Which noun is the direct object in this sentence?

Pyramids have four sides.

Sides is the direct object. It tells what the pyramids have.

Exercise 1

Find the noun used as a direct object in each sentence. The verb in each sentence is in italics.

1. Pharaohs *ruled* ancient Egypt.
2. The word *pharaoh means* "king."
3. Nefertiti *married* a pharaoh.
4. Nefertiti and her husband, Akhenaten, *ruled* the country.
5. Sculptors *carved* her portrait in stone.
6. For a time history *forgot* the queen.
7. Then scientists *located* the lovely sculpture.
8. Scientists now *may have found* her actual mummy.

Exercise 2

Find the noun used as a direct object in each sentence.

1. Let's explore the Nile River.
2. Egyptians celebrated the river.
3. The Nile brought wealth.
4. Its water helped farmers.
5. Every year the waters flooded its banks.
6. It left rich, black soil for the farmers.
7. The farmers raised food for the pharaoh.

Practice Power

Write three sentences about a leader that you've heard of or have read about. The person may be a pharaoh, for example, a president, or a coach. Use a noun as a direct object in each sentence. Underline each direct object.

Example: Many people liked <u>President Kennedy</u>.

Nouns as Subject Complements

A **subject complement** gives information about the subject. A subject complement follows a linking verb, such as the verb *be* and its various forms (*am, is, are, was, were*).

A noun can be a subject complement. A noun used as a subject complement renames the subject.

> Ramona Quimby is a young *girl.*
> Snoopy is a *dog.*

Girl and *dog* are nouns used as subject complements. Each noun follows a linking verb and renames the subject of the sentence.

> Ramona Quimby = girl
> Snoopy = dog

What noun is the subject complement in this sentence?

> Keiko was a whale.

You are right if you said the subject complement is *whale.* It is a noun that follows the linking verb *was.* It renames the subject, *Keiko.*

Find the subject complement in this sentence.

> Beverly Cleary is an author.

The subject complement is *author.* It renames the subject, *Beverly Cleary,* and it follows the linking verb *is.*

Exercise 1

Tell what the subject complement is in each sentence.

1. *The Secret Garden* is a work of fiction.
2. The account of Achilles is a myth.
3. The tales about Paul Bunyan are amusing yarns.
4. The contents of *Where the Sidewalk Ends* are poems.
5. The story of Rip Van Winkle is a legend.
6. Anne Shirley was a troublemaker.
7. *The Autobiography of Ben Franklin* is a famous book.
8. *Webster's* is a fine dictionary.
9. *Charlotte's Web* is a story about a spider and a pig.
10. *Chasing Vermeer* is a mystery.

Exercise 2

Complete each sentence with a subject complement.

1. Bozo is a _____.
2. Pretzels are a _____.
3. Soccer is a _____.
4. The Soviet Union was a _____.
5. Dinosaurs were _____.
6. Math is a _____.
7. Eagles are _____.

Practice Power

Write three sentences that tell about family members. Use a noun as a subject complement in each sentence.

Example: Margot is the baby.

Noun Challenge

Read the paragraph and answer the questions.

1. Newfoundlands are dogs that are famous for rescuing people in distress. 2. They can swim and reach people in trouble in the water. 3. One dog named Star carried a rope out to a boat in trouble. 4. A crowd on shore then pulled the craft to safety. 5. The passengers' lives were saved. 6. A Newfoundland is a special breed. 7. The dog's webbed feet make it a good swimmer. 8. Its strong body is a powerhouse. 9. It swims the breaststroke rather than the dog paddle. 10. These dogs will dive into really deep water and can swim through high waves. 11. Clubs exist for Newfoundland owners.

1. Which noun is the subject of sentence 1?

2. Find a common noun and a proper noun in sentence 3.

3. Find a collective noun in sentence 4.

4. In sentence 4 what noun is the direct object?

5. In sentence 5 what is the singular possessive of *passengers' lives?*

6. In sentence 6 which noun is a subject complement?

7. In sentence 7 what is the singular form of *feet?*

8. What noun is the subject of sentence 7?

9. In sentence 10 which is the noncount noun?

10. In sentence 11 what kind of noun is *clubs?*

Pronouns

Personal Pronouns: Part I

A **personal pronoun** is a word that takes the place of a noun. Here is a list of personal pronouns.

I	she	he	we	it	you
me	her	him	us	its	yours
mine	hers	his	ours		

In the second sentence below, *they* takes the place of *peasants;* *him* takes the place of *king.*

> The *peasants* cheered for the *king.*
> *They* cheered for *him.*

Pronouns help to avoid repeating nouns, and they make your writing sound smoother. Read this paragraph.

> The Middle Ages occurred between AD 500 and 1500. During that time nobles lived in castles. Nobles were powerful. Nobles were under a king's rule. Nobles promised to serve their king and country.

Now read the paragraph with pronouns. What are they?

> The Middle Ages occurred between AD 500 and 1500. During that time nobles lived in castles. They were powerful. Nobles were under a king's rule. They promised to serve their king and country.

You are right if you said *they.* In the third and fifth sentences *they* takes the place of the noun *nobles.*

Exercise 1

Find all the personal pronouns in these sentences.

1. You can see objects from the Middle Ages at a museum.

2. They include things such as swords, armor, and tapestries.

3. The guide told me about life in the Middle Ages.

4. She said it was difficult.

5. We asked how a man became a knight.

6. He had to have enough money to buy armor and a horse.

7. I saw armor for a horse when I went to the museum.

8. For a class project we made a model of a castle.

Exercise 2

Tell what personal pronoun can take the place of each group of words in italics.

1. *A lord* might have several manors.

2. *A manor* usually included a castle, a village, and a church.

3. *Peasants* lived in the village.

4. *A woman* could be seen spinning wool.

5. *A man* might be in the field planting crops.

6. *Children* also worked.

7. *A common house* was made of mud.

Practice Power

Write four sentences, each using one of these words: *castle, knight, lady, horse, moat,* or *peasants.* Then rewrite each sentence, using a pronoun to replace the noun.

Example: Castles were made from stone.
        They were made from stone.

Personal Pronouns: Part II

Personal pronouns refer to the person speaking; the person spoken to; or the person, place, or thing spoken about. They are **first person, second person,** or **third person.**

	Singular	Plural
First person	I, me, mine	we, us, ours
Second person	you, yours	you, yours
Third person	he, him, his	they, them, theirs
	she, her, hers	
	it, its	

- First person pronouns refer to the person speaking.
  I like to paint.   *We* like to paint.

- Second person pronouns refer to the person spoken to.
  You should paint a picture.

- Third person pronouns refer to the person, place, or thing spoken about.
  Elsa painted *her.*

Which sentence has a pronoun in the third person?

  A. I wore a smock.
  B. You paint well.
  C. They painted portraits.

You are right if you said C. *They* names the persons spoken about. *They* is a third person pronoun. Sentence A has a pronoun in the first person—*I,* and sentence B has a pronoun in the second person—*you.*

Exercise 1

Tell whether each pronoun in italics is in the first, second, or third person.

1. Painting is fun for *us.*

2. Andrea asked *him* for the yellow paint.

3. *He* painted a golden retriever.

4. Why did *you* paint a dog?

5. *I* painted a picture of my favorite cat.

6. Matt gave the picture to *her.*

7. *We* display our finished works in the school halls.

8. Where is *yours*?

Exercise 2

Complete each sentence with a pronoun in the first, second, or third person. Use the directions in parentheses.

1. _____ used a lot of blue paint. (second person)

2. _____ painted landscapes. (third person)

3. _____ entered the collages in the art contest. (first person)

4. _____ won first prize. (third person)

5. _____ made papier-mâché masks. (first person)

6. _____ produced a sculpture from old cans. (third person)

7. _____ drew a self-portrait. (second person)

8. The judges congratulated _____. (first person)

Practice Power

Write three sentences in the first person that tell about art class.

Example: We made ceramic vases last year.

Singular Pronouns and Plural Pronouns

A **singular personal pronoun** refers to one person, place, or thing. A **plural personal pronoun** refers to more than one person, place, or thing.

Singular	Plural
I, me, mine	we, us, ours
you, yours	you, yours
he, him, his	they, them, theirs
she, her, hers	
it, its	

Singular

Angela recycles paper.
She recycles paper.

Plural

Conserving water and paper is important to Mom and Dad.
Conserving water and paper is important to *them.*

The pronoun *she* is singular. It refers to one person. The pronoun *them* is plural. It refers to more than one person.

Which sentence has a plural personal pronoun?

    A. It is a gigantic tomato.
    B. She doesn't use pesticides.
    C. They grow vegetables.

You are right if you said sentence C. *They* is a plural pronoun.

Exercise 1

Tell whether the pronoun in italics is singular or plural.

1. *I* set up a recycling program.

2. He asked me, "How can I help *you*?"

3. *He* told other students about the program.

4. *They* brought many things to recycle.

5. I put *ours* in the bin.

6. Molly had a bag with 20 plastic bottles in *it.*

7. *She* said the bag wasn't heavy.

8. *We* collected newspapers, soda cans, and milk bottles.

Exercise 2

Rewrite each sentence. Replace the word or words in italics with the correct personal pronoun. Tell whether that pronoun is singular or plural.

1. *The students* worked to help save the environment.

2. *Shana* walks to school.

3. *Jacques* turns off the lights in empty rooms.

4. *Marie, Michelle, and David* planted trees.

5. Mr. Li told *Kay and me* about energy-saving light bulbs.

6. Nisha taught *Jane* about endangered animals.

7. *Dina* reuses the plastic bags from the grocery store.

8. Ted helped *Amy and Curt* separate the plastic bottles.

Practice Power

Write five sentences about protecting the environment. Use a pronoun in each sentence. Tell whether each pronoun is singular or plural.

Example: <u>She</u> recycles glass. singular

Subject Pronouns

A personal pronoun may be used as the subject of a sentence. The subject tells what the sentence is about. It tells who or what does something. **Subject pronouns** are used as subjects.

Singular	Plural
I	we
you	you
he, she, it	they

I shiver.   *She* shivers.   *We* shiver.

I, she, and *we* are subject pronouns. They answer the question *Who shivers?*

To find the subject of a sentence, ask *who* or *what* before the predicate. Can you find the subjects in these sentences? Which subjects are pronouns?

A. We like cold weather.
B. The Ice Age happened long ago.
C. It had extremely cold weather.

Sentence A has a pronoun for a subject. Ask, *Who likes cold weather?* The answer is *we.* For sentence B ask, *What happened a long time ago?* The answer is the noun *Ice Age.* For sentence C ask, *What had extremely cold weather?* The answer is *it,* a pronoun.

Exercise 1

Find the pronoun used as a subject in each sentence.

1. Do you know about the most recent Ice Age?

2. It started about 70,000 years ago.

3. We learned about it from our teacher.

4. She told us many things about ice ages and glaciers.

5. Did you know that ice covered a third of the earth?

6. We learned that there was an ice age more than three million years ago.

7. It led to a series of warm and cold cycles when glaciers grew bigger or smaller.

8. We don't know the specific reasons for the beginnings and the endings of ice ages.

Exercise 2

Use a subject pronoun to take the place of the word or words in italics.

1. *Steve* asked about ice-age animals.

2. *Mrs. Alvarez* told the class about the saber-toothed tiger.

3. *The saber-toothed tiger* had teeth up to seven inches long.

4. *Simon and I* asked about mastodons.

5. *Mastodons* had curved tusks and long, furry coats.

6. *Human hunters* may have caused the mastodons' extinction.

Practice Power

Tell what you and your friends would have done if you had lived during one of the major ice ages. Write four sentences. Use a subject pronoun in each of them.

Example: We would have lived in caves.

Pronouns in Compound Subjects

Two or more nouns or subject pronouns can be used together as a **compound subject.** They are connected by *and* or *or*. The subject pronouns are *I, you, we, he, she, it,* and *they*. Study these compound subjects.

> *Angela* and *Hector* went to the city. (two nouns)
> *Angela* and *he* went to the city. (a noun and a pronoun)
> *She* and *Hector* went to the city. (a pronoun and a noun)
> *She* and *he* went to the city. (two pronouns)

Which sentence has a compound subject with two pronouns?

> **A.** You and I went to New York.
> **B.** I rode on the subway.
> **C.** Carrie and Nancy visit him in the city.

You are right if you said sentence A. *You and I* is a compound subject with two pronouns.

Which pronoun correctly completes the sentence?

> Angela and (I me) flew in an airplane.

You are correct if you said *I*. The pronoun *I* is a subject pronoun. It is part of the compound subject.

In speaking and writing, it is polite to put *I* after other subject words that refer to people.

> She and I can talk about the trip.

Exercise 1

Find the compound subject in each sentence. Name all the subject pronouns.

1. My mother and I talked with the travel agent.
2. She and he arranged for plane tickets.
3. My family and I took a taxi from the airport.
4. Tom and he ran through Central Park.
5. He and she planned to meet on Fifth Avenue.
6. She and I waved to a police officer.
7. My dad and she bought hot dogs from a street vendor.
8. Jody and I mailed postcards to friends.

Exercise 2

Rewrite each sentence, using a compound subject. Use subject pronouns from the list to complete each sentence.

I	he	she	we	they

1. Laura and _____ saw the Empire State Building.
2. _____ and _____ walked through Central Park.
3. Patrick and _____ fed the ducks.
4. _____ and _____ rode the subway.
5. Mindy and _____ saw a Broadway play.
6. _____ and _____ love to visit New York.

Practice Power

Tell about a place that you and your family have been. Write five sentences. Use compound subjects with pronouns.

Example: My family and I went to Washington, D.C.

Object Pronouns

A personal pronoun may be used as the direct object in a sentence. Ask *whom* or *what* after the verb to find the direct object. **Object pronouns** are used as direct objects.

Singular	Plural
me	us
you	you
him, her, it	them

The reporter questioned *Roberto.*
The reporter questioned *him.*

Roberto is the answer to the question *The reporter questioned whom? Roberto* is a proper noun used as the direct object of the sentence. The noun can be replaced by the object pronoun *him*, as shown in the second sentence. *Him* acts as the direct object.

Which sentence uses a pronoun as a direct object?

   A. The politician gave a speech.
   B. He used note cards.
   C. He dropped them.

You are right if you said sentence C. The word *them* comes after the verb and is the direct object. It answers *He dropped what?*

Pronouns can be part of compound direct objects.

   The governor told *the class and me* about his job.

Exercise 1
Find the pronoun used as a direct object in each sentence.

1. Mrs. Pringles teaches us about state government.

2. The governor heads it.

3. Voters elected him and the state representatives.

4. We saw them when we visited the state capital.

5. He called her.

6. He invited us.

7. We visited him and her in the state capital.

8. He questioned Kathy and me about our studies.

Exercise 2
Use an object pronoun to take the place of the word or words in italics.

1. Matt told *Sharon* about the voting age.

2. The candidate gave *many speeches.*

3. The politician thanked *the voters.*

4. The politician won *the election.*

5. Sheila asked *her dad* about the election.

6. Mom helped *Sheila and me* with our civics assignment.

7. The losing candidate congratulated *his opponent.*

8. Reporters questioned *the senator* about the proposed law.

Practice Power

Write six sentences about the state you live in. Use object pronouns in some of the sentences. Underline the object pronouns.

Possessive Pronouns

A **possessive pronoun** shows ownership or possession. Possessive pronouns stand alone.

> The snake is *Wendy's.* (possessive noun)
> The snake is *hers.* (possessive pronoun)

	Singular	Plural
First person	mine	ours
Second person	yours	yours
Third person	his, hers, its	theirs

A possessive pronoun can take the place of the person and the object owned.

Noun Phrase	Possessive Pronoun
My pet is gray.	*Mine* is gray.
Your pet is gray.	*Yours* is gray.
Ching Mae's pet is gray.	*Hers* is gray.
Tim's and Tom's pets are gray.	*Theirs* are gray.

Which sentence uses a possessive pronoun?

A. I fed your dog.
B. Nick fed biscuits to the dog.
C. Terri fed hers.

You are right if you said sentence C. *Hers* is a possessive pronoun that tells about something that belongs to Terri.

Exercise 1
Find the possessive pronoun in each sentence.

1. Hers has white paws.
2. What special features does yours have?
3. Mine is black all over.
4. Theirs is a Persian cat.
5. I think hers is a calico cat.

Exercise 2
Change each sentence so that it has a possessive pronoun. Remember that a possessive pronoun stands alone.

Example: *Tanita's cat* is black.
  Hers is black.

1. *My dog* likes to play with a Frisbee.
2. The chihuahua is *Tammy and Tony's.*
3. Did you feed *your canary*?
4. *Gus's guinea pig* is friendly.
5. We built a special house for *our German shepherd.*
6. *Angela's parrot* has a huge cage.
7. *My gerbils* have a cage with a wheel.
8. Will you describe *Jan's and Jacob's pets,* please?

Practice Power

Describe several pets of neighbors, relatives, and friends. Write several sentences that use possessive pronouns. Be sure the pronouns stand alone.

Example: His has spots.
  Theirs wears a collar.

Possessive Adjectives

A **possessive adjective** shows who owns something. A possessive adjective goes before a noun. It does not stand alone.

Here is a list of possessive adjectives.

	Singular	Plural
First person	my	our
Second person	your	your
Third person	his, her, its	their

<u>My</u> bicycle is fast.
<u>Her</u> bicycle is red.
<u>Their</u> bicycle has two seats.

The words *my, her,* and *their* are adjectives. They are used before the noun *bicycle* to show who owns each bicycle.

Which sentence uses an adjective to show ownership?

- **A.** I like bicycles.
- **B.** Tim's bicycle has bent handlebars.
- **C.** His bicycle has wide tires.
- **D.** The bicycle with narrow tires is hers.

You are right if you said sentence C. The word *his* describes the noun *bicycle.* Notice that sentence D has a possessive (*hers*), but *hers* is a pronoun. Sentence B also has a possessive (*Tim's*), but *Tim's* is a possessive noun.

Exercise 1
Find the possessive adjective in each sentence.

1. I rode my bicycle to a friend's house.

2. His bicycle was in the garage.

3. He pumped air into its tire.

4. We pedaled our bicycles down the path.

5. The bicycle had a holder for his water bottle.

6. Our bike ride was long.

7. His mom made lemonade for us.

8. Did you always wear your helmet?

Exercise 2
Complete each sentence with a possessive adjective.

1. Moira packed _____ gear.

2. Thomas brought _____ compass.

3. Did you put a map in _____ bag?

4. We made _____ lunches.

5. Did you bring _____ canteen?

6. Mario wore _____ thick socks.

7. The hikers lost _____ way.

8. Thomas helped us find _____ route.

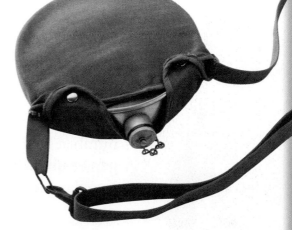

Practice Power

Pretend you are going for a bicycle ride or a hike with friends. Write four sentences about the things that you and your friends will need. Use a possessive adjective in each sentence. Remember that a possessive adjective goes before a noun.

Pronouns and Antecedents

Personal pronouns have antecedents. An **antecedent** is the word that the pronoun replaces. The pronouns *he, him,* and *his* refer to male antecedents. *She, her,* and *hers* refer to females. *It* and *its* refer to animals and things.

> Marco Polo lived in the 1200s. Marco Polo was a famous explorer.
>
> Marco Polo lived in the 1200s. *He* was a famous explorer.

In the second set of sentences, the personal pronoun *he* is used instead of the noun *Marco Polo. He* takes the place of the noun *Marco Polo* and avoids repetition of that term. *Marco Polo* is the antecedent of *he.*

A pronoun and its antecedent must agree in person and number. In the example above, the pronoun *he* is third person singular. Its antecedent *Marco Polo* is third person singular. *He* is used because Marco Polo was a man.

What is the antecedent of the pronoun *them* in this sentence?

> The video on explorers helped us learn about them.

You are right if you said *explorers.* The pronoun *them* is third person plural. The antecedent *explorers* is third person plural.

Exercise 1

Find the pronoun and its antecedent in each sentence.

1. Mrs. Gott remarked that explorers really interested her.

2. Marco Polo lived in Venice, but he is most famous for a trip elsewhere.

3. Venice's merchants were adventurous, and they traded with many different countries.

4. Ships carried spices from the East, bringing them to Venice.

5. Marco, his father, and an uncle planned the trip they would take.

6. The Polos' destination was China; the men knew it had many inventions that did not exist in Europe at the time.

Exercise 2

Complete each sentence by choosing the correct pronoun. Make sure that it agrees with the antecedent in italics.

1. The *students* were studying Marco Polo, and (they he) did projects on people, places, and events of his times.

2. Chinese *inventions* interest me, so I chose (it them) for my project.

3. Sue had a *book* on China, and she lent (it them) to me.

4. Our *teacher* gave a slide presentation on China, and (he they) showed pictures of the country's historic places.

Practice Power

Tell about something interesting that you have learned in school. Write five compound sentences like those in Exercise 2. Circle the pronouns and underline their antecedents.

I, Me, We, and *Us*

First person pronouns refer to the speaker.

• Use the words *I* and *me* to talk about yourself. Use *I* as the subject of a sentence. Use *me* after the verb as a direct object.

• Use *we* and *us* to talk about yourself and at least one other person. Use *we* as the subject of a sentence. Use *us* after the verb as a direct object.

Subject			Object
I	play sports.	Sports interest	me.
We	like sports.	Sports thrill	us.

These pronouns may be part of compound subjects and compound objects. Be sure to check how the compound is used.

Jake and I like sports. (compound subject)
Sports thrill *Jake and me.* (compound direct object)

Which sentences are correct in their use of the pronouns?

A. I play soccer.
B. Karen and me play soccer.
C. Karen's dad invited me to the game.
D. Karen's dad took her and I to the game.

You are right if you said A and C. In sentence A, *I* is used correctly as the subject, and in sentence C, *me* is used correctly as the direct object. *Me* is used incorrectly as part of a compound subject in sentence B, and in sentence D, *I* is used incorrectly as part of a compound direct object.

380 • Section 3.10

Exercise 1

Use _I_ or _me_ to complete each sentence.

1. My friend and ____ are forwards on the soccer team.

2. My friend accidentally tripped ____ in practice.

3. The coach taught my friend and ____ about kicking.

4. ____ thanked him for his help.

5. ____ scored the winning goal in the last game.

6. My teammates joined ____ on the field in celebration.

7. Marguerite and Hans applauded ____.

8. ____ can't wait for the next game.

Exercise 2

Use _we_ or _us_ to complete each sentence.

1. ____ played volleyball.

2. The other team beat ____ before.

3. The coach told ____ about trying hard.

4. ____ were inspired.

5. ____ scored many points.

6. ____ won the game.

7. The fans applauded ____.

8. ____ celebrated our win.

Practice Power

Tell about your favorite sports. Write four sentences. Use _I, me, we,_ and _us._ Choose from these sports or any others you are familiar with.

softball	**ice skating**	**swimming**
hockey	**football**	**running**

Pronouns and Contractions

Personal pronouns can be joined with some verbs to form contractions. An apostrophe (') replaces the missing letter or letters in a contraction.

Here is a list of common contractions with pronouns:

I'm = I am   I've = I have
you're = you are   you've = you have
he's = he is *or* he has   she's = she is *or* she has
it's = it is *or* it has   we're = we are
we've = we have   they're = they are
they've = they have

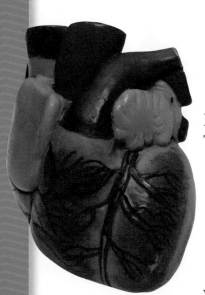

I've read about the heart. = *I have* read about the heart.
It's a muscular pump. = *It is* a muscular pump.

Possessive adjectives are often confused with contractions. They express possession and do not contain apostrophes.

Pronoun + Verb	Possessive Adjective
You're = You are breathing.	*Your* heart is important.
It's = It is beating.	*Its* role is important.
They're = They are organs.	*Their* role is important.

Which choice correctly completes the sentence?

(Your You're) able to see a large model of a heart at the museum.

You are correct if you chose *you're.* The sentence means *You are able to see a large model of a heart at the museum.*

Exercise 1

Tell whether the word in italics is a possessive adjective or a contraction. Name the two words that make up each contraction.

1. An important part of *your* body is the circulatory system.

2. *It's* essential because it carries food to the body.

3. *Its* job is to carry blood to cells.

4. *They're* the smallest parts of our bodies.

5. *You've* got a heart, veins, and arteries.

6. *Their* roles in the circulatory system are different.

7. *We've* got arteries.

8. *They've* got the job of carrying blood to cells.

Exercise 2

Rewrite each sentence. Choose the correct possessive adjective or contraction.

1. (You're Your) veins are part of the circulatory system.

2. (They're Their) vessels that carry blood back to the heart.

3. After the food and oxygen have been removed from the blood, (it's its) color in the veins is dark red.

4. The heart is an important part of your body; (it's its) the key part of the circulatory system.

5. (It's Its) always pumping blood into the arteries.

6. (You're Your) heart may beat more than 100,000 times a day.

Practice Power

Write six sentences on any topic, showing the correct use of these words: *your, you're, they're, their, its, it's.*

Pronoun Challenge

Read the paragraph and answer the questions.

1. Bicycles have really changed since they were invented in the 1790s. 2. You walked the first bicycles along because they had no pedals. 3. Today, mine has pedals, brakes, and gears. 4. Dad, Mom, and I bike often. 5. He and she used to race bikes. 6. They tell me all about their favorite courses. 7. Even though certain types of racing bikes have neither brakes nor multiple gears, I want them on my bike. 8. Our town has a bike path through the forest preserve. 9. It's used a lot in nice weather.

1. In sentence 1 what is the antecedent of the pronoun *they?*

2. In sentence 2 which pronoun is in the second person?

3. In sentence 3 what kind of pronoun is *mine?*

4. In sentence 4 which word is a subject pronoun?

5. What is the subject of sentence 5?

6. In sentence 6 what are the two pronouns?

7. In sentence 6 which pronoun is used as a subject?

8. In sentence 7 to what does *them* refer?

9. What word shows ownership in sentence 8? Is it a pronoun or an adjective?

10. Is the first word of sentence 9 a contraction or a possessive pronoun?

Adjectives

Descriptive Adjectives

Adjectives describe or point out nouns. A **descriptive adjective** gives more information about a noun. It can tell how a thing looks, tastes, sounds, feels, or smells. It can tell about size, number, color, shape, or weight.

Here are some descriptive adjectives:

> green   itchy   delicious   fragrant   loud

Here are those adjectives used to describe nouns.

> *green* hat   *delicious* pizza   *loud* noise
> *itchy* socks   *fragrant* roses

Descriptive adjectives often come before the nouns they describe.

> The *blue* <u>waves</u> reach the *sandy* <u>shore</u>.

Blue and *sandy* are descriptive adjectives. They give more information about the nouns *waves* and *shore*.

What are the descriptive adjectives in this sentence? What nouns do they describe?

> The noisy children are making huge castles in the sand.

You are right if you said *noisy* and *huge*. *Noisy* tells how the children sound. *Huge* describes the size of the castles.

Exercise 1

Find the descriptive adjective in each sentence. Tell the noun it describes.

1. Reefs are warm habitats in the ocean.

2. They occur in shallow water.

3. The massive structure of a reef often contains coral.

4. Coral is formed from tiny animals.

5. When they die, the skeletons add to the stony structure.

6. Reefs provide safe homes for animals.

7. Colorful sea urchins live there.

Exercise 2

Add a descriptive adjective before each noun.

1. _____ flamingo

2. _____ orchid

3. _____ parrot

4. _____ fish

5. _____ tree

6. _____ island

Exercise 3

Add a noun that could be described by each pair of adjectives.

1. big, friendly

2. large, noisy

3. fresh, crunchy

4. dark, gloomy

5. delicate, graceful

6. old, creaky

Practice Power

Write five sentences about a beautiful place, such as a park or a mountain. Use a descriptive adjective in each sentence.

Example: The <u>orange</u> sun set over the cliff.

Proper Adjectives

A common noun names any one member of a group of persons, places, or things. A proper noun names a particular person, place, or thing. An adjective formed from a proper noun is called a **proper adjective.** A proper adjective begins with a capital letter.

Proper noun: *Ireland* is famous for its wool.
Proper adjective: *Irish* sheep have soft wool.

Here are some proper nouns and the adjectives formed from them.

Proper Noun	Proper Adjective
Africa	African
Canada	Canadian
Egypt	Egyptian
Germany	German
Poland	Polish
Spain	Spanish
Vietnam	Vietnamese

Which sentence includes a proper adjective?

  A. I eat linguini.
  B. Pasta is good.
  C. I like Italian food.

You are right if you said sentence C. *Italian* is a proper adjective. It is formed from the proper noun *Italy.*

Exercise 1

Find the proper adjective in each sentence. Tell the noun it describes.

1. Belgian chocolate is rich and creamy.

2. We ate French pastries in Paris.

3. Mrs. Patel made a spicy Thai curry.

4. I drank Chinese tea.

5. Mexican cocoa is usually made with cinnamon.

6. Swedish meatballs are popular with my friends.

Exercise 2

Rewrite each sentence, adding a proper adjective formed from the proper noun in parentheses. Check a dictionary for the correct spellings.

1. The _____ bouzouki looks like a guitar. (Greece)

2. The sitar is the best-known _____ instrument. (India)

3. The _____ didgeridoo looks like a bassoon. (Australia)

4. _____ bagpipes are difficult to play. (Scotland)

5. Some _____ music uses steel drums. (Jamaica)

6. A _____ musician plays the flute. (Peru)

Practice Power

Imagine that you are planning a trip around the world. Write a few sentences about the places you'll visit. Use proper adjectives in some of your sentences.

Example: I will go to Ireland and eat some <u>Irish</u> soda bread.

Articles

The **articles** are *a, an,* and *the.* Articles point out nouns.

- *A* and *an* are **indefinite articles.** They point out any one of a class of people, places, or things.

    a dollar   a president   an engraving

- Use *a* before a word that begins with a consonant sound. Use *an* before a word that begins with a vowel sound.

    a quarter   a uniform   an hour   an ancient coin

- *The* is the **definite article.** It points out a specific person, place, or thing.

    the postman   the San Francisco mint   the coffee mug

Can you find the articles in this sentence? What noun does each point out?

    The San Francisco mint survived an earthquake.

The definite article *the* points out the noun *mint.* The indefinite article *an* points out the noun *earthquake.*

Which one of these sentences uses the definite article?

- **A.** The money we collected is missing.
- **B.** We put coins in a quart jar.
- **C.** I have an ancient penny.

You are right if you said sentence A. *The* is the definite article.

Exercise 1

Find all the articles in each sentence. Name the noun each points out.

1. The first mint in the United States was created in 1792.

2. A man named David Rittenhouse was the director of the mint.

3. The mint's coins were made of gold, silver, or copper.

4. Until 1873 the mint was an independent agency.

5. The first Lincoln penny was coined in 1909.

6. Since then, a mint has been located in each of four cities: San Francisco, Denver, Philadelphia, and Washington, D.C.

7. A mark on each coin identifies the city where it was made.

8. Each coin has an initial on it.

Exercise 2

Add the indefinite article *a* or *an* before each noun.

1. ____ nickel

2. ____ eagle

3. ____ dime

4. ____ olive branch

5. ____ eye

6. ____ quarter

7. ____ portrait

8. ____ coin

Practice Power

Think about coins or other things you carry in your pocket. Write four sentences about one of these objects. Underline each article you use.

Examples: I see <u>a</u> shiny penny.

<u>The</u> penny has Lincoln's picture on one side.

Demonstrative Adjectives

A **demonstrative adjective** points out a specific item or items. The demonstrative adjectives are *this, that, these,* and *those.* They come before nouns.

- *This* and *that* point out one person, place, or thing.
- *These* and *those* point out more than one person, place, or thing.
- *This* and *these* point out items that are near.
- *That* and *those* point out items that are farther away.

Near: *This* turkey is big. (singular)
              These turkeys are small. (plural)

Far away: *That* turkey seems too big for us. (singular)
              Those turkeys seem to be the right size. (plural)

Which sentence has a demonstrative adjective?

A. The turkey is done.
B. These mashed potatoes are wonderful.
C. Put some gravy on the turkey.

You are right if you said sentence B. *These* points to mashed potatoes that are near and plural in form.

Exercise 1
Identify the demonstrative adjective in each sentence.

1. This letter from Edward Winslow is a record of the first Thanksgiving.

392 • Section 4.4

2. These drawings show the colonists at Plymouth.

3. Those colonists shared the first Thanksgiving feast with the Wampanoag Indians.

4. The holiday is somewhat different these days.

5. People ate venison and waterfowl at that first dinner.

6. Nowadays we generally eat turkey for this holiday.

7. Aunt Dana made those sweet potatoes.

Exercise 2

Complete each sentence with a correct demonstrative adjective. Choose from *this, that, these,* and *those.* Then write whether the noun is near or far.

1. I'll set _____ table.

2. Let's use _____ tablecloth.

3. _____ cranberries are tart.

4. Put some of _____ vegetables on your plate.

5. I didn't care for _____ brussels sprouts.

6. May I have a slice of _____ pumpkin pie?

7. Is there any more of _____ stuffing?

8. Put _____ flowers on the table.

9. Dad always falls asleep in _____ chair after dinner.

10. You should use _____ pitcher for the water.

Practice Power

Imagine you have invited a friend to share a special meal. Write a few sentences to tell about the meal. Use a demonstrative adjective in each sentence.

Example: These cupcakes are Mom's specialty.

Adjectives That Tell How Many

Some adjectives tell exactly how many or about how many. They come before nouns.

Exactly how many: *Three* polar bears were in the den.
About how many: *Several* polar bears were in the den.

Numbers can be used as adjectives to tell exactly how many.

one iceberg   *three* zookeepers

These words can be used as adjectives to tell about how many: *few, many, several, some.*

many zoos   *some* animals

Which sentence has an adjective that tells about how many?

A. Polar bears live in the Arctic.
B. Some polar bears live in zoos.
C. Polar bears are white.

You are right if you said sentence B. The adjective *some* tells about how many polar bears. *Some* is not an exact amount.

Exercise 1

Find the adjective that tells how many in each sentence. Does it tell exactly how many or about how many?

1. I have seen many programs on polar bears on TV.

2. Polar bear cubs weigh an average of one pound at birth.

3. A mother polar bear usually has two cubs.

4. When the cubs leave the den, each generally weighs 30 pounds.

5. The mother shows the cubs some ways to hunt seals.

6. A polar bear can smell a seal 20 miles away.

7. It takes the cubs a few years to learn how to hunt well.

8. A polar bear may have several sets of cubs in a lifetime.

Exercise 2

Complete each sentence with an adjective that tells how many. Use the word in parentheses to help you choose.

1. We saw _____ polar bears at the zoo. (about how many)

2. _____ polar bears were eating. (exactly how many)

3. A polar bear ate _____ fish. (exactly how many)

4. Polar bears are quite an attraction at our zoo, and _____ people visit them daily. (about how many)

5. Polar bears' big paws are like _____ huge paddles. (exactly how many)

6. _____ different kinds of animals are food for polar bears, including seals, fish, and ducks. (about how many)

Practice Power

Write five sentences about an animal you like. Use adjectives that tell how many in each sentence.

Subject Complements

An adjective that comes after a linking verb acts as a **subject complement.** A subject complement tells something additional about the subject of a sentence. It describes the noun or pronoun that is the subject of the sentence.

The most common linking verb is *be* and its various forms: *is, are, was,* and *were.*

> E. B. White is *famous.*
> His books for children are *popular.*

Famous and *popular* are adjectives used as subject complements. *Famous* follows the linking verb *is* and describes the subject, *E. B. White. Popular* is an adjective that follows the linking verb *are* and describes the subject, *books.*

Which sentence has an adjective subject complement? What does it tell about?

> **A.** E. B. White created the character Stuart Little.
> **B.** Stuart Little was a mouse.
> **C.** White's characters are likable.

You are right if you said sentence C. *Likable* is a subject complement that describes the subject, *characters. Likable* follows a linking verb—*are.* Sentence B has a linking verb, *was,* but the word that follows it, *mouse,* is a noun.

Exercise 1

Find the adjective used as a subject complement in each sentence. Tell the noun it describes.

1. The story is famous.
2. The pig was afraid.
3. Wilbur was small.
4. The spider was friendly.
5. Charlotte was clever.
6. Her webs were delicate.
7. The words in the web were wonderful.
8. People were curious about the words.
9. Wilbur was safe.
10. *Charlotte's Web* is great!

Exercise 2

Complete each sentence with an adjective used as a subject complement.

1. Computer games can be _____.
2. Pizza is _____.
3. Amusement parks are _____.
4. Heroes are _____.
5. The spider is _____.

Practice Power

Write five sentences about a book you have read and the characters in it. Use an adjective as a subject complement in each sentence.

Adjectives That Compare

Adjectives can be used to make comparisons. To compare two people, places, or things, *-er* may be added to an adjective. To compare three or more people, places, or things, *-est* may be added to an adjective.

Adjective:	November is *cold.*
Compare two things:	December is *colder* than November.
Compare three or more things:	January is the *coldest* month of all.

Find the sentence with an adjective that compares.

A. Ponce de Leon was an explorer.
B. Columbus was braver than Ponce de Leon.
C. Columbus was an explorer and sailor.

In sentence B, *braver* compares two explorers.

Here are some spelling rules for adding *-er* and *-est.*

- If the adjective ends in *e,* drop the *e* and add the ending.
  safe   safer   safest

- If the adjective ends in *y* following a consonant, change the *y* to *i* and add the ending.
  sunny   sunnier   sunniest

- If the adjective ends in a single consonant following a single vowel, double the consonant and add the ending.
  big   bigger   biggest

Exercise 1

Copy and complete the chart.

Adjective	Compare Two Things	Compare Three or More Things
1. tall	_____	_____
2. scary	_____	_____
3. wide	_____	_____
4. great	_____	_____
5. cute	_____	_____
6. hot	_____	_____
7. dusty	_____	_____
8. fat	_____	_____

Exercise 2

Find the adjective that compares in each sentence.

1. Exploration is one of the oldest human activities.

2. Early explorers of the North and South poles may have been the bravest explorers of all.

3. Their voyages were harder than those of other explorers.

4. The weather is harsher at the poles than in other places.

5. Robert Peary was one of the earliest explorers of the poles and is credited with reaching the North Pole in 1909.

6. Roald Amundsen was luckier than Robert Scott, reaching the South Pole first.

Practice Power

Write sentences with six of the adjectives you wrote in Exercise 1.

Irregular Adjectives That Compare

Some adjectives that compare are not formed by adding -er or -est. They are **irregular adjectives.** Two common irregular adjectives are *good* and *bad*.

Adjective	Compare Two Things	Compare Three or More Things
good	better	best
bad	worse	worst

I make *good* brownies.
My mother's brownies are *better* than my brownies.
My big brother makes the *best* brownies of all.

Which sentence uses an irregular comparative adjective?

A. The bakery sells cookies.
B. This is the best bakery in town.
C. All the cookies have sprinkles.

You are right if you said sentence B. *Best* is a form of *good*, and it is used in comparing all the bakeries in the town.

Which choice correctly completes the sentence?

The green candy tastes (worse worst) than the red candy.

The correct answer is *worse*. It is used to compare two sets of items. Note that *better* and *worse* are often used with *than*.

Exercise 1

Choose the correct adjective to complete each sentence. Use *good, better,* or *best.*

1. I have a _____ idea.

2. Let's see who bakes the _____ cookies.

3. Jane made _____ chocolate chip cookies.

4. Mark baked _____ cookies than Jane.

5. These are _____ sugar cookies.

6. I think oatmeal cookies are _____ than sugar cookies.

7. We've had a _____ time eating these.

8. Moira's gingersnaps are the _____ cookies of all.

Exercise 2

Choose the correct adjective to complete each sentence. Use *bad, worse,* or *worst.*

1. My first cooking experience was _____.

2. It was even _____ than my attempt to bake a pie.

3. My cooking left a _____ smell in the kitchen.

4. Mom said it was the _____ odor ever in her kitchen.

5. I think my cooking is _____ than that of my little brother.

6. The results of my cooking are the _____ eating experience a person can have.

Practice Power

Think of your favorite and your least favorite foods. Write four sentences about those foods. Use *good, better, best, bad, worse, worst.*

Example: I think peas taste better than beans.

More, Most

Some adjectives that compare use *more* and *most*. Usually the adjectives are longer than the adjectives that use *-er* and *-est*. *More* is used in comparing two things. *Most* is used in comparing three or more things.

Adjective	Compare Two Things	Compare Three or More Things
dishonest	more dishonest	most dishonest
intelligent	more intelligent	most intelligent

- Use *more* or *most* with adjectives of three or more syllables.

  This is a *popular* exhibit.
  Snakes are usually *more popular* than birds.
  The bat house is our *most popular* exhibit this year.

- Use *more* or *most* with some two-syllable adjectives.

  It's quite *humid* today.
  Today is *more humid* than yesterday.
  August is the *most humid* month of the year.

Check a dictionary if you are unsure of how the comparative forms of an adjective are formed—by adding *-er* and *-est* or by using *more* and *most*.

Which choice correctly completes the sentence?

  I think that a rain forest is (more beneficial most beneficial) than a coral reef.

You are correct if you chose *more beneficial*. The word *beneficial* is more than two syllables, two items are being compared, and *than* is used in the comparison.

Exercise 1

Find the adjectives that compare in each sentence.

1. The most extensive rain forests are in South America.

2. The plants and animals of the tropical rain forests are more diverse than those of any other ecosystem.

3. Evergreen trees are more common than any other trees.

4. Insects are the most numerous species.

5. I think that the animals and plants of the rain forest are more beautiful than those in other ecosystems.

6. Parrots and butterflies are among the most colorful animals.

7. Some of the most important rain-forest products are chocolate and spices.

Exercise 2

Choose the correct adjective that compares in each sentence.

1. Preserving the rain forest has become (more critical most critical) than ever before.

2. This is one of our (more serious most serious) problems.

3. Rain forests are (more important most important) than people may think: they produce much of our oxygen.

4. Rain-forest plants are among the (more useful most useful) plants because of their medicinal value.

5. We should be (more careful most careful) with the earth's resources than we have been.

Practice Power

Write three sentences using these adjectives. Add *more* or *most* to each: *interesting, beautiful, important.*

Less, Least and Fewer, Fewest

The comparative adjectives *fewer* and *fewest* are used with plural count nouns. *Less* and *least* are used with noncount nouns.

Count nouns name things that can be counted: *players, games, hits.* They generally have plural forms ending in *-s.* Noncount nouns name things that cannot be counted: *water, food, patience.* They do not have plural forms ending in *-s.*

In these sentences *fewer* and *fewest* are used with the plural noun *sports.*

> That park offers *fewer* sports than the one nearby.
> This park offers the *fewest* sports of all the city parks.

In these sentences, *less* and *least* are used with the noncount noun *progress.*

> We made *less* progress than the other team.
> We made the *least* progress of any team.

Which choice correctly completes the sentence?

> (Fewer Less) students tried out for the team this year.

You are right if you said *fewer. Students* is a plural count noun, and so *fewer* is the correct choice.

Exercise 1

Copy this chart. Identify each word as a count or a noncount noun. Then write phrases to show whether you should use *fewer, fewest* or *less, least* with each noun.

Example: hits—count   fewer hits, fewest hits

Noun	Count or Noncount?	Fewer, Fewest or Less, Least?
1. sunshine	_____	_____
2. cloud	_____	_____
3. bat	_____	_____
4. humidity	_____	_____
5. knowledge	_____	_____

Exercise 2

Choose the correct adjective to complete each sentence.

1. Our team has won (fewer less) games this year than last year.

2. We have (fewer less) good hitters this year than last.

3. We have had (fewer less) time for practice this year.

4. There was (fewer less) rain last year than this year.

5. We've scored (fewer less) runs this year.

6. In fact, we've scored the (fewest least) runs of all the teams in the league.

7. Our best pitcher, Rita, has allowed the (fewest least) hits of all the pitchers in the league.

Practice Power

Write sentences for four of the phrases that you wrote in the chart in Exercise 1.

Position of Adjectives

Many adjectives come before nouns. Adjectives used as subject complements, however, come after the nouns they describe. These adjectives come after linking verbs, such as the verb *be* and its various forms.

> The *tiny* puppy trembled. (before noun)
> The puppy was *tiny.* (after linking verb)

In the first sentence the adjective *tiny* comes before the noun *puppy.* In the second sentence the adjective *tiny* comes after the linking verb *was.* It describes the subject *puppy.* It is a subject complement.

In which sentence does the adjective come after the noun it describes?

A. Animals can have unusual defenses.
B. Some jellyfish are poisonous.
C. Snakes in the rain forest use their green skin as camouflage to hide among the trees.

You're correct if you chose sentence B. The adjective *poisonous* follows the linking verb *are.* It describes the subject, *jellyfish.*

In sentence A the adjective *unusual* comes before the noun *defenses.* In sentence C the adjective *green* comes before the noun *skin.*

Exercise 1

Find the descriptive adjective in each sentence. Tell whether the adjective comes before the noun or whether it is a subject complement.

1. The frightened octopus is defending itself.

2. Its long tentacles spread out.

3. The octopus is huge to predators.

4. A scared turtle hides in its shell.

5. Its shell is protective.

6. The wood louse rolls into a tight ball.

7. The porcupinefish is spiny.

Exercise 2

Draw one line under the descriptive adjectives that come before nouns. Draw two lines under the descriptive adjectives that are subject complements.

Snakes are reptiles. Reptiles include turtles, alligators, crocodiles, and lizards. Snakes are legless. A snake has scaly skin. Its body is flexible and can roll into a ball. It has a narrow, forked tongue. The eggs of snakes are soft and fragile. Most snakes are harmless, though a few are poisonous.

Practice Power

Write four sentences to tell about a time when you were afraid of an animal or about an animal that might scare you if you crossed its path. Use adjectives that come before nouns and adjectives that are used as subject complements.

Example: The dog's sharp teeth showed as it snarled.
Its bark was scary.

Adjective Challenge

Read the paragraph and answer the questions.

1. A beaver is a furry animal that has a wide, flat tail. 2. North American beavers use their strong teeth to cut down and eat trees. 3. Are they the busiest of all animals? 4. Many observers think so. 5. The beaver's tail is one of its most interesting features. 6. The tail can be 12 inches long, six inches wide, and about one inch thick. 7. A beaver's tail has scaly skin. 8. Beavers use their tails to steer when they swim, to send a warning message when they are frightened, and to prop themselves up when they eat. 9. These animals are not welcome in some places. 10. Some farmers say that they cause flooding and wish that there were fewer beavers.

1. In sentence 1 name all the adjectives.

2. In sentence 2 find a proper adjective.

3. In sentence 3 what is the adjective that compares?

4. In sentence 4 does *many* tell exactly how many or about how many?

5. In sentence 5 what is the adjective that compares?

6. In sentence 7 what is the article? Is it definite or indefinite?

7. In sentence 7 what is the descriptive adjective? Does it come before the noun or is it a subject complement?

8. In sentence 9 find a demonstrative adjective.

9. In sentence 10 why is *fewer* rather than *less* used to describe *beavers*?

Verbs

Action Verbs

Many verbs express action. An **action verb** tells what someone or something does.

> Aesop *wrote* many fables.
> His fables *teach* lessons.

Wrote and *teach* are action verbs. *Wrote* tells what Aesop did. *Teach* tells what the fables do.

Here are some more action verbs.

bring	eat	talk
brush	give	throw
copy	laugh	touch
draw	sing	watch
drive	stir	write

Which sentences have action verbs?

A. The students read books of folktales.
B. The students are in the library.
C. The students talk about the books.

You are right if you said sentences A and C. *Read* and *talk* are both action verbs that tell what the students do.

Exercise 1

Find the action verb in each sentence.

1. In one fable by Aesop, a fox fell into a deep well.
2. The fox shouted for help.
3. A goat walked by.
4. It heard the fox's shout.
5. The fox gave the goat false information.
6. The goat jumped into the well for water.
7. The fox climbed onto the goat's back.
8. The fox then scrambled out of the well.
9. The goat remained in the well.
10. In this way the fox tricked the goat.

Exercise 2

Complete each sentence, using an action verb.

1. A slimy worm _____ up my arm.
2. Who _____ the salad?
3. The herons _____ on the beach.
4. Jerome _____ the paper dragon.
5. Terry _____ the cellar door with a gasp.

Practice Power

Write a sentence for each noun below, using an action verb.

Example: trucks

Trucks rumble down the highway.

1. astronauts	3. waves	5. singer
2. wind	4. worm	6. waiter

Being Verbs

Not all verbs show action. A **being verb** shows what someone or something is.

Action Verbs

The sun *shines.*
The earth *revolves* around the sun.

Being Verbs

The sun's rays *are* warm.
Too much sun *is* dangerous.

The action verbs *shines* and *revolves* tell what the sun and the earth do. *Are* and *is* are being verbs. They do not express action; they simply tell something about what the rays and the sun are.

Here is a list of some being verbs:

am	is	are	was	were
has been	had been	have been	will be	

Which sentence has a being verb?

   A. The sun sets at 8:00 p.m.
   B. The sunset is beautiful.
   C. The sun rises in the east.

You are right if you said sentence B. The verb *is* is a being verb.

Exercise 1

Find the verb in each sentence. Tell whether it is an action verb or a being verb.

1. My teacher told us many things about astronomy.
2. The information was extremely interesting.
3. Hot stars send off a blue glow.
4. Red is the color of cooler stars.
5. Yellow stars are in-between.
6. A smaller star is a dwarf.
7. Our sun is a yellow dwarf.
8. Scientists study the sun to learn more about the stars.
9. The sun is our major source of light and energy.
10. My science report gives many details about the sun.

Exercise 2

Complete each sentence, using a being verb from the list on page 412.

1. The sun _____ hot today.
2. I _____ in the sun too long.
3. My skin _____ reddish.
4. I _____ uncomfortable.
5. I _____ more careful.

Practice Power

Write about the place you are in now or a place where you have been or will be. Describe it in four sentences with being verbs.

Examples: I have been to the library today.
The library was very quiet.

Linking Verbs

A being verb can be a linking verb. A **linking verb** joins the subject of a sentence to a subject complement.

The subject complement renames or describes the subject of the sentence. It can be a noun, a pronoun, or an adjective.

Subject	Linking Verb	Subject Complement
The pretzels	*are*	a snack. (noun)
The person who brought pretzels	*was*	she. (pronoun)
A pretzel	*is*	salty. (adjective)

In the first sentence the linking verb *are* joins the subject *pretzels* with the noun *snack.* In the second sentence the subject *person* and the pronoun *she* are joined by the linking verb *was.* In the third sentence the linking verb *is* joins the subject *pretzel* with the adjective *salty. Snack, she,* and *salty* are subject complements.

Which sentences have linking verbs?

    A. The pretzel was delicious.
    B. The person who ate the last pretzel was he.
    C. Charlie ate the pretzel.

You are correct if you said sentences A and B. Both sentences have the linking verb *was.* In sentence A, *was* is followed by an adjective. In sentence B, *was* is followed by a pronoun.

Exercise 1

The linking verb in each sentence is in italics. Find the subject complement that is linked to the subject. Tell whether it is a noun, a pronoun, or an adjective.

1. A monk *was* the inventor of the pretzel.

2. The first pretzel *was* leftover bread dough.

3. Its shape, like arms folded in prayer, *was* special.

4. The first pretzels *were* soft.

5. Hard pretzels *were* originally a mistake by a baker.

6. The person who cooked the pretzels too long *was* he.

7. People, however, *were* delighted.

8. The new pretzels *were* tasty and crunchy.

Exercise 2

Complete each sentence with a linking verb that makes sense. Choose from the list of being verbs on page 412.

1. Pretzel baking _____ an art.

2. The first pretzels _____ handmade.

3. In 1879 two men _____ the first people to make a machine to twist pretzels.

4. I _____ a pretzel fan.

5. Pretzels _____ popular for a long time to come.

Practice Power

Choose one of the foods listed below. Write three sentences about it. Use a linking verb in each sentence.

waffles   tacos   pizza   nachos

Example: Nachos are cheesy and very tasty.

Helping Verbs

A verb can have two parts—a **helping verb** and a main verb. A helping verb always comes before another verb.

Here are some helping verbs:

am	was	do	has	will	could
is	were	did	have	would	should
are	had	can	must		

Study how helping verbs are used in these sentences.

Without a Helping Verb

The children *play* jacks.

With a Helping Verb

The children *can* play jacks.
The children *should* learn the rules of jacks.
The children *are* learning the game of jacks.
I *have* played jacks with Mom.

Which of these sentences does not have a helping verb?

A. I will teach you the game.
B. Jessie should bounce the ball.
C. She grabbed two jacks.

You are right if you said sentence C. In sentence A, *will* is a helping verb that goes with the verb *teach*. In sentence B, *should* is a helping verb that goes with the verb *bounce*.

Exercise 1

Find the helping verb in each sentence.

1. Mom and Dad had played jacks as children.

2. We can try several games.

3. Mom was explaining how to play onesies.

4. The jacks are scattered on the floor.

5. The ball is tossed in the air.

6. The ball may bounce once.

7. The player must grab a jack.

8. A player should catch the ball in the same hand.

Exercise 2

Tell whether the verb in italics in each sentence is a helping verb or a linking verb.

1. Jacks *are* fun.

2. Amanda's jacks *were* colorful.

3. We *are* making our own rules.

4. I *will* bounce the ball high in the air.

5. She *has* missed one jack.

6. The last jack *is* purple.

7. Cal *should* grab that jack.

8. We *can* play again.

Practice Power

Write four sentences about a game you like to play. Use a helping verb in each sentence.

Example: I have played chess.

Verb Phrases

A **verb phrase** is made up of one or more helping verbs and a main verb.

Helping verbs: I *should have* given you the funny cartoon.

Main verb: I should have *given* you the funny cartoon.

Verb phrase: I *should have given* you the funny cartoon.

What is the verb phrase in this sentence?

The cartoonist can draw funny characters.

A. can

B. can draw

C. draw

You are right if you said B. *Can draw* is the verb phrase. It is made up of the helping verb *can* and the main verb *draw.* A has only the helping verb *can,* and C has only the main verb *draw.*

Can you find the verb phrase in this sentence?

The newspaper will be delivered before 7 a.m.

You are correct if you said *will be delivered. Will* and *be* are helping verbs, and *delivered* is the main verb. *Be, been,* and *being* can be helping verbs that follow other helping verbs in verb phrases.

Exercise 1

The verb phrases in these sentences are shown in italics. Find the helping verb or verbs and the main verb in each sentence.

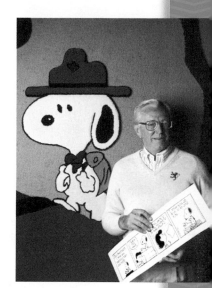

1. I *am reading* a book of Peanuts cartoons.

2. Charles Schulz's cartoons *have become* world famous.

3. Schulz's family *had been given* a dog.

4. That dog *would inspire* Schulz's most famous character.

5. The cartoon dog *would be given* the name Snoopy.

6. An early sketch by the young Schultz *was printed* in a local paper.

7. Schulz *was paid* little money for his first efforts.

8. Since then his comic strip *has appeared* in some 2,600 newspapers.

Exercise 2

Add a helping verb to complete the verb phrase in each sentence. Identify the complete verb phrase you form.

1. I _____ seen the comics this morning.

2. You _____ read these when I finish.

3. Wendy _____ share the section with me.

4. We _____ laughing about this one.

5. The dog in the cartoon _____ writing a novel!

6. We _____ read the newspaper every day.

Practice Power

Think of a newspaper or TV cartoon you like. Write four sentences about the cartoon. Use a verb phrase in each sentence.

Example: I have seen a Charlie Brown movie on TV.

Principal Verb Parts

A verb has four **principal parts: present, present participle, past,** and **past participle.**

Present	Present Participle	Past	Past Participle
play	playing	played	played
learn	learning	learned	learned
bake	baking	baked	baked

- The present participle is formed by adding *-ing* to the present. The present participle is often used with a form of the helping verb *be* (*am, is, are, was,* and *were*).

  Some artists *paint* outdoors. (present)
  The artist *is painting* flowers. (present participle)

- The past and the past participle are formed by adding *-d* or *-ed* to the present. The past participle is often used with the helping verb *has, have,* or *had.*

  The artist *painted* flowers. (past)
  The artist *has painted* flowers. (past participle)

- To form the present participle of verbs ending in *e,* drop the final *e* and add *-ing*: *use + ing = using.*

- To form the present or past participle of a verb ending in a consonant following a vowel, double the consonant before adding *-ing* or *-ed*: *plug + ing = plugging, tag + ed = tagged.*

Exercise 1

Tell whether the verb in italics is the present, present participle, past, or past participle part of the verb. Look for forms of the verb _be_ before present participles and _has, have,_ or _had_ before past participles.

1. The painter *sketched* the man's wrinkled face.

2. Veronica had *posed* for a portrait.

3. A sculptor *molds* clay.

4. Some artists *work* with metal.

5. That student is *painting* with watercolors.

6. Doug had *used* pastels in the drawing of the lily.

7. She is *using* charcoal for her sketch of the park.

8. Lesley *prepared* the canvas.

Exercise 2

Complete each sentence with the form of the verb in parentheses.

1. We always _____ the local art fair. (visit—present)

2. Artists are _____ their works. (show—present participle)

3. Li is _____ an artist paint. (watch—present participle)

4. Li _____ a lot by watching the painter. (learn—past)

5. That artist has _____ an original style. (develop—past participle)

6. The judges _____ him first prize. (award—past)

Practice Power

Choose one of the verbs in Exercise 2. Use the verb in four sentences. In each sentence use a different principal verb part: present, present participle, past, or past participle.

Irregular Verbs

The past and the past participle of a regular verb end in *-d* or *-ed*. The past and the past participle of an **irregular verb** are not formed this way.

Begin, break, and *know* are irregular verbs. The chart shows the principal parts of these irregular verbs. Remember that the present participle and the past participle are often used with a helping verb.

Present	Present Participle	Past	Past Participle
begin	beginning	began	begun
break	breaking	broke	broken
know	knowing	knew	known

We *begin* class at 8:30. (present)
We *are beginning* now. (present participle—with the helping verb *are*)
We *began* class at 9:30 yesterday. (past)
We *have begun* class at 8:30 today. (past participle—with the helping verb *have*)

Which word correctly completes the sentence?

Justin (begin begins) class at 8:00.

You're right if you said *begins.* For the present with a singular subject, use the present form ending in *-s.*

Exercise 1

Complete each sentence with the correct part of *begin.*

1. The class _____ the lesson on gravity last week.

2. The teacher _____ class as soon as the bell rings.

3. We are _____ to understand the concepts.

4. I have _____ my experiment on gravity already.

Exercise 2

Complete each sentence with the correct part of *break.*

1. Tyrone _____ his arm last week.

2. He had _____ his toe last year.

3. He is _____ lots of things because he can use only one arm.

4. He said he has _____ a vase at home as well.

Exercise 3

Complete each sentence with the correct part of *know.*

1. Martina had _____ a lot about gravity before studying it in class.

2. We plan to work together on a project; she _____ about a gravity experiment with a ramp.

3. My brother _____ about Galileo's experiment on gravity before he studied it in sixth grade.

4. I now _____ something about gravity too.

Practice Power

Write four sentences. Use a different form of the verb *break* in each one.

More Irregular Verbs

Choose, do, and *teach* are **irregular verbs.** The chart shows the principal parts of these verbs.

Present	Present Participle	Past	Past Participle
choose	choosing	chose	chosen
do	doing	did	done
teach	teaching	taught	taught

We generally *choose* seats in the front. (present)
We *are choosing* our seats. (present participle—with the helping verb *are*)
We *chose* our seats. (past)
We *have chosen* our seats. (past participle—with the helping verb *have*)

Note that *does* is a present form used with singular noun subjects and the pronouns *he, she,* and *it.*

Arlene always *does* the supper dishes.

Which form of the verb correctly completes the sentence?

Have you ever (did done do) a collage?

You're right if you chose *done.* The past participle form is needed with the helping verb *have.*

Exercise 1

Complete each sentence with the correct part of _choose_.

1. Chloe _____ pink socks to match her shirt today.

2. The coaches are _____ players.

3. I have _____ a new book from the library.

4. I never _____ to do dishes if I can do another chore.

5. Last night I _____ to vacuum the rug.

Exercise 2

Complete each sentence with the correct part of _do_.

1. Who is _____ a computer slide show presentation?

2. Pat _____ his homework every Friday night.

3. Kelly _____ her assignment last Sunday night.

4. Fred and Tom have _____ their presentations.

5. They always _____ their work on time.

Exercise 3

Complete each sentence with the correct part of _teach_.

1. My mother is _____ me chess.

2. At first she _____ me the names of the pieces.

3. She already has _____ me the basic rules.

4. She and my father are also _____ me Scrabble.

5. My aunt _____ chess at the local park.

Practice Power

Write four sentences, using the present, the present participle, the past, and the past participle parts of _do_.

Simple Present Tense

The tense of a verb shows when an action or a state of being takes place. A verb in the **simple present tense** tells about something that is always true or about an action that happens again and again.

> Whales *swim* in the ocean.
> Whales *eat* fish.
> A whale *leaps* from the water.

The verbs *swim, eat,* and *leaps* are in the simple present tense. The verbs tell things that are true about whales. They tell about actions a whale does again and again.

A verb in simple present tense ends in *-s* when the subject is a singular noun or the pronoun *he, she,* or *it.* A verb in the simple present tense does not end in *-s* when the subject is plural.

Which sentence is in the simple present tense?

> **A.** Amy always watches for whales at the aquarium.
> **B.** I saw a whale at the aquarium.

You are right if you said sentence A. *Watches* is in the simple present tense. Sentence B tells about something that took place in the past.

Exercise 1

Choose the correct verb to complete each sentence.

1. Bottlenose dolphins (live lives) in groups called pods.

2. A calf (stay stays) with its mother for three to six years.

3. Dolphins (jump jumps) up to 16 feet in the air.

4. A bottlenose dolphin ordinarily (swim swims) at speeds of 3 to 7 miles per hour.

5. Every so often its usual speed (increase increases).

6. Scientists (record records) dolphin speeds of up to 22 miles per hour.

Exercise 2

Complete each sentence with the correct form of the verb in parentheses. Be sure the subject and the verb agree.

1. Dolphins _____ through the water. (slide)

2. A powerful tail fin _____ a dolphin. (propel)

3. This fin _____ up and down. (move)

4. A dolphin _____ through a blowhole. (breathe)

5. It _____ its breath while under water. (hold)

6. A dolphin's dive _____ up to 10 minutes. (last)

7. Oceans _____ a home for most dolphins. (provide)

Practice Power

Write four sentences about dolphins or other interesting animals you have seen. Use the simple present tense in your sentences.

Simple Past Tense

A verb in the **simple past tense** tells about something that happened in the past.

> Dinosaurs *lived* thousands of years ago.
> Last year we *studied* about dinosaurs.
> The teacher *showed* a video about *T. rex.*

The verbs *lived, studied,* and *showed* are in the simple past.

Most past tense verbs end with *-ed.* Remember that irregular verbs in the past do not end in *-ed.*

> We *discussed* dinosaurs in class. (regular verb)
> I *read* a book on dinosaurs last year. (irregular verb)

Here are some spelling rules for *-ed* endings.

* If a verb ends in *e,* just add *-d: name + d = named.*
* If a verb ends in *y* following a consonant, change the *y* to *i* and add *-ed: try + ed = tried.*
* If a verb ends in a consonant following a vowel, double the consonant and add the ending: *wrap + ed = wrapped.*

Which sentence shows the simple past tense?

> **A.** The class is learning about fossils.
> **B.** We learn about fossils in science.
> **C.** We learned about dinosaur fossils.

You are right if you said sentence C. The *-ed* ending on *learned* indicates a past action.

Exercise 1

Write the simple past tense of each verb. Be careful! Some verbs are irregular. Check a dictionary if you need to.

1. sing
2. chew
3. stomp
4. serve
5. growl

6. smell
7. grab
8. dry
9. grow
10. walk

Exercise 2

Complete each sentence with the verb in parentheses. Use the simple past tense. Some verbs are irregular.

1. Dinosaurs _____ out about 65 million years ago. (die)

2. Paleontologists recently _____ a *Titanosaur* skull and skeleton together. (find)

3. Most skulls _____ over the centuries. (disappear)

4. The scientists _____ carefully to remove this rare fossil from the ground. (work)

5. *Titanosaurs* _____ plants. (eat)

6. They _____ to the group of dinosaurs called sauropods. (belong)

7. They _____ long necks. (have)

8. Scientists also _____ *Titanosaur* eggs. (discover)

Practice Power

Write four sentences about dinosaurs. Use the simple past tense in each.

Future Tenses

The word *will* and the phrase *going to* are ways to express something that will take place in the future. Both forms are used to talk about predictions and to express **future tense.**

> Many families *will donate* food to the food pantry.
> The supermarket *is going to be* busy tomorrow.

The helping verb *will* is used with the present to form a future tense; for example, *will + help = will help.* The helping verb *will* is often used when someone agrees to do something soon.

> I *will go* to the supermarket with my parents.

When the future is expressed with *going to,* the verb *am, is,* or *are* precedes *going to,* which is followed by the present form of the verb; for example, *is + going to + make = is going to make.* The form *going to* is often used when someone wishes to express an action that has already been planned.

> He *is going to buy* canned goods.

Which sentence expresses the future?

> **A.** Sam's family helps out at the food pantry.
> **B.** Sam bought cereal at the supermarket.
> **C.** Sam will donate boxes of cereal.

You are right if you said sentence C shows the future. *Will donate* is in the future tense and indicates something that will happen in the future.

Exercise 1

Identify the verb or verb phrase in each sentence. Tell the tense of each verb.

1. We will make a shopping list.
2. We are going to walk to the store.
3. Sonny found a cart.
4. I am going to put apples in it.
5. Pam wants doughnuts.
6. Mom is going to say no.

Exercise 2

Rewrite each sentence in the future tense, using *will*.

1. I volunteer at St. Mary's food pantry.
2. My family shops for groceries.
3. We donate the food.
4. We put the food into bags.

Exercise 3

Rewrite each sentence in the future tense, using *going to*.

1. Who brings the groceries to the food pantry?
2. Dad delivers the food.
3. I ride with him.
4. We bring food twice a month.

Practice Power

Write five sentences about things you could do to help people in need. Use the future tense with *will* or *going to*.

Example: I will donate several items of clothing.

Progressive Tenses

A verb in the **present progressive tense** tells about an action that is happening now. The present progressive tense is formed with *am, is,* or *are* and the present participle.

A verb in the **past progressive tense** tells what was happening over a period of time in the past. The past progressive tense is formed with *was* or *were* and the present participle.

> Lucy *is brushing* her teeth. (present progressive)
> Lucy *was brushing* her teeth when her dad shouted, "Hurry up!" (past progressive)

Which sentences are in a progressive tense?

   A. Marcus brushes his teeth after dinner.
   B. He is plugging in his electric toothbrush.
   C. Marcus was searching for his cinnamon-flavored toothpaste this morning.

You are right if you said sentences B and C. *Is plugging* is in the present progressive tense. *Was searching* is in the past progressive tense.

Exercise 1

Write the present progressive tense and the past progressive tense of each verb. Use the pronoun in parentheses as the subject of the verb phrase.

Example: sleep (I)   I am sleeping   I was sleeping

1. rinse (you)
2. wash (we)
3. scrub (he)
4. chew (they)
5. comb (she)
6. floss (they)
7. change (we)
8. bathe (I)

Exercise 2

Find the verb phrase in each sentence. Tell whether it is in the present progressive tense or the past progressive tense.

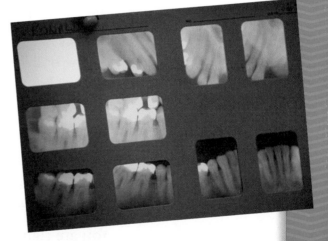

1. Felicity was flossing her teeth.
2. The dentist was examining my teeth.
3. The hygienists were cleaning teeth.
4. He is polishing Jake's teeth.
5. She was taking X-rays.
6. Dr. Palazzo is telling me about tooth care.
7. She was showing me how to brush.
8. Are you taking good care of your teeth?

Practice Power

Be a reporter! Imagine you are at a concert, a sporting event, or a parade. Write four sentences about what is going on around you. Use the present progressive tense in your sentences. Then rewrite the sentences, using the past progressive tense.

Present Perfect Tense

A verb in the **present perfect tense** tells about an action that happened at some indefinite time in the past. It can also tell about an action that started in the past and continues into the present.

The present perfect tense is formed with *has* or *have* and the past participle.

> Lucy *has traveled* to many states.
> She and her family *have taken* a long road trip each year.
> Lucy *has kept* a diary of her travels since she was seven.

Which sentence uses the present perfect tense?

A. I have read a book about South Dakota.
B. I read a book about South Dakota last week.
C. I will read a book about South Dakota soon.

You are right if you said sentence A uses the present perfect tense. It means that I read the book at some indefinite time in the past.

Exercise 1

Write the present perfect tense of each verb. Be careful. Some verbs are irregular. Use the pronoun in parentheses as the subject of the verb phrase.

Example: leave (I)   I have left

1. pack (you)
2. buy (we)
3. drive (he)
4. ask (they)

5. take (it)
6. eat (they)
7. try (she)
8. forget (I)

Exercise 2

Complete each sentence, using the verb in parentheses in the present perfect tense.

1. I _____ to South Dakota with my family. (travel)
2. We _____ to Mount Rushmore. (be)
3. I _____ the huge faces of the four presidents! (see)
4. The amazing sculpture _____ for more than 80 years! (exist)
5. Millions of tourists _____ it during that time. (visit)
6. People _____ the addition of a fifth face—that of Susan B. Anthony, an advocate of women's rights. (propose)
7. I _____ photos from my trip on my Web site. (put)
8. _____ you ever _____ to South Dakota? (be)

Practice Power

Write four sentences about places you have been and things you have seen there.

Past Perfect Tense

A verb in the **past perfect tense** tells about an action that was finished before something else happened in the past.

The past perfect tense is formed with *had* and the past participle.

> I *had finished* my report before I called my friend.
> After I *had chosen* Elizabeth Blackwell as the topic of my report, I went to the library to find books about her life.

Which sentence uses the past perfect tense?

A. I think Elizabeth Blackwell was strong and courageous.
B. I had read two books about Blackwell before I started to write my report.
C. The library has several books about Blackwell.

You are right if you said sentence B uses the past perfect tense. *Had read* means I read the books before I did something else—started to write the report.

Which action in this sentence took place first?

Before Elizabeth Blackwell studied to become a doctor, she had worked as a teacher.

You are right if you said *had worked*. The past perfect tense indicates that one action (working) preceded another action (studying) in the past.

Exercise 1

Write the past perfect tense of each verb. Use the pronoun in parentheses as the subject of the verb.

Example: play (I)   I had played

1. visit (you)
2. look (we)
3. talk (he)
4. lose (they)
5. help (she)
6. fall (it)

Exercise 2

Rewrite each sentence, using the past perfect tense of the verb in italics. Some verbs are irregular.

1. Before Elizabeth Blackwell, no woman in the United States _____ as a doctor. (graduate)

2. She _____ to 29 medical schools before one accepted her as a student. (apply)

3. Once she _____ her medical degree, she couldn't get a job in the United States and went to Europe for work. (earn)

4. After she _____ to the United States, she opened her own clinic for poor people. (return)

5. Because Blackwell _____ the way, it was easier for other women to become doctors. (pave)

Practice Power

Write four sentences in the past perfect tense about things you did yesterday. Include two actions in each sentence.

Example: After I had cleaned my room, I played computer games.

Future Perfect Tense

A verb in the **future perfect tense** tells about an action that will have been completed at some time in the future. The future perfect tense is formed by adding *will have* to the past participle of the verb.

> Corinne *will have saved* enough money to go to the movie by Saturday.

Will have saved tells that Corinne will have completed the action (saving money) before some time in the future (Saturday).

Which sentence uses the future perfect tense?

A. She will have eaten dinner by 7:00 p.m.
B. He eats dinner every night.
C. We will have dinner at 6:30 tonight.

You are right if you said sentence A uses the future perfect tense. *Will have eaten* tells us that she will have completed the action (eating dinner) before some time in the future (7:00 p.m.).

Exercise 1

Write the future perfect tense of each verb. Some verbs are irregular. Use the pronoun in parentheses as the subject of the verb phrase.

Example: speak (I)   I will have spoken

1. pack (you)
2. schedule (we)
3. drive (he)
4. arrive (they)
5. stop (it)
6. wait (they)
7. move (it)
8. sit (I)

Exercise 2

Rewrite each sentence, using the future perfect tense of the verb in parentheses. Some verbs are irregular.

1. Wanda _____ the tickets to us by tomorrow. (give)
2. We're late! Trudy _____ by the time we arrive. (dance)
3. Terrance _____ by now. (sing)
4. The play _____ by then. (start)
5. We _____ the first act. (miss)
6. Andrew _____ by the final act. (doze)
7. Some people _____ before the end of the play. (leave)
8. My family _____ back home before 10:00 p.m. (arrive)

Practice Power

Imagine you are leaving for a trip. Write four sentences that tell the things that will have happened by the time you leave. Use future perfect tense in each sentence.

Example: Before I leave, I will have taken the cat to my neighbor's house.

Subject-Verb Agreement

A subject and verb must agree, whether the verb is a helping verb or the main verb.

	Present	Past
I	am, do	was, did
you, we, they	are, do	were, did
he, she, it	is, does	was, did

Singular Subject	Verb
The *girl*	*is* petting the dog.
That *dog*	*does* tricks.

Plural Subject	Verb
Kevin and Kurt	*are* brushing the dog.
They	*were* at the dog show.

Which verb completes this sentence correctly?

Several breeds _____ shown at the dog show.

A. is

B. are

C. was

You are right if you said B. The subject *breeds* is plural and needs the verb *are*.

A collective noun is considered a singular noun even though it refers to more than one person or thing.

The *litter* of puppies includes one solid-black pup.

Exercise 1

Choose the verb that agrees with the subject.

1. We (is are) bringing our dogs to the dog show.

2. Our wolfhound (was were) a winner last year.

3. He (do does) all sorts of tricks.

4. I (am is) nervous.

5. (Does Do) you know where to go?

6. The girls (is are) grooming their dogs.

Exercise 2

Complete each sentence correctly with _am, is, are, was, were, do,_ or _does._

1. The dog show _____ at the kennel club every year.

2. The toy dogs _____ fun to watch—they looked cute.

3. A funny dachshund _____ in line after them as they paraded across the stage.

4. _____ this collie follow commands?

5. _____ you think our spaniel will win?

6. Those Great Danes _____ large dogs. Do you see them?

7. Rex _____ a mixed breed, but I love him.

8. _____ you coming to the show next year?

Practice Power

Use _am, is, are, was, were, do,_ or _does_ in four sentences about dogs. Make sure subjects and verbs agree.

Examples: Some dogs are guides.
I am the owner of a collie.

There Is and *There Are*

When a sentence starts with *there is, there are, there was,* or *there were,* the subject follows the verb. The verb must still agree with the subject.

	Verb		Singular Subject	
There	*is*	a	*sea*	around Japan.

	Verb		Plural Subject	
There	*are*	many	*islands*	in Japan.

In the first sentence the singular subject *sea* comes after the verb *is*. In the second sentence the plural subject *islands* comes after the verb *are*.

What is the subject in this sentence? Which verb correctly completes it?

> There _____ noisy monkeys called macaques in Japan.
>
> **A.** is
> **B.** are
> **C.** was

You are right if you said B. *Monkeys* is the subject, and it is plural. The verb *are* is needed to agree with it.

Exercise 1

Find the subject and the verb in each sentence. Tell whether the subject is singular or plural.

1. There are four main islands in Japan.

2. There is a beautiful mountain, Mount Fuji, an inactive volcano.

3. There are many people in Japanese cities.

4. There was much pollution in the past.

Exercise 2

Complete each sentence with *there is, there are, there was,* or *there were.* Make sure the subjects and verbs agree.

1. _____ emperors in Japan in the past.

2. _____ still an emperor today.

3. _____ a prime minister too.

4. _____ once fierce warriors in Japan called samurai.

5. _____ tea at nearly every meal in Japan even today.

6. _____ raw fish in some sushi, a popular Japanese food.

7. _____ arcades with games in Tokyo.

8. _____ a big festival every year for New Year's.

9. _____ many earthquakes in Japan.

Practice Power

Write four sentences about things in your town. Begin your sentences with *There is, There are, There was,* or *There were.*

Verb Challenge

Read the paragraph and answer the questions.

1. This fall our class went on a field trip to a farm. 2. It was the first time many of us had visited a farm. 3. First we took a hayride. 4. Our host told us about the farm crops while we were riding through the fields on a wagon pulled by a tractor. 5. Next we walked through a maze in a corn field. 6. There was a winding path between tall stalks of corn. 7. I was the first out, but next time I'm going to find the way out even faster! 8. The best part of the trip was a stop at the pumpkin patch. 9. We each chose a pumpkin to take home. 10. My mom has helped me carve mine, and the jack-o-lantern is sitting on a table in our front window. 11. Maybe we can return to the farm for our spring field trip.

1. In sentence 1 is *went* an action, a being, or a helping verb?

2. In sentence 2 what is the tense of the verb *had visited*?

3. In sentence 3 is *took* a regular or irregular verb? What are its principal parts?

4. In sentence 4 what is the tense of the verb *were riding*?

5. In sentence 5 is *walked* a regular or irregular verb? What are its principal parts?

6. In sentence 6 what is the verb? What is the subject?

7. In sentence 7 what is the verb phrase in the future tense?

8. In sentence 8 what is the linking verb?

9. In sentence 10 what is the tense of the verb phrase *has helped*?

10. In sentence 10 what is the tense of the verb phrase *is sitting*?

11. In sentence 11 what is the helping verb?

Adverbs and Conjunctions

Adverbs of Time and Place

An **adverb** tells more about a verb. An adverb can tell when, how often, or where.

- An **adverb of time** answers the question *when* or *how often*.
- An **adverb of place** answers the question *where*.

When:	He will bring his lunch *tomorrow.*
How often:	I *always* bring my lunch.
Where:	She ate *outside.*

Study the lists of some common adverbs of time and place.

Adverbs of Time	Adverbs of Place
again	above
already	ahead
always	away
before	back
immediately	below
late	down
never	far
now	forward
often	here
sometimes	in
soon	inside
then	near
today	out
tomorrow	overhead
usually	there
yesterday	up

Exercise 1

Tell whether each adverb tells *when, how often,* or *where*.

1. immediately
2. below
3. far
4. now
5. above

6. near
7. always
8. never
9. up
10. sometimes

Exercise 2

Find the adverb of time or place in each sentence.

1. Yesterday my sister and I decided to make apple pancakes.
2. We had never made them.
3. We got the ingredients out.
4. Soon we started mixing ingredients.
5. Then I knocked over the bag of flour.
6. The flour flew everywhere.
7. We immediately started to clean.
8. We didn't have any flour left to make a batter again.
9. We put everything back.
10. We went to a restaurant and ate apple pancakes there.

Practice Power

Think of an activity you like to do with your family, your friends, or your class. Write about it, using adverbs of time and place. Circle the adverbs you use.

Adverbs of Manner

An adverb can tell how an action takes place. An **adverb of manner** answers the question *how* about the verb. Many adverbs of manner end in *-ly*, but some—such as *fast, well,* and *hard*—do not.

> The wind blew *strongly.* (How did the wind blow?)
> The kite flew *gracefully.* (How did the kite fly?)
> We ran *fast* across the field. (How did we run?)

Strongly, gracefully, and *fast* answer the question *how.* They are adverbs of manner.

Study the list of some common adverbs of manner.

Adverbs of Manner		
carefully	forcefully	rapidly
clearly	happily	slowly
easily	kindly	patiently

Which sentence uses an adverb of manner?

A. The string hung loosely.
B. The string is white.
C. The string tangled again.

You are right if you said that sentence A has an adverb of manner. *Loosely* tells how the string hung.

Which of the following is not an adverb of manner?

A. fast   **B.** greedily   **C.** recently

You are right if you said C. *Recently* is an adverb of time.

Exercise 1

Identify the adverb of manner in each sentence.

1. Chuck ran quickly.

2. He held the kite string tightly.

3. A breeze blew lightly across the veranda.

4. He hastily tossed the kite into the air.

5. It floated gently to the ground.

6. Chuck ran fast the next time.

7. He launched the kite excitedly.

8. It flew perfectly.

Exercise 2

Complete each sentence with an adverb of manner. Choose from the following adverbs. Use each one once.

patiently	attentively	enthusiastically
lightly	strongly	similarly

1. Mr. Ellerbruch _____ explained how kites work.

2. The students listened _____.

3. Kites work _____ to sailboats.

4. The wind should not blow too _____ or too _____.

5. Heather and Sally talked _____ about kite flying.

Practice Power

Make a list of things you like to do. Then think of one or more adverbs that tell how you do each thing.

Example: I play soccer.
I play soccer skillfully, intelligently, and enthusiastically.

Adverbs That Compare

Many adverbs can be used to make comparisons. Adverbs can compare the actions of two or more persons or things. To compare the actions of two people or things, *-er* is often added to an adverb. To compare three or more people or things, *-est* is often added to an adverb.

Juanita wakes up early.

Comparing the Actions of Two People

Juanita wakes up *earlier* than her brother.

Comparing the Actions of More Than Two People

Of all the family members Mom wakes up *earliest.*

Earlier compares the actions of Juanita and her brother. It compares the actions of two people. Note that *-er* forms are often used with *than. Earliest* compares Mom's action to those of all the other members of the family.

Which sentence uses an adverb that compares an action?

    A. Mom takes a shower first.
    B. Dad showers fastest of all the family members.
    C. Juanita always sings in the shower.

You are right if you said sentence B. The adverb *fastest* compares Dad's action to those of the other family members.

Exercise 1

Complete the chart.

Adverb	Compares Actions of Two	Compares Actions of Three or More
1. deep	_____	_____
2. high	_____	_____
3. hard	_____	_____
4. fast	_____	_____
5. late	_____	_____
6. long	_____	_____

Exercise 2

Underline the adverb that compares in each sentence.

1. The wind was great for kite flying yesterday: It blew harder than it had the day before.

2. Ali arrived earliest at the field for a kite-flying lesson.

3. To launch his kite Ali ran fastest of all the learners.

4. His kite rose higher than mine did.

5. Once up, it stayed in the air longest.

6. Ali held his string tightest of all the kite flyers.

7. He tried harder than the other learners to master the principles of kite flying.

Practice Power

Use three adverbs from Exercise 1 in sentences that compare.

More Adverbs That Compare

Some **adverbs** that compare are not formed by adding *-er* or *-est.* Instead, these adverbs use *more* or *most* to make comparisons.

- Use *more* or *most* for adverbs ending in *-ly.*
  clearly   more clearly   most clearly

- Use *more* or *most* for adverbs of three or more syllables.
  clumsily   more clumsily   most clumsily

More is used when the actions of two people or things are compared. Adverbs with *more* are often used with *than.* *Most* is used when the actions of three or more people or things are compared.

> Jennie stood *more steadily* on the balance beam than Katie did. (compares the actions of two people)
> Of all the gymnasts Amelie stood on the balance *most steadily.* (compares the actions of three or more people)

Which sentence uses an adverb that compares?

- **A.** David tumbled most frequently of all.
- **B.** David did well on the rings.
- **C.** David practiced frequently.

You are right if you said sentence A. *Most frequently* compares David's actions to those of two or more other gymnasts.

Exercise 1

Complete the chart.

Adverb	Compares Actions of Two	Compares Actions of Three or More
1. diligently	_____	_____
2. thoughtfully	_____	_____
3. tirelessly	_____	_____
4. easily	_____	_____
5. quietly	_____	_____
6. loudly	_____	_____
7. brightly	_____	_____

Exercise 2

Choose the correct adverb that compares to complete each sentence.

1. Of all the campers Connie tells a ghost story (more effectively most effectively).

2. Rita can put up a tent (more quickly most quickly) than Alison can.

3. Jane and Jessica row across the lake (more rapidly most rapidly) than any other pair.

4. Dorothy paddles a kayak (more skillfully most skillfully) of all.

5. Of all the archers Kevin hits the target (more frequently most frequently).

Practice Power

Use three adverbs from Exercise 1 in sentences that compare.

Good and *Well;* Negatives

The word *good* is an adjective; it describes a noun. It usually tells *what kind.* The word *well* is an adverb; it describes a verb. It tells *how.*

Margo made a *good* meal. (tells what kind of meal)
Margo cooks *well.* (tells how Margo cooks)

Well can be used as an adjective, but only in reference to a person's health.

Arnie wasn't *well* enough to play today.

A **negative** idea can be formed in one of several ways.

- By using *never* or *not* before the verb. *Not* is sometimes a part of a contraction: *didn't, won't, wouldn't.*
I *never* eat candy.
Let's *not* make pizza.

- By adding *no* before a noun.
We have *no* ice cream.

Use only one negative word in a sentence to express a negative idea. Is this sentence correct?

I don't never eat ice cream.

The sentence is incorrect because it has two negative words, *don't* and *never.* To correct it, remove one of the negative words: *I don't eat ice cream* or *I never eat ice cream.*

Exercise 1

Complete each sentence with *good* or *well*.

1. My sister bakes _____.

2. Her homemade bread is very _____.

3. I can make smoothies _____.

4. I operate the blender _____.

5. I mix the ingredients _____.

6. Everyone says that my smoothies are _____.

Exercise 2

These sentences are incorrect because they contain more than one negative word. Rewrite each to correct it.

1. Angie doesn't never eat rutabagas.

2. I don't never bring my lunch to school.

3. Candice doesn't never have pizza for breakfast.

4. The cafeteria doesn't have no ice cream today.

5. I don't put no bananas on my cereal.

6. My friends don't never get their lunches from the cafeteria.

7. We don't never have pizza on Monday.

8. I don't have no money to buy a drink.

Practice Power

Write three sentences about things that you like to do or things that you don't like to do. Use *good* and *well* in at least one sentence.

Examples: I don't like to dance.
I don't dance well.
I may practice to become a good dancer.

Coordinating Conjunctions

A **coordinating conjunction** joins two words or groups of words. The words *and, but,* and *or* are coordinating conjunctions. They are used to join words or word groups that are similar.

And:	Patty <u>buys</u> *and* <u>trades</u> baseball cards.
But:	Horatio <u>plays football</u> *but* <u>collects baseball cards</u>.
Or:	Do you like <u>football</u> *or* <u>baseball</u>?
	Do you keep your cards <u>in boxes</u> *or* <u>in bags</u>?

In these sentences the similar words and groups of words connected by the coordinating conjunctions are underlined.

Which sentences have coordinating conjunctions? What do the conjunctions join?

A. Michael and Rhonda like photography.
B. I want to take a picture too!
C. Lennon smiled but blinked during the shot.

You are right if you said A and C. In sentence A *and* joins *Michael* and *Rhonda*. In sentence C *but* joins *smiled* and *blinked*.

Exercise 1

Find the coordinating conjunction in each sentence. Identify the words or groups of words the conjunction joins.

Example: Some stamps are <u>rare</u> *and* <u>valuable</u>.

1. Stamp collecting can be an exciting but expensive hobby.

2. People collect new or used stamps.

3. Many stores buy and sell stamps.

4. You can get used stamps from letters or from packages.

5. After you remove a stamp with water, dry and press it.

6. Many stamps show flowers or birds.

7. Is this stamp common or rare?

8. Keep your stamps in envelopes or in albums.

Exercise 2

Rewrite each sentence with a coordinating conjunction that makes sense.

and	but	or

1. Knitting is fun _____ difficult.

2. Tanya knitted mittens _____ a scarf.

3. She will use the purple _____ the green yarn.

4. She finished the scarf _____ didn't wear it.

5. Should I make a blanket _____ a sweater?

Practice Power

Write some sentences about a hobby. Use the conjunctions *and, but,* and *or* in your sentences.

Example: Cooking is difficult but fun.

Adverb and Conjunction Challenge

Read the paragraph and answer the questions.

1. Finally the wild animal acts were completed. 2. Now it was time for the main event of the circus. 3. The new act was exciting but dangerous. 4. The famous acrobat would swing skillfully above the heads of the crowd. 5. She approached the ladder, climbed up quickly, and smiled down at the vast audience. 6. The drums rolled loudly and then were silent. 7. The figure grasped the bar tightly, swung forward, and then let go. 8. She gracefully twirled in the air, seemed to hang momentarily suspended in space, and then smoothly reached for the trapeze at the other side. 9. The crowd breathed easily again. 10. They applauded more enthusiastically for her than for any other circus performer.

1. In sentences 1 and 2 find the adverbs of time.

2. In sentence 3 what is the coordinating conjunction? What two words does it connect?

3. In sentence 4 what is the adverb of manner?

4. In sentence 5 what are the two adverbs of place?

5. Name the two adverbs in sentence 6. What kind is each?

6. Name the adverb of place in sentence 7.

7. Name the two adverbs of time in sentence 8.

8. Name the two adverbs in sentence 9. What kind is each?

9. Find the adverb that compares in the paragraph.

Punctuation and Capitalization

End Punctuation

End punctuation helps make writing clear. It indicates where one sentence ends and the next one begins.

- A declarative sentence makes a statement. Use a period at the end of a declarative sentence.

  Michael Jordan played basketball.

- An imperative sentence gives a command. Use a period at the end of an imperative sentence.

  Throw the ball to me.

- An interrogative sentence asks a question. Use a question mark at the end of an interrogative sentence.

  Did she make the basket?

- An exclamatory sentence expresses strong or sudden feeling or emotion. Use an exclamation point at the end of an exclamatory sentence.

  What a shot he just made!

Which punctuation mark goes at the end of this sentence?

  There are five players on a
  basketball team

You are right if you said a period. The sentence, which makes a statement, is a declarative sentence. It must end with a period.

Exercise 1

Tell whether each sentence makes a statement, gives a command, asks a question, or expresses a strong feeling or emotion. Use the end punctuation as a clue.

1. James Naismith invented basketball.

2. Let's give three cheers for James Naismith!

3. Why did he invent the game?

4. He wanted a game that could be played indoors during winter.

5. Tell us how he did it.

Exercise 2

Rewrite these sentences, using the correct end punctuation.

1. Naismith used a soccer ball and put up two peach baskets for hoops

2. That was clever

3. Please, don't stop telling the story of James Naismith

4. When did he invent basketball

5. He invented it in 1891

6. What a great game basketball is

Practice Power

Tell about a sport you have played or seen. Write four sentences, one of each type. Be sure to use the three kinds of end punctuation.

Examples: The Tour de France takes place every summer.
Where is it held?
Look at that bike.
Wow, it's amazing!

Capital Letters

A sentence begins with a **capital letter.**

Some words always begin with a capital letter.

- The first word in a sentence

- Names of people and pets

Jane **G**oodall	**B**enjamin **F**ranklin
Aunt **M**ary	**R**ex
General **A**nderson	**K**oko

- Names of streets, cities, states, and countries

Market **S**treet	**P**ennsylvania
Philadelphia	**C**anada

- Names of days, months, and holidays

Thursday	**A**ugust	**C**olumbus **D**ay

- The personal pronoun *I*

Which word group needs capital letters?

A. a day at the beach

B. thanksgiving day in new york city

C. brunch with the family

You are right if you said B. *Thanksgiving Day* and *New York City* need capital letters. These word groups name a specific holiday and a specific city.

Exercise 1

Tell why each word or word group needs one or more capital letters.

1. Janice
2. September
3. Carroll Avenue
4. Valentine's Day
5. Tuesday
6. Moscow
7. Oregon
8. Nigeria
9. New Year's Day
10. my cat, Buttercup

Exercise 2

Rewrite each sentence, adding capital letters where they are needed.

1. the first monday in september is labor day.
2. canadians celebrate thanksgiving in October.
3. my family and i once celebrated pioneer day with relatives in utah.
4. we learned that flag day is in june.
5. in japan children's day is celebrated on may 5.
6. a marathon race is held in boston on patriot's day.
7. My cousin ed ran in the marathon last april.
8. in vietnam tet, the holiday that marks the start of a new year, is celebrated in late january or early february.

Practice Power

Write a few sentences about what you and your family members do on holidays. Use capital letters correctly.

Titles of Works

There are special rules for writing the titles of books, poems, and other published works.

- Each important word in the title begins with a capital letter.

- The first word and the last word of a title always begin with a capital letter.

- Some short words, such as *of, to, for, a, an,* and *the,* are not capitalized unless they are the first or last word in the title. Verbs such as *is* and pronouns such as *it* are capitalized.

- Titles of books and magazines are italicized when they are typed and underlined when they are handwritten.

- Titles of poems, stories, and magazine articles have quotation marks around them.

Book: *Super Fudge* (or <u>Super Fudge</u>) by Judy Blume
Magazine: *National Geographic for Kids* (or <u>National Geographic for Kids</u>)
Poem: "The Pickety Fence" by David McCord
Short Story: "The Happy Prince" by Oscar Wilde
Article: "Explore the Fantastic Forest!" by Peter Mandel

Which of these is a poem? How do you know?

A. *Abel's Island* by William Steig
B. *Saffy's Angel* by Hilary McKay
C. "Until I Saw the Sea" by Lilian Moore

You are right if you said C. The title of a poem has quotation marks around it.

Exercise 1

Tell whether each is the title of a book or a poem.

1. *Ginger Pye* by Eleanor Estes

2. "Fog" by Carl Sandburg

3. *How to Eat Fried Worms* by Thomas Rockwell

4. "Paul Revere's Ride" by Henry Wadsworth Longfellow

5. *Amber Brown Wants Extra Credit* by Paula Danzinger

6. "The Lesson for Tonight" by John Ciardi

Exercise 2

Write each of these titles correctly.

1. clarence by Shel Silverstein (poem)

2. scary sharks by Ruth Musgrave (article)

3. best school year ever by Barbara Robinson (book)

4. the further adventures of toad by Kenneth Grahame (story)

5. every time i climb a tree by David McCord (poem)

6. miracles on maple hill by Virginia Sorensen (book)

Practice Power

Make a list of some books and poems you have read. Remember to underline book titles and put quotation marks around poem titles. Be sure to capitalize all important words.

Examples: <u>Pippi Longstocking</u> by Astrid Lindgren
"Flies" by Ogden Nash

Abbreviations

A short form of a word is called an **abbreviation.**
Abbreviations usually end with periods.

Days of the Week

Sunday—Sun.	Thursday—Thurs.
Monday—Mon.	Friday—Fri.
Tuesday—Tues.	Saturday—Sat.
Wednesday—Wed.	

Months of the Year

January—Jan.	September—Sept.
February—Feb.	October—Oct.
March—Mar.	November—Nov.
April—Apr.	December—Dec.
August—Aug.	

May, June, and *July* are not abbreviated.

Addresses

Street—St.	Avenue—Ave.	North—N.	East—E.

Units of Measure

inch—in.	pint—pt.	bushel—bu.
yard—yd.	ounce—oz.	mile—mi.

Abbreviations for units of measure do not begin with
capital letters. Periods are not used in metric measures.

liter—l	kilometer—km	centimeter—cm

Postal Abbreviations for States

Alaska—AK	Kentucky—KY

Postal abbreviations have two capital letters and no
periods.

Exercise 1

Write the word each of these abbreviations stands for.
Use a dictionary or other reference book if you need help.

1. Wed.

2. l

3. Blvd.

4. S.

5. Jan.

6. IL

7. km

8. qt.

9. Apr.

10. Ave.

11. E.

12. CA

Exercise 2

Rewrite each word group, using the abbreviation for each word in italics.

1. *South* Third *Avenue*

2. one *pint* of ice cream

3. Miami, *Florida*

4. *Thursday, April* 15

5. a *yard* of cloth

6. one *liter* of soda

7. *North* Front *Street*

8. Austin, *Texas*

9. Peterson *Boulevard*

10. *Friday, February* 10

Practice Power

Look for abbreviations in things you read over the next few days. Write them down and report back to the class. Are all of them correct? Check in a dictionary if you are not sure what an abbreviation stands for.

Personal Titles

Titles such as *Mr., Mrs., Ms., Dr., Sgt.,* and *Gov.* are abbreviations that go in front of people's names. Each one begins with a capital letter and ends with a period.

Mr. Mark Holzer	Dr. Mary Carter
Mrs. Juanita Cruz	Sgt. Phil Harmon
Ms. Fern Beamon	Gov. Ron Adams

A person may use an initial in place of a name. An initial is a capital letter followed by a period.

John F. Kennedy	J. R. R. Tolkien
Robert E. Lee	J. K. Rowling

Some countries and organizations occasionally use initials in place of a name. The initials are usually followed by periods.

U.S.A.	United States of America
B.S.A.	Boy Scouts of America

Which name is not written correctly?

A. Doctor Susan O'Malley

B. Dr. S O'Malley

C. Dr. S. O'Malley

You are right if you said B. A period is needed after the initial *S.*

Exercise 1
Rewrite these names, using periods and capital letters where needed.

1. dr simon a cook

2. cpl sue t marks

3. mrs susan k pruess

4. mr h r ruiz

5. pres w wayne noble

6. dr jill m greef

7. ms lily k wisdom

Exercise 2
Rewrite these sentences. Use the correct initials for the italicized words.

1. John *Fitzgerald* Kennedy was the 35th *United States* president.

2. *Phineus Taylor* Barnum ran a circus.

3. William *Dickson* Boyce was the founder of the *Boy Scouts of America.*

4. *Elwyn Brooks* White wrote about a pig and a spider.

5. *Clive Staples* Lewis wrote fables and fairy tales for children.

Practice Power

Think of people you know about who use initials in their names. Write four names, using initials, and tell who the people are.

Commas

A **comma** is used to separate words and groups of words so that they are easier to read and understand.

A comma is used

- before *and, or,* or *but* to separate two sentences joined into a compound sentence

  Petra raised her hand, but Tim shouted the answer.

- to separate words in a series

  Ana, Christopher, and Barton raised their hands.

- in direct address, to separate the name of the person spoken to from the rest of the sentence

  Kate, please hand in your paper.

- after the word *yes* or *no* when it introduces a sentence

  Yes, you are correct.

Which sentence does not use commas correctly?

  A. Carmelo, have you been to Chicago?
  B. Jenny went to Boston but she had wanted to go to Florida.
  C. We visited Atlanta, Detroit, and Seattle.

You are right if you said B. A comma is missing before *but* to separate the two parts of this compound sentence.

Exercise 1

Rewrite these sentences, adding commas where needed.

1. For a long time the family had wanted to go to England and they planned their trip carefully.

2. Yes she packed an umbrella a raincoat and a waterproof hat.

3. No she didn't forget her boots.

4. Louisa we want to visit London Oxford and Cambridge.

5. The tourists visited Big Ben Buckingham Palace and Windsor Castle.

6. We tried to visit the British Museum but it was closed.

7. The restaurant served tea scones and a variety of jams.

8. Yes a scone is somewhat like a biscuit with raisins in it.

9. Brenda are you still hungry?

Exercise 2

Rewrite the sentences so that they use commas correctly.

1. We did not have good weather but we still had a good time.

2. We had fog, rain and sleet, on the same day.

3. We traveled by taxi bus, and boat.

4. Yes a highlight of the trip was taking the London Eye.

5. It is like a giant Ferris wheel but its cars are big glass booths.

Practice Power

Write about a trip you took. Tell about places you visited, what you did and saw, and what you ate. Use commas correctly.

Apostrophes

An **apostrophe** is used

- to form the possessive of a noun

  The room belongs to Tim.
  It is *Tim's* room. (possessive noun)

  Adding an apostrophe and the letter *s* to the name *Tim* shows that the room is his.

- to show that one or more letters are left out of a contraction

  Melvin will not clean his room.
  Melvin *won't* clean his room.

  Common contractions are *isn't, aren't, wasn't, weren't, doesn't, didn't, can't, won't,* and *I'll.*

Which sentence uses an apostrophe to show possession? How are the other apostrophes used?

  A. Sandy's room is messy.
  B. She couldn't find her shoes.
  C. She doesn't know where to look.

You are right if you said A. The apostrophe and -*s* added to the name *Sandy* shows that the room belongs to her. Both B and C use apostrophes in contractions.

Exercise 1

Tell whether the apostrophe in each sentence shows possession or helps make a contraction.

1. Larry's brother sleeps on the top bunk.

2. His brother didn't make his bed.

3. Please don't leave dirty socks on the floor.

4. All the toys and rumpled clothes are under Dillon's bed.

5. Doesn't my room look nice?

Exercise 2

Rewrite the sentences, adding apostrophes where they are needed.

1. Lets rearrange our bedroom.

2. Well need help to move the furniture.

3. Sams desk should go here.

4. I dont want my computer over there.

5. Please be careful with the hamsters cage.

6. I cant move the heavy bookcase.

7. Dads old globe looks good on the desk.

8. Im also going to clean my closet.

Practice Power

Write five sentences about how you might rearrange your classroom or another room in the school building. Use a word with an apostrophe in each sentence.

Addresses

Capital letters and commas are used in writing addresses. An address is written like this:

> Name
> Street Address, Apartment or Unit Number
> City, State Abbreviation ZIP Code

In an address capitalize the first letter of every title, word, and abbreviation. Capitalize both letters of a state's postal abbreviation.

> Dr. Charles Turner
> 1312 E. Main St., Apt. 2
> Gatesville, TX 76528

If there is an apartment or a floor number, it is separated from the street address by a comma. A comma always separates the names of the city and the state, but there is never a comma between the state abbreviation and the ZIP Code.

Is this address written correctly?

> Jamie Jones
> 6700 N. Arrowhead Drive, Apt. 12
> Urbana, IL 61820

You are right if you said yes. The first letter of each word is capitalized. Both letters of the postal abbreviation are capitalized. Commas are used between the street address and the unit number and between the city and the state names.

Exercise 1

Rewrite each address, using capital letters where needed.

mr. tom gannon
100 vahalla st., apt. 6A
cordale, ga 31015

mrs. becky ritter
10 n. cherry blvd.
towanda, pa 18848

Exercise 2

Rewrite each address, using commas and capital letters where needed.

mr. antonio p. rodriguez
5500 reflections blvd.
lutz fl 33558

dr. shelly klickstein
10 e. jackman ave. apt. 3
Benton ak 72015

Practice Power

Pretend you have written a letter to a friend. Draw an envelope. Write your name and address in the upper left corner for the return address. Write your friend's name and address for the mailing address.

Direct Quotations

A **direct quotation** contains the exact words a person says. Quotation marks are used before and after the words of a speaker. A comma is used to set off what is said from the rest of the sentence.

Comma	Direct Quotation

Lucy said, "I know some interesting facts about Russia."

Direct Quotation	Comma

"Please tell us something about Russia," requested Louis.

The name of the person speaking can go in the middle of a direct quotation. Two sets of quotation marks and two commas set off a divided quotation.

"The capital of Russia," remarked Terry, "is Moscow."

Which sentence tells Lucy's exact words?

A. Lucy said that Russia is the largest country.
B. Lucy said, "Russia is the largest country."
C. Lucy says her grandparents miss Russia.

You are right if you said sentence B. This sentence includes a direct quotation. Lucy's exact words are inside the quotation marks. A comma sets off what she said from the rest of the sentence.

Exercise 1

Rewrite each sentence. Use a comma to separate what is said from the rest of the sentence.

1. Mr. Thompson said "More than a hundred languages and dialects are spoken in Russia."

2. "Russian, however, is the official language" he added.

3. Susie exclaimed "That's a great many languages!"

4. Chris asked "Does anyone speak most of the languages?"

5. "That's an interesting question" Mr. Thompson replied.

Exercise 2

Rewrite each sentence. Put quotation marks around the exact words of the speaker.

1. Some students in our school come from Russia, said Mr. Thompson.

2. He asked, Mikhail, will you tell the class about Russia?

3. The summer months are beautiful, Mikhail said.

4. Tina exclaimed, I thought it was freezing in Russia!

5. Many places here can be just as cold, said Mikhail.

6. The daylight in summer, he continued, lasts a long time.

Practice Power

Pretend you are having a conversation with someone from another country. Write four sentences that contain that person's exact words. Use commas and quotation marks correctly.

Section 7 Review

Correct punctuation and capitalization help make sentences clear.

Periods
- end sentences that make statements or give commands
- are used with most abbreviations

Question Marks
- end sentences that ask questions

Exclamation Points
- end sentences that express strong or sudden feeling

Commas
- are used before *but, or,* or *and* in a compound sentence
- separate words in a series
- are used in direct address
- are used after *yes* or *no* at the start of a sentence
- set off a direct quotation

Apostrophes
- are used in possessive nouns
- mark where a letter is missing in a contraction

Capitalize
- the first word in a sentence and in a direct quotation
- initials in names
- the pronoun *I*
- most words in titles of published works

Exercise 1

Tell whether each sentence uses correct punctuation and capitalization. If a sentence is incorrect, rewrite it correctly.

1. Who wrote *the wizard of oz.*

2. I cant remember.

3. L. Frank Baum is the author.

4. Robert E Lee was a general.

5. "yes I knew that" said Colleen.

6. The label read 3 qt. 9 oz.

7. M. A. Jackson lives at 212 W 83rd St.

8. Kieran please share your notes.

Exercise 2

Rewrite each sentence, using correct punctuation and capitalization.

1. did you know that a a milne wrote *winnie the pooh*

2. c s lewis wrote these three children's books: prince caspian the silver chair and the last battle

3. clarissa i love that book

4. youll read it soon in school

5. tomas take this package to 321 main street said Mr. Jones

6. is that an apartment a condominium or a house tomas asked

7. thats my cousins house, said eli.

8. what an amazing coincidence said tomas

Practice Power

Write a few sentences about one of your favorite books. Use punctuation and capitalization correctly.

Section 7 Challenge

Read the paragraph and answer the questions.

1. It was Monday afternoon at Jefferson Elementary School. 2. Jerry listened carefully as their guest speaker, Mr. Mark Gray, told the class about birds of prey. 3. "Birds of prey come in all shapes and sizes," the speaker said. 4. "They're amazing creatures." 5. Jerry discovered that birds of prey include falcons, hawks, eagles, and vultures.

6. "Mr. Gray, are owls also birds of prey?" Jerry asked.

7. "Yes, they are," Mr. Gray answered.

8. Jerry then learned that owls are the only birds of prey that hunt primarily at night. 9. He was amazed that the wingspan of some birds of prey is almost ten feet. 10. Did you know that birds of prey have three eyelids? 11. Yes, Jerry and his class learned a great deal about those magnificent birds.

1. In sentence 1 why do *Monday* and *Jefferson Elementary School* begin with capital letters?

2. What kind of sentence is sentence 2?

3. In sentence 3 why are quotation marks used?

4. In sentence 4 why is an apostrophe used?

5. In sentence 5 why are commas used?

6. In sentence 6 name a noun in direct address.

7. In sentence 7 what are the exact words of Mr. Gray?

8. In sentence 7 why is a comma used after the word *are*?

9. What kind of sentence is sentence 10?

10. In sentence 11 why is the comma used?

SECTION 8

Diagramming

Subjects, Verbs, and Direct Objects

A **diagram** is a drawing that shows how the parts of a sentence are related. The most important parts of a sentence are the subject and the predicate. The simple subject of a sentence is a noun or a pronoun. The simple predicate is a verb. The direct object is the noun or pronoun that completes the action of the verb.

A sentence with a simple subject, a simple predicate, and a direct object is diagrammed in this way.

subject	verb	direct object

Let's do an example: **Monkeys climb trees.**

1. Draw a horizontal line.
2. Write the predicate—the verb *climb*—on the line.
3. Think: *Who or what climbs? Monkeys* is the subject. Write *Monkeys* on the line in front of *climb*.
4. Draw a vertical line to separate the subject and the predicate. This vertical line goes through the horizontal line.

5. Next think: *Monkeys climb what? Trees* is the answer. It is the direct object. Write *trees* on the line after *climb*. Draw a vertical line to separate the predicate and direct object but do not draw it through the horizontal line.

| Monkeys | climb | trees |

Exercise 1

Complete each diagram with a direct object. Choose from these direct objects.

| milk | oatmeal |

1. | Cows | give |

2. | Janet | dislikes |

Exercise 2

Diagram each sentence.

1. We played checkers.
2. Yolanda delivers newspapers.
3. Octopuses squirt ink.
4. Kris wears sunglasses.
5. Pioneers built cabins.

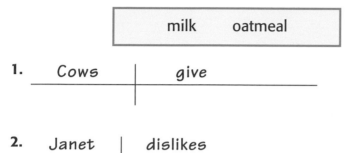

Practice Power

Write three sentences about people you know and what they do. Use a subject, a predicate, and a direct object. Diagram each sentence.

Example: Amy writes poems.

Possessives and Adjectives

A possessive noun shows who possesses, or owns, something. Possessive nouns end in *-'s* or just in an apostrophe: the *baby's* toy, the *babies'* toys. The noun that follows a possessive noun names the thing that is owned.

In a sentence diagram a possessive noun is placed on a slanted line under the noun it goes with.

Let's do an example: **Kate's horse trots.**

1. Write the predicate *trots* and the simple subject *horse* on the line with a vertical line between them.

2. Think: *Who owns the horse?* Kate owns the horse. It is Kate's horse. Write *Kate's* on a slanted line under *horse*.

An **adjective** describes a noun. An adjective can tell how much or how many. The articles *a, an, the*—which point out nouns—are also adjectives. In a diagram an adjective is placed on a slanted line under the noun it goes with.

Let's do an example: **Wild horses gallop.**

1. Write the predicate *gallop* and the subject *horses* on the line with a vertical line between them.

2. Think: *What kind of horses gallop? Wild* is an adjective that tells more about horses. Write *wild* on a slanted line under *horses.*

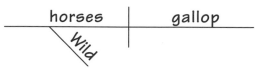

Exercise 1
Complete each diagram with the possessive or adjective given.

1. Tanya's

balloon	popped

2. Red

Exercise 2
Diagram each sentence.

1. Sam's bike broke.

2. Busy bees buzz.

3. Ralph likes warm pretzels.

4. Andrea's act received loud applause.

5. A frog eats insects.

Practice Power

Write two sentences with possessive nouns and two with adjectives. Then diagram them.

Example: Shirley's dog has black spots.

Adjective Complements

A subject complement comes after a linking verb. Some linking verbs are *is, are, was,* and *were.* An adjective can be a subject complement. An adjective used as a subject complement describes the subject of the sentence.

In a diagram an adjective used as a subject complement is positioned on the horizontal line to the right of the verb. A slanted line that points back to the subject separates the verb and the subject complement.

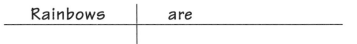

subject | verb \ subject complement

Let's do an example: **Rainbows are colorful.**

1. Write the linking verb and the subject on the horizontal line.

Rainbows | are

2. Think: *What are rainbows?* Rainbows are *colorful. Colorful* is an adjective that tells more about the subject, *rainbows.* Draw a slanted line that points back to *rainbows* after the verb *are.* Write *colorful* on the line after the verb.

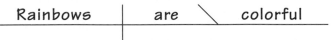

Rainbows | are \ colorful

Exercise 1

Copy each diagram. Finish it by adding the adjective provided as a subject complement.

1. sandy

Beaches	are

2. fluffy

Clouds	are

Exercise 2

Diagram each sentence.

1. Mountains are beautiful.
2. Hikes are enjoyable.
3. The path is steep.
4. The trails were rocky.
5. Shauna was weary.
6. The fire was warm.
7. The stars are bright.
8. This cocoa is delicious.

Practice Power

Write two sentences about an interesting place. Use adjectives as subject complements to describe the place. Diagram each sentence.

Examples: New York City is lively.
The streets are noisy.

Noun Complements

A noun can be a subject complement. A noun used as a subject complement follows a linking verb—such as *is, are, was,* and *were*—and renames the subject.

In a diagram a noun used as a subject complement is placed on the horizontal line to the right of the predicate. Just as with an adjective used as a subject complement, a slanted line after the verb points back to the subject. The noun is written to the right of the slanted line.

subject	predicate \ subject complement

Let's do an example: **Lassie is a dog.**

1. Write the linking verb and the subject on the horizontal line.

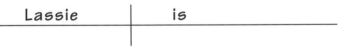

Lassie	is

2. Think: *What is Lassie?* Lassie is a *dog. Dog* is a noun that renames the subject *Lassie.* Draw a slanted line that points back to *Lassie* after the verb *is.* Write *dog* on the horizontal line after the linking verb. The article *a* is an adjective that goes with the noun *dog* and therefore is positioned on a slanted line under *dog.*

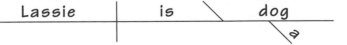

Exercise 1

Copy each diagram. Finish it by adding the noun provided as a subject complement.

1. fruit

   | Oranges | are |

2. gems

   | Diamonds | are |

Exercise 2

Diagram each sentence.

1. Whales are mammals.
2. The trees were cypresses.
3. Mom's specialty is cornbread.
4. The supermarket was a busy place.
5. A submarine is a sandwich.

Practice Power

Write three sentences about people or animals you know. Use a noun as a subject complement to tell more about each person or animal. Diagram each sentence.

Example: Javier is a teammate.

Tip is Grandpa's dog.

Adverbs

An adverb tells more about a verb. An adverb tells *when, how often, where,* or *how.* Add an adverb to a diagram by writing it on a slanted line under the verb that it tells more about.

Let's do an example: **Jess walked quickly.**

1. Write the predicate and the subject on the line.

   | Jess | walked |

2. Think: *How did Jess walk?* The answer is *quickly. Quickly* is an adverb that tells how about the verb *walked.* Write *quickly* on a slanted line under *walked.*

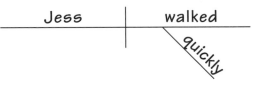

Here is another example. Can you tell how each word is used? Is it the subject, verb, or direct object? Is it an adjective, an adverb, or a possessive noun?

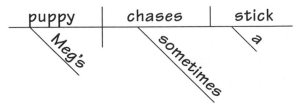

Exercise 1

Copy each diagram. Finish it by adding the adverb given.

1. badly

2. often

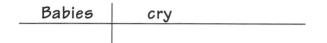

Exercise 2

Diagram each sentence.

1. The flowers wilted quickly.

2. I often eat raspberries.

3. The North Star shines brightly.

4. The turtle crawled inside.

5. Julie cautiously petted the horse.

Practice Power

Write four sentences about what people do on weekends. Use an adverb to tell where, when, how often, or how they do what they do. Diagram each sentence.

Examples: **People sleep late.**
We eat dinner early.
We sometimes play basketball.
We play aggressively.

Compounds: Part I

A sentence may have more than one subject. A sentence may also have more than one predicate. These are called compound subjects and compound predicates. In a diagram they are placed on separate parallel lines that are connected by a dashed line for the conjunction.

Let's do an example: **Airplanes and helicopters fly.** (compound subject)

1. Draw two short, parallel horizontal lines. Write a subject on each line.

2. Connect the subjects as shown. Write the conjunction *and* on the dashed line. Complete the diagram.

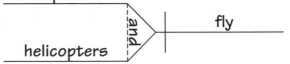

Let's do an example: **She smiled and waved.** (compound predicate)

1. Draw a short horizontal line. Write the subject on the line.

2. Draw a vertical line to separate the subject from the predicate. Draw two short, parallel horizontal lines, one for each verb.

3. Connect the lines as shown. Write the conjunction *and* on the dashed line.

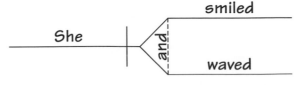

Exercise 1

Copy each diagram. Finish it by adding the compound subject or predicate given.

1. Catchers and pitchers

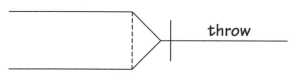

2. float and bob

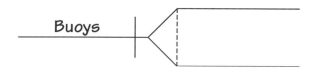

Exercise 2

Diagram each sentence.

1. T. J. swims and bikes.

2. Sarah and I swim.

3. Carrots and pretzels crunch.

4. Carlos and Ann swept and dusted.

5. Lewis and Clark were explorers.

Practice Power

Write four sentences, two with compound subjects and two with compound predicates. Diagram your sentences.

Examples: The players and the coaches arrived.
The crowd stood and cheered.

Compounds: Part II

A sentence may have more than one direct object. A direct object completes the action of the verb. To find the direct object or direct objects in a sentence, ask *whom* or *what* after the verb. In a diagram a compound direct object is placed on parallel horizontal lines connected by a dashed line for the conjunction.

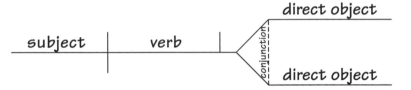

Let's do an example: **We cooked eggs and pancakes.**

1. Write the verb and the subject on the line with a vertical line between them.

2. Think: *What did we cook?* The answer is *eggs* and *pancakes.* The two nouns form a compound direct object. Write *eggs* and *pancakes* on two short, parallel horizontal lines after the verb *cooked.* Put the conjunction *and* on a dashed line between the nouns. Insert a vertical line between the verb and the compound direct object.

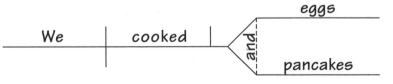

Exercise 1

Copy the diagram. Finish it by adding the compound direct object given.

tulips and daffodils

Exercise 2

Diagram each sentence.

1. Bob likes soccer and basketball.
2. I often eat pizza or spaghetti.
3. The acrobats juggled balls and rings.
4. Lilian wore jeans and a T-shirt.
5. Jacob plays the guitar and the piano.
6. We study math and science.
7. Mom bought apples and grapes.
8. My sister writes stories and poems.

Practice Power

Complete these sentences with compound direct objects. Then diagram the sentences.

Examples: I like reading and painting.
I often eat . . .
I usually wear . . .
I play . . .

Compounds: Part III

A sentence may have more than one noun used as a subject complement. In a diagram a compound subject complement is placed on parallel, horizontal lines connected by a dashed line for the conjunction.

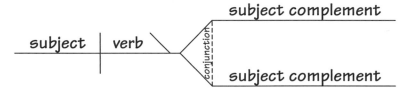

Let's do an example: **Popular sports are baseball and football.**

1. Write the linking verb and the subject on the line.

2. Think: *What are popular sports?* The answer is *baseball* and *football*. The nouns form a compound complement that renames the subject *sports*. Draw a slanted line that points back to the subject after the linking verb. Then draw two parallel horizontal lines after the predicate *are*. Write *baseball* and *football* on the lines and connect them with a dashed line on which to write the conjunction *and. Popular* is an adjective that describes *sports.* Put *popular* on a slanted line under the noun.

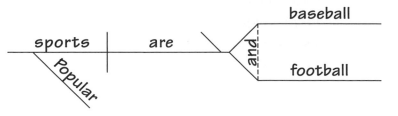

Exercise 1

Copy the diagram. Finish it by adding the nouns given as a compound subject complement.

dancers and singers

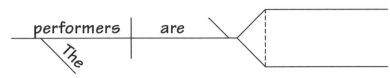

Exercise 2

Diagram each sentence.

1. The main characters are a frog and a toad.

2. The topic is birds or flowers.

3. The partners are Jason and Alex.

4. The books are mysteries and biographies.

5. Tomie de Paola is an author and an illustrator.

6. My cousins are skaters and skiers.

7. Jenna's pets are a frog and some fish.

8. Her gifts were a sweater and a scarf.

Practice Power

Complete these sentences with compound noun complements. Diagram them.

Examples: Students' favorite foods are pizza and hot dogs.

Popular games are . . .

Two good writers are . . .

My good friends are . . .

Compounds: Part IV

A sentence may have more than one adjective used as a subject complement. In a diagram a compound adjective complement is placed on parallel horizontal lines connected by a dashed line for the conjunction.

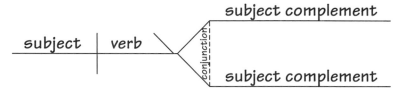

Let's do an example: **Cheetahs are sleek and fast.**

1. Diagram the subject and the linking verb.

2. Think: *What are cheetahs?* Cheetahs are *sleek* and *fast*. *Sleek* and *fast* are adjective complements that describe the subject *cheetahs*. Draw a slanted line that points back to the subject *cheetahs*. Then draw a line for each adjective as shown. Connect these lines with a dashed line for the conjunction *and*.

Exercise 1

Copy the diagram. Finish it by adding the adjectives given as a compound subject complement.

sugary and sweet

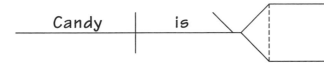

Exercise 2

Diagram each sentence.

1. Elephants are big but gentle.

2. The soup was hot and salty.

3. The cave was dark and gloomy.

4. Frogs' skin is green or brown.

5. The gems were small but expensive.

6. The sky was gray and cloudy.

7. The bonfire was warm and colorful.

8. Paul's kitten is cute and curious.

Practice Power

Write two sentences about a vacation. Use a compound adjective complement in each sentence. Then diagram each sentence.

Examples: Our vacation was long and enjoyable.
The weather was cold and snowy.

Compound Sentences

A compound sentence consists of two smaller sentences. A compound sentence is diagrammed as two independent simple sentences, with each sentence on a separate horizontal line, one above the other. The lines are connected by a dashed line for the conjunction *and, or,* or *but.*

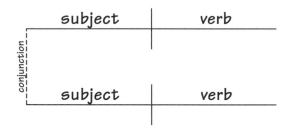

Let's do an example: **Callie sleeps late, but Colin wakes early.**

1. Diagram each simple sentence on a horizontal line. Put one horizontal line above the other. Be sure to place each adverb under the appropriate verb.

2. Draw a dashed line to connect the sentences. Write the conjunction *but* on the dashed line.

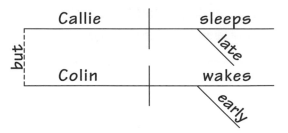

Exercise 1

Copy the diagram. Finish it by adding the sentence given. Use the conjunction _but_.

Veronica watches TV.

Exercise 2

Diagram each sentence.

1. Simon is happy, but Sherry is sad.

2. Temperatures soared, and we went outside.

3. I play the guitar, but I rarely practice.

4. Kara finished the book, and she then wrote a report.

5. A chameleon is a lizard, and it changes color.

6. Tom was excited, but Leo was bored.

7. Mom cleaned the garage, and Dad washed the car.

8. Carrie made hamburgers, and we ate outdoors.

Practice Power

Write two compound sentences. Exchange your sentences with a partner. Diagram each other's sentences.

Diagramming Practice

You have learned to diagram sentences that have compound parts. Can you match the correct diagram with each of these sentences? The diagrams do not include describing words.

1. Mira had a cold, and she ate hot soup.
2. Homemade soup is delicious and healthful.
3. Martha and Mary make good pies.

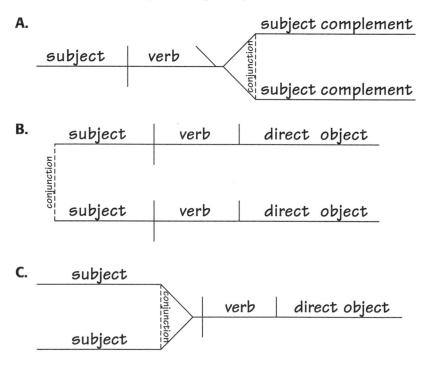

A.

subject | verb
subject complement
conjunction
subject complement

B.

subject | verb | direct object
conjunction
subject | verb | direct object

C.

subject
conjunction
subject
verb | direct object

You are right if you matched sentence 1 with B, sentence 2 with A, and sentence 3 with C.

Exercise 1

Match each sentence with one of the diagrams on page 502— A, B, or C.

1. Louis and Thomas feed the hamsters.
2. Dogs are friendly and affectionate.
3. We wanted snow, but we got rain.
4. The supermarket was busy and crowded.
5. Edison and Frank collect coins.

Exercise 2

Diagram each sentence. Be careful. Some of the sentences do not fit in the diagrams on page 502.

1. Jane peeled potatoes and cucumbers.
2. Dogs and cats are good pets.
3. The happy fans clapped and cheered.
4. The robot mopped the floor, and it made supper.
5. Zebras' stripes are black and white.
6. The children ate cookies and drank lemonade.
7. My new skateboard is red and black.
8. Actors and actresses learn their parts.

Practice Power

Write three sentences about food and meals. Diagram each sentence.

Examples: **Dori likes chocolate, but I like vanilla.**
Donuts are sweet.

Diagramming Challenge

Study the diagram and answer the questions.

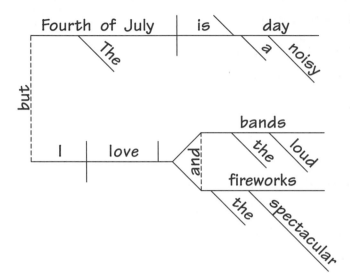

1. Is this a simple or a compound sentence?

2. What are the subjects? What are the predicates?

3. What compound sentence part is there?

4. What are the adjectives and articles? What noun does each describe or point out?

5. What is the subject complement? How do you know?

6. What are the direct objects? How do you know?

7. Write out the sentence.

504

Grammar and Mechanics Handbook

Grammar

ADJECTIVES

An adjective points out or describes a noun.

Adjectives That Compare

Adjectives can be used to make comparisons. To compare two people, places, or things, *-er* is often added to an adjective. To compare three or more people, places, or things, *-est* is often added to an adjective.

> A horse is *taller* than a deer.
> A moose is *bigger* than a horse.
> An elephant is the *largest* land animal.

Some adjectives that compare have special forms.

> Vanilla ice cream is *good*.
> Strawberry ice cream is *better* than vanilla.
> Chocolate ice cream is the *best* flavor of all.

> The baby had a *bad* cold on Sunday.
> The cold was *worse* on Monday.
> It was the *worst* cold she'd ever had.

Some adjectives that compare use *more* and *most*. *More* and *most* are used with adjectives of three or more syllables and with some adjectives of two syllables.

> Carla is a *more careful* worker than Luis.
> Marta is the *most intelligent* student in class.

The comparison adjectives *fewer* and *fewest* are used with plural count nouns. The comparison adjectives *less* and *least* are used with noncount nouns.

> I have *fewer* pencils than Jody does.
> I have *less* paper too.
> Mark has the *fewest* pens.
> Carmen has the *least* chalk.

Adjectives That Tell How Many

Some adjectives tell how many or about how many.

> Only *six* members came to the meeting.
> A *few* members were sick.

Some adjectives tell numerical order.

> I finished reading the *sixth* chapter.

Articles

Articles point out nouns. *The, a,* and *an* are articles. *The* is the definite article. It points out a specific person, place, or thing. *A* and *an* are indefinite articles. They point out any one of a group of people, places, or things. Use *a* before a consonant sound and *an* before a vowel sound.

> *The* man ate *a* peach and *an* apple.

Demonstrative Adjectives

Demonstrative adjectives point out or tell about a specific person, place, or thing. The demonstrative adjectives are *this, that, these,* and *those.*

Singular	Plural
this flower	*these* bushes
that flower	*those* bushes

This and *these* point out things or persons that are near. *That* and *those* point out things or persons that are farther away.

> *This* flower is red. (singular and near)
> *Those* bushes are tall. (plural and far)

Descriptive Adjectives

A descriptive adjective tells more about a noun. It can tell how something looks, tastes, sounds, feels, or smells. It can tell about size, number, color, shape, or weight.

A descriptive adjective often comes before the noun it describes.

> A *tall* tree stood near the *red* barn.

A descriptive adjective can follow a linking verb as a subject complement. It describes the subject of the sentence.

> The tree near the red barn was *tall*.

Possessive Adjectives

A possessive adjective shows who or what owns something. A possessive adjective is used before a noun. The possessive adjectives are *my, your, his, her, its, our,* and *their.*

> I have *my* camera, and Lucy has *her* phone.

Proper Adjectives

Proper adjectives are formed from proper nouns. A proper adjective always begins with a capital letter.

> When we went to China, I ate *Chinese* food.

ADVERBS

An adverb tells more about a verb. Many adverbs end in *-ly.*

An adverb of time tells when or how often an action takes place.

> I went to the mall *yesterday*.
> I *sometimes* go to the toy store.

An adverb of place tells where an action takes place.

> I went *outside* after dinner.
> I played *there* until it was dark.

An adverb of manner tells how an action takes place.

> My new skateboard goes *fast*.
> I ride it *gracefully*.

Adverbs That Compare

An adverb can compare the actions of two or more persons or things. To compare the actions of two persons or things,

-er is often added to an adverb. To compare the actions of three or more persons or things, *-est* is often added to an adverb.

> Sam went to bed *later* than Henry.
> Luke went to bed *latest* of us all.

Some adverbs that compare use *more* and *most.* Use *more* and *most* with adverbs ending in *-ly* and with adverbs of three or more syllables.

> Sam answered *more sleepily* than Henry.
> Luke answered *most sleepily* of us all.

Negatives

Some adverbs form negative ideas. Use *not, n't* for *not* in a contraction, or *never* to express a negative idea. Do not use more than one negative word in a sentence.

> He will *not* be ready on time.
> He *can't* find his sneakers.
> He *never* remembers where he left them.

ANTECEDENTS

The noun to which a pronoun refers is its antecedent. A pronoun must agree with its antecedent in person and number. The pronouns *he, him,* and *his* refer to male antecedents. The pronouns *she, her,* and *hers* refer to female antecedents. The pronouns *it* and *its* refer to animals or things.

CONTRACTIONS

A contraction is a short way to write some words. An apostrophe (') is used to show where one or more letters have been left out of a word.

Many contractions are formed with the word *not*.

do not = don't
cannot = can't
was not = wasn't
will not = won't

Many contractions are formed with personal pronouns.

I am = I'm
you are = you're
he is = he's
we have = we've

COORDINATING CONJUNCTIONS

A coordinating conjunction joins two words or groups of words that are similar. The words *and, but,* and *or* are coordinating conjunctions.

My dad *and* I went to the pool.
I can swim *but* not dive.
The pool is never too hot *or* crowded.

DIRECT OBJECTS

The direct object in a sentence is the noun or pronoun that receives the action of the verb. To find the direct object, ask whom or what after the verb. Two or more direct objects joined by *and* or *or* form a compound direct object.

My mom made *pasta* and *salad.*
I helped *her.*

NOUNS

A noun is a word that names a person, a place, or a thing. See NUMBER.

Collective Nouns

A collective noun names a group of people or things.

> My *class* saw a *herd* of buffalo.

Common Nouns

A common noun names any one member of a group of persons, places, or things.

> My *cousin* saw a *dog* run down the *street*.

Count Nouns

Count nouns name things that exist as individual units. You can count them. A count noun has a singular and a plural form.

> The *girls* are wearing *boots* and *mittens*.

Noncount Nouns

Noncount nouns name things that cannot be counted. A noncount noun has only a singular form.

> We could smell *rain* in the *air*.

Plural Nouns

A plural noun names more than one person, place, or thing. Most plurals are formed by adding *-s* or *-es* to the singular form. Some nouns have irregular plural forms. Some nouns have the same form in the singular and plural.

> The *children* have some *turtles* and some *fish*.

Possessive Nouns

The possessive form of a noun shows possession or ownership.

A singular possessive noun shows that one person owns something. To form the singular possessive, add an apostrophe (') and the letter *s* to a singular noun.

friend	friend's book report
baby	baby's bottle
Tess	Tess's soccer ball
woman	woman's purse

A plural possessive noun shows that more than one person owns something. To form the regular plural possessive, add an apostrophe (') after the plural form of the noun.

friends   friends' book reports
babies   babies' bottles
the Smiths   the Smiths' house

To form the plural possessive of an irregular noun, add an apostrophe and *s* ('*s*) after the plural form.

women   women's purses
mice   mice's cheese

Proper Nouns

A proper noun begins with a capital letter and names a particular person, place, or thing.

Meg saw *Shadow* run down *Pine Street.*

Singular Nouns

A singular noun names one person, place, or thing.

The *girl* has a *kite* and a *skateboard.*

NUMBER

The number of a noun or pronoun indicates whether it refers to one person, place, or thing (singular) or more than one person, place, or thing (plural).

PERSON

Personal pronouns and possessive adjectives change form according to person—whether they refer to the person speaking (first person), the person spoken to (second person), or the person, place, or thing spoken about (third person).

PREDICATES

The predicate of a sentence tells what the subject is or does.

Complete Predicates
The complete predicate of a sentence is the simple predicate and any words that go with it.

> Tom *rode his new bike.*

Compound Predicates
Two predicates joined by *and, but,* or *or* form a compound predicate.

> Karen *got a glass* and *poured some milk.*

Simple Predicates
The simple predicate of a sentence is a verb, a word or words that express an action or a state of being.

> The boys *ran* noisily down the street.
> They *were* happy.

PRONOUNS

A pronoun is a word that takes the place of a noun. See NUMBER, PERSON.

Personal Pronouns
A personal pronoun refers to the person speaking or to the person or thing that is spoken to or about. In this sentence, *I* is the person speaking, *you* is the person spoken to, and *them* are the people spoken about.

> *I* heard *you* calling *them.*

Object Pronouns

An object pronoun can be the direct object of a sentence. The object pronouns are *me, you, him, her, it, us,* and *them.* Two or more object pronouns can be joined by *and* or *or* to form a compound direct object.

> Karen will help *them.*
> Chris will help *her* and *me.*

Plural Pronouns

A plural pronoun refers to more than one person, place, or thing.

> *They* are helping *us.*

Possessive Pronouns

A possessive pronoun shows ownership or possession. A possessive pronoun takes the place of a noun. It takes the place of the owner and the thing that is owned. The possessive pronouns are *mine, yours, his, hers, its, ours,* and *theirs.*

> My cap is here, and your cap is over there.
> *Mine* is here, and *yours* is over there.

Singular Pronouns

A singular pronoun refers to one person, place, or thing.

> *I* gave *it* to *her.*

Subject Pronouns

A subject pronoun can be used as the subject of a sentence. The subject pronouns are *I, you, he, she, it, we,* and *they.* Two or more subject pronouns can be joined by *and* or *or* to form a compound subject.

> *She* is a great tennis player.
> *She* and *I* play tennis often.
> *She* and Tom like to play video games.

SENTENCES

A sentence is a group of words that expresses a complete thought. Every sentence has a subject and a predicate. Every sentence begins with a capital letter.

Compound Sentences

Two sentences joined by a comma and *and, but,* or *or* form a compound sentence.

> Ming is eating, but Lili is sleeping.

Exclamatory Sentences

An exclamatory sentence expresses strong or sudden emotion. It ends with an exclamation point (!).

> How cold it is today!

Imperative Sentences

An impcrative sentence gives a command or makes a request. The subject of an imperative sentence is generally *you,* which is often not stated. A command ends with a period (.).

> Please wear your jacket.

Interrogative Sentences

An interrogative sentence asks a question. It ends with a question mark (?).

> Are you ready?
> Where is your jacket?

Declarative Sentences

A declarative sentence makes a statement. It tells something. A statement ends with a period (.).

> Your jacket is in the closet.

SUBJECT COMPLEMENTS

A subject complement follows a linking verb in a sentence. It is a noun or a pronoun that renames the subject or an adjective that describes the subject. Two or more subject complements joined by *and, but,* or *or* form a compound subject complement.

> That police officer is a *hero.*
> His actions were *brave* and *skillful.*
> The officer with the medal for bravery was *he.*

SUBJECTS

The subject of a sentence is who or what the sentence is about. The subject can be a noun or a pronoun.

Complete Subjects
The complete subject is the simple subject and the words that describe it or give more information about it.

> *The little gray kitten* is playing.

Compound Subjects
Two or more subjects joined by *and* or *or* form a compound subject.

> *Bob* and *Lisa* went to the movies.
> *Norman* or *I* will sweep the floor.

Simple Subject
The simple subject is the noun or pronoun that a sentence tells about.

> His little *dog* likes to chase balls.
> *It* runs very fast.

SUBJECT-VERB AGREEMENT

A subject and verb must agree, whether the verb is a main verb or a helping verb.

> I *like* chocolate ice cream.
> My brother *likes* peach ice cream.
> Our parents *like* strawberry ice cream.

> I *am building* a birdhouse.
> He *is building* a shed.
> They *are building* a garage.

A collective noun is generally considered a singular noun though it means more than one person or thing; therefore, the verb agrees with the singular form.

> Our *class is entering* the contest.

When a sentence starts with *there is, there are, there was,* or *there were,* the subject follows the verb. The verb must agree with the subject.

> There *is a book* on the desk.
> There *were some pencils* in the drawer.

TENSE

The tense of a verb shows when the action takes place.

Future Tense
The future tense tells about something that will happen in the future.

One way to form the future tense is with a form of the helping verb *be* plus *going to* plus the present form of a verb.

> I *am going to make* toast.
> Dad *is going to butter* it.
> They *are going to eat* it.

Another way to form the future tense is with the helping verb *will* and the present form of a verb.

> Our class *will go* to the museum.
> The guide *will explain* the exhibits.

Future Perfect Tense

The perfect future tense tells about an action that will have been completed by some time in the future. The future perfect tense is formed with *will* plus *have* plus the past participle of a verb.

> I *will have finished* my homework by dinnertime.
> I *will have made* a salad by that time too.

Past Perfect Tense

The past perfect tense tells about an action that was finished before another action in the past. The past perfect tense is formed with *had* and the past participle of a verb.

> She *had come* straight home after school.
> She *had finished* her homework before dinner.

Past Progressive Tense

The past progressive tense tells what was happening in the past. The past progressive tense is formed with *was* or *were* and the present participle of a verb.

> I *was feeding* the cat.
> My parents *were reading*.

Present Perfect Tense

The present perfect tense tells about an action that happened at some indefinite time in the past or about an action that started in the past and continues into the present. The present perfect tense is formed with a form of *have* and the past participle of a verb.

> He *has finished* his homework.
> They *have lived* in that house for three years.

Present Progressive Tense

The present progressive tense tells what is happening now. The present progressive tense is formed with *am, is,* or *are* and the present participle of a verb.

> We *are watching* TV.
> I *am eating* popcorn.
> My sister *is drinking* juice.

Simple Past Tense

The simple past tense tells about something that happened in the past. The simple past tense of regular verbs is formed by adding *-d* or *-ed* to the present form of a verb.

> We *cooked* breakfast this morning.
> Mom *fried* the eggs.

Simple Present Tense

The simple present tense tells about something that is always true or something that happens again and again. The present part of a verb is used for the present tense. If the subject is a singular noun or *he, she,* or *it, -s* or *-es* must be added to the verb.

> Prairie dogs *live* where it's dry.
> A prairie dog *digs* a burrow to live in.

VERBS

A verb shows action or state of being. See TENSE.

Action Verbs

An action verb tells what someone or something does.

> The girl *is singing*.
> Dogs *bark*.

Being Verbs

A being verb shows what someone or something is. Being verbs do not express action.

> The girl *is* happy.
> The dog *was* hungry.

Helping Verbs

A verb can have more than one word. A helping verb is a verb added before the main verb that helps make the meaning clear.

We *will* go to the movie.
We *might* buy some popcorn.

Irregular Verbs

The past and the past participle of irregular verbs are not formed by adding *-d* or *-ed*.

Present	Past	Past Participle
sing	sang	sung
send	sent	sent
write	wrote	written

Linking Verbs

A linking verb joins the subject of a sentence to a subject complement. Being verbs can be linking verbs.

My aunt *is* a professional writer.
Her stories *are* excellent.
The winner of the writing award *was* she.

Principal Parts

A verb has four principal parts: present, present participle, past, and past participle. The present participle is formed by adding *-ing* to the present. The past and the past participle of regular verbs are formed by adding *-d* or *-ed* to the present.

Present	Present Participle	Past	Past Participle
walk	walking	walked	walked
wave	waving	waved	waved

The past and the past participle of irregular verbs are not formed by adding -d or -ed to the present.

Present	Present Participle	Past	Past Participle
do	doing	did	done
fly	flying	flew	flown
put	putting	put	put

The present participle is often used with forms of the helping verb *be*.

We *are walking* to school.
I *was doing* my homework

The past participle is often used with forms of the helping verb *have*.

We *have walked* this way before.
He *has done* his homework.

Regular Verbs

The past and the past participle of regular verbs are formed by adding -d or -ed to the present.

Present	Past	Past Participle
jump	jumped	jumped
paste	pasted	pasted

Verb Phrases

A verb phrase is made up of one or more helping verbs and a main verb.

I *should have shown* you my drawings.
I *am entering* them in the art contest.
You *can see* them there.

Mechanics

CAPITAL LETTERS

Use a capital letter to begin the first word in a sentence.

> Tomorrow is my birthday.

Use a capital letter to begin the names of people and pets.

> Aunt Peg let me play with her ferret, Nibbles.

Use a capital letter to begin the names of streets, cities, states, and countries.

> I live on Roscoe Street.
> My cousin lives in Guadalajara, Mexico.

Use a capital letter to begin the names of days, months, and holidays.

> Christmas is on Monday, December twenty-fifth.

Use a capital letter to begin a proper adjective.

> I love to eat Chinese food.

Use a capital letter to begin people's titles.

> Mrs. Novak
> Dr. Ramirez
> Governor Charles Ryan

Use a capital letter to begin the important words in the title of a book or poem. The first and last words of a title are always capitalized. Short words such as *of, to, for, a, an,* and *the* are not capitalized unless they are the first or last word of the title.

The Secret Garden
"Sing a Song of Cities"

The personal pronoun *I* is always a capital letter.

PUNCTUATION

Apostrophes

Use an apostrophe to form possessive nouns.

Keisha's skateboard
the children's lunches
the horses' stalls

Use an apostrophe to replace the letters left out in a contraction.

didn't   can't   wasn't

Commas

Use a comma to separate the words in a series.

Mark, Anton, and Cara made the scenery.
They hammered, sawed, and nailed.

Use a comma or commas to separate a name in direct address.

Carl, will you help me?
Do you think, Keshawn, that we will finish today?

Use a comma before the coordinating conjunction when two short sentences are combined in a compound sentence.

Dad will heat the soup, and I will make the salad.
Dad likes noodle soup, but I like bean soup.

Use a comma to separate the names of a city and state.

She comes from Philadelphia, Pennsylvania.

Use a comma or commas to separate a direct quotation from the rest of the sentence.

"Hey," called Mario, "where are you going?"
"I'm going to the movies," Juana answered.

Use a comma after the word *yes* or *no* that introduces a sentence.

No, I can't go to the movies tonight.

Exclamation Points
Use an exclamation point after an exclamatory sentence.

We won the game!

Periods
Use a period after a declarative or an imperative sentence.

The cat is hungry.
Please feed it.

Use a period after most abbreviations.

Sun.	Sept.	ft.	yd.
Ave.	St.	gal.	oz.

Periods are not used after abbreviations for metric measures.

km   cm

Use a period after a personal title.

Mr. Frank Cummings
Mrs. Joanna Clark
Dr. Hilda Doolittle
Sgt. Barry Lindon

Use a period after an initial.

John F. Kennedy   U.S.A.
J. K. Rowling   B.S.A.

Question Marks

Use a question mark after an interrogative sentence.

Where are you going?

Quotation Marks

Use quotation marks to show the exact words a person says in a direct quotation.

Carla said, "I can't find my markers."
"Where," asked her mother, "did you leave them?"

Use quotation marks around the title of a poem, story, or magazine article. Titles of books and magazines are italicized when they are typed and underlined when they are handwritten.

"Paul Revere's Ride"
Harry Potter and the Half-Blood Prince
Mr. Popper's Penguins

Index

A

Acknowledgments

Illustration

Marla Baggetta: Illustrations: 9, 10, 19, 52, 65, 98, 107, 129, 146, 153, 214, 222, 226, 227, 230, 231, 232, 233, 243, 273

Dave LaFleur: Illustration: 289

Photography

Alamy: 360

Corbis: 14, 175, 201, 205, 209, 239, 328, 355, 396, 419, 436, 458

Getty: 23, 25, 44, 94, 106, 126, 144, 172, 200, 213, 217, 220, 237, 252, 272, 277, 280, 281, 283, 288(t), 292, 295, 296, 369, 383, 384, 442

Hans Hong: 340(l)

Phil Martin Photography: 6, 7, 12, 13, 18, 21, 29, 35, 37, 39, 43, 44, 48, 49, 51, 57, 59, 60, 61, 66, 68, 71, 72, 73, 74, 75, 76, 77, 78, 79, 80, 81, 83, 90, 95, 96, 100, 102, 108, 113, 117, 120, 121, 122, 130, 134, 139, 142, 144(r), 149, 150, 151, 157, 161, 162, 163, 169, 174, 180, 183, 189, 195, 196, 202, 203, 206, 208, 218, 221, 225, 229, 233, 235,259, 265, 271, 282, 286, 290, 297, 302, 303, 309, 381, 414, 417, 422

Northwind Picture Archive: 14, 22, 50, 54, 86, 123(t), 127, 132, 137(t), 274, 276, 279, 284

Stock Montage: 8, 30, 64(t), 82, 89(b), 102, 140, 158, 160, 166(t), 170, 182, 234, 240, 251, 254, 258

Loyola Press has made every effort to locate the copyright holders for the cited works used in this publication and to make full acknowledgment for their use. In the case of any omissions, the Publisher will be pleased to make suitable acknowledgments in future editions.